CREATIVE CITIES

Cultural Industries, Urban Development and the Information Society

CREATIVE CITIES

Cultural Industries, Urban Development and the Information Society

Edited by Jan Verwijnen and Panu Lehtovuori

University of Art and Design Helsinki UIAH

Photo credits:
Cleo Bade: pages 30, 44, 78, 116, 119, 144, 147
Valtteri Bade: 22, 38, 47, 57, 130, 270, 271, 272
Stefan Bremer: 220, 225, 232
Ralf Collaris: 185
Edina Dufala: 235, 236
The Finnish Museum of Architecture: 218
Panu Lehtovuori: 22, 29, 67, 73, 80, 89, 120, 258, 260, 269
Livady: 232
Mikko Mälkki: 236, 237
Saku Paasilahti: 260, 267, 268
Doina Petrescu/RDS: 151, 152, 154, 159
Pekka Piippo: 11, 21, 49, 80, 89, 106, 113, 135, 144, 262, 265
Ilona Törmikoski: 44, 111, 144
Jan Verwijnen: 44, 215
pages 240, 242 source: Girald, Greg., City of darkness – life in the Kowloon Walled City, 1993

Publication series of University of Art and Design Helsinki UIAH B 56
Edited by Jan Verwijnen and Panu Lehtovuori
Graphic design: Cleo Bade and Valtteri Bade
© UIAH and the authors
Proofreading of the articles by Valtasana Oy
Printed at Gummerus Printing
Jyväskylä 1999
ISBN 951–558–023–4
ISSN 0782–1778

Distribution
University of Art and Design Helsinki UIAH
UIAH Publishing Unit
Hämeentie 135 C
FIN–00560 Helsinki
Finland

Contents

Jan Verwijnen	**Preface**	6
Pekka Korpinen	**Helsinki Needs to Sharpen its Cultural Profile**	8

Introduction

Jan Verwijnen	**The Creative City's New Field Condition**	12
	Can Urban Innovation and Creativity Overcome Bureaucracy and Technocracy?	
Peter Hall	**The Creative City in the Third Millennium**	36

Aspects of the Creative City

Bert Mulder	**The Creative City or Redesigning Society**	60
Justin O'Connor	**Popular Culture, Reflexivity and Urban Change**	76
Geoff Mulgan	**Programming Creativity**	102
	Public Policy in an Information Age	
L.van den Berg, I.Bramezza, E. Braun and J.van de Meer	**Urban Management in a Creative City**	114
	The Case of Rotterdam	
Jennifer Williams	**Making Space for Creativity**	128
	The Changing Responsibilities of Arts Organisations and Artists in Contemporary Communities	
Jean Schneider	**The City Furnished**	142
Doina Petrescu	**Inform(ing) City**	148
Ron Kenley	**From SimCity to Our City**	162

Projects

Hans Mommaas	**The Tilburg Pop Cluster**	176
	New Strategies of Urban Development	
Phil Wood	**Kirklees**	190
	The Development of a Creative Milieu	
Riitta Vesala	**Gardens of Anchor**	200
	Urban Pilot Project Proposal for the City of Lahti	
	The Creative Lahti Study	208
Panu Lehtovuori	**Two Creative Cases**	212
	The Cable Factory and the Glass Palace Media Centre	
Edina Dufala	**Culturing the Mall**	234
	A Design Museum in the Heart of the City	
Jackie Kwok & Michael Siu	**Kowloon City**	238
	Destruction of the Wall of Identity. (Re)construction of a Public Place of Consumption	
Carl Gardner	**Urban Lighting in the 21st Century**	256
	New Strategies for New Uses	

JAN VERWIJNEN

Preface

The idea of the Creative City Conference goes back to Charles Landry, who proposed it and was a co-producer. As founder of Comedia, Britain's leading cultural planning consultancy, he has not only undertaken numerous projects and studies but also more or less invented the notion of the Creative City.

> *Historically, creativity and innovation have been the lifeblood of cities. Yet there are special reasons for thinking about the problems of cities today in terms of creativity and innovation – or the lack of it. Today many of the world's cities are facing agonising periods of transition. Old industries are disappearing – value added in cities is created less through what we manufacture and more through the application of new knowledge to products, processes and services. The factors that once shaped city development – transport, rivers, proximity of raw materials – have become less relevant.*
>
> *As we approach the 21st century there is a widespread understanding that it will be the creativity and innovativeness of our cities that will determine the future success of Europe and elsewhere. But surprisingly little is known about the conditions for creativity and innovation to emerge: the informal as well as formal structures that have helped Silicon Valley or Hollywood, Barcelona, the Third Italy around Emilia Romagna, the advanced technology enclaves surrounding Tokyo or Glasgow develop world reputations for creativity and the creation of new businesses and services.*
>
> *The modern urban malaise is a complex crisis, which cannot be solved by traditional urban planning and policy. The hard sciences of urban planning need to be reformed and enriched by mobilising the experiences of different disciplines and people currently marginalised from decision making – many of these might come from the cultural arena. Culture is crucially important. It is the often forgotten glue that may hold things together in cities. It is in the cultural arena that the battles of the future will be fought – won and lost. Thus a cultural perspective needs to move centre stage in the planning of our cities.*
>
> —— CHARLES LANDRY, CONFERENCE PRESENTATION

This Creative City publication interprets 'urban innovation and creativity' particularly towards creating new workplaces through the potential of information and communication structures. A key question becomes how urban development can promote the interaction between cultural industries and technical innovation and foster an "innovative milieu" (see Peter Hall's contribution). The preceding publication *Managing Urban Change* was more preoccupied with the links between the *strategic planning* debate as an alternative to traditional master planning and the British *cultural planning* debate introduced by Franco Bianchini. The Urban Pilot Projects (UPP) introduced in this publication attempt to illustrate this link.

In the context of the Creative City Conference the programmatic development of an area in the immediate vicinity of the University of Art and Design Helsinki called Arabianranta (85 ha for 7000 inhabitants and 8000 new working places) has to be mentioned. The University has been an important actor in planning the 'Art and Design Centre', a design industry oriented business core of the area. Arabianranta, too, became the subject of an Urban Pilot Project application submitted in April 1996. It is part of a larger redevelopment of the whole eastern waterfront of Helsinki – a several kilometres long industrial belt along the shoreline. In the middle of the project lies the huge Arabia factory complex, in which porcelain production is gradually making way for other programmes. The University of Art and Design, which was founded in 1871, moved in a decade ago. The idea of the 'Design City' is to locate a number of existing, but also to create a number of new businesses focusing on design related services. Like in a science park the University has set up a business incubator for these cultural industries. Design is no longer simply concerned with products and spaces, but increasingly involved with audio-visual industry. Design for film and TV is a growth industry with a tremendous potential, thus a new audio-visual centre of the University, which includes an auditorium/cinema, screening rooms, studio theatres, exhibition galleries and a broad-band fibre network supporting digital production, will be the first building of the 'Art and Design Centre' to be completed in 1999. As the traditional roles of the home and of the workspace are being questioned, a demand for new kinds of homes and schools is created. Arabianranta as a new housing area has the ambition to establish a creative relationship between information technology, cultural production (design, music) and urban innovation.

Pekka Korpinen
Deputy Mayor, City of Helsinki

Helsinki Needs to Sharpen its Cultural Profile

For a small country with an obscure language, culture is a crucial factor in competition for foreign investments. Even if Helsinki's arts scene is richer than in other parts of the country, by international standards Helsinki does not cut a very impressive figure.

Cinema is usually regarded as one of Helsinki's strong points; it is, after all, fairly easy to import and subtitle a foreign-made film. However, while the average person in Helsinki goes to the cinema five times a year, the corresponding average in Dublin and Edinburgh is roughly ten and seven even in Copenhagen. Although Helsinki has three symphony orchestras, every third city resident goes to a concert only once a year. In Zurich the figure is more than twice that, and in relative terms even Stockholm has twice as many concert-goers as Helsinki. To take one more example, although theatre is the Finn's favourite cultural attraction, the average theatre attendance for Stockholm is more than twice that of Helsinki. Only in terms of borrowings from libraries does Helsinki come quite near the top in Europe.

Now that Helsinki has been chosen as one of Europe's cultural capitals for the year 2000, one would hope to see a permanent shift towards a greater appreciation of culture, also when measured by public expenditure. In order to create a lasting cultural base, we must take a long-term perspective without lapsing into populism. A century ago there were, per resident, nearly as many theatres and triple the number of classical orchestras as there are in present-day Helsinki. At the end of last century, there were a few more museums per capita in Helsinki than now. In a hundred years only the number of art galleries and art museums has risen substantially.

When Finland was striving for independence, a dedicated effort was made to advance Finnish culture. The fledgling nation found roots and a solid basis for self-esteem in its arts and culture. Now as we prepare for a new millennium, culture may once again become a source of strength. Otherwise the pressures of internationalization and the EU may prove too great for us. Taking the lead, Helsinki has enough driving force to benefit the whole country.

INTRODUCTION

The Creative City's New Field Condition
Can Urban Innovation and Creativity Overcome Bureaucracy and Technocracy?

JAN VERWIJNEN

Professor, University of Art and Design Helsinki

[1] A more precise account can be found in the contribution of Justin O'Connor later in this publication entitled *Popular Culture, Reflexivity and Urban Change*: cities are now beginning to address the problems of promoting knowledge intensive industrial growth in conjunction with cultural policies aimed at providing a creative milieu. (O'Connor 1999)

[2] The concept of the 'innovative milieu' was first developed by Philippe Aydalot; more recently it has been connected to post-Fordist networked production. A 'creative' milieu has the necessary hard and soft infrastructure for cultural industries. Particularly important for such a milieu is 'soft' infrastructure, the system of social networks and human interactions that facilitate the flow of ideas.
(Peter Hall unpublished manuscript, Castells 1996)

The notion of the creative city draws our attention to the fact that beyond the traditional forms of urban renewal and urban regeneration, cities show a growing interest in creating districts imbued with a climate of innovation and creativity[1]. It expresses a will to make part of downtown or a depressed neighbourhood an innovative milieu[2] that can meet the challenges of the future. Once reserved for science parks, innovation is now seen as an ingredient connected to the formation of new cultural industries. Until recently, gentrification has been the main tool to renew abandoned industrial areas – generally meaning projects on the level of a sanitised and often unified, upper-middle-class taste through a stylish form of retail space and housing. But the actors in the new cultural industries that are increasingly inhabiting these former industrial areas reject this gentrified style of 'revitalisation', preferring instead a different cultural landscape. These industries generally consist of a multitude of small offices and studios that increasingly operate with multimedia content, rely on information technology and are heavily networked. They are now considered to be an important if not the main source of new employment (O'Connor 1998). This article questions if cities, at the very moment they discover this new potential for their economic revival, realise that they are not well equipped to plan for an environment that attracts these types of people and companies.

Will, in the wake of the 'Network Society', traditional technocratic and bureaucratic planning tools be able to deal with the cultural forces carried by a new wave of urban innovation and creativity? Evidence for this new wave of urban innovation based on information and communication technology is given by Peter Hall's contribution to this publication, *The Creative City in the Third Millennium*. Further, Justin O'Connor in his article *Popular Culture, Reflexivity and Urban Change* draws attention to the importance of the local context for actors in the new cultural industries[3], which urban development decision makers seem to neglect. This article will introduce the notion of urban 'field conditions', which points to the necessity of a more fluid bottom-up approach in designing for the kind of cultural landscape that attracts new cultural industries. Finally, the fact that our society is becoming increasingly networked and that information technology is connecting everything to everything else makes the content of these connections become cultural. If the production of culture by new cultural industries thus becomes pervasive in the Network Society, then the specific 'culture of production' – the condition in which the actors of these industries operate – must be acknowledged by the creative city. This is no longer a question of replacing a few aging civil servants by younger ones with the 'right feeling', but of a fundamental shift of the urban decision-making system towards an evolutionary and networked mode.

[3] With 'new' cultural industries is meant an area of multimedia design and music production strongly connected to Internet based activities beyond the sales, marketing, advertising, public relations, fashion, decoration etc. of the late 1970s and 1980s that make up the metropolitan new petite bourgeoisie classified by Bourdieu. It is this MSE (micro and small enterprises) sector which is a major driver for innovation and creativity, operating in complex interaction with the big culture industry production and distribution companies such as Sony, Time Warner, Bertelsmann etc. (O'Connor 1999).

Culture-Driven Urban Renewal

In the last two decades the usefulness of arts- and culture-driven urban regeneration has generally been acknowledged. Following the American examples of specifically Boston and Baltimore and their waterfront redevelopment, which included new convention centres, aquariums and the invention of festival shopping centres, the European cities also started initiatives driven by cultural policy (Landry et al. 1996). They developed policies encompassing cultural animation, festivals, pedestrianisation, revitalisation of the evening economy, the creation of cultural centres, etc., generally to attract tourists and local residents alike.

The transformation of historical and/or waterfront areas into retail/leisure and residential developments was based around 'upmarket' consumption with a high cultural input. This could include cultural animation programmes, artists' residences, subsidised workshops and a public art that fitted well with a new 'postmodern' aesthetic.
— O'CONNOR 1999

But as Landry et al. (1996) point out in their study of urban renewal through cultural activity, much of the resources allocated to culture initiatives were commonly sidetracked into building programmes that actually supported the construction industry rather than cultural activities. Further, the on-going funding of the initial investment into building arts centres is usually inadequate, so that gross under-staffing and under-maintenance follow – meaning that the buildings rarely develop their potential. Particularly in the UK, the community arts movement developed a different cultural perspective based on socially motivated art and cultural activity. It has taken a lead in developing people's interest in the local environment and is using the arts to create a forum for discussion between urban planners and residents. Although community arts can be of great local importance, they are economically not operating with the same kind of vibrancy as the new cultural industries.

The cultural sector has grown remarkably since the beginning of the 1980s in terms of the economic importance of this sector for the cities. Zukin (1995) draws attention to the new symbolic economy of culture for cities:

As a set of architectural themes, it plays a leading role in urban redevelopment strategies based on historic preservation or local 'heritage'. With the disappearance of local manufacturing industries and periodic crises in government and finance, culture is more and more the business of cities – the basis of their tourist attractions and their unique, competitive edge. The growth of cultural consumption (of art, food, fashion, music, tourism) and the industries that cater to it fuels the city's symbolic economy, its visible ability to produce both symbols and space.
— ZUKIN 1995: 1–2

At first cultural policies were mainly used to upgrade a city's image and promote city marketing for business investment[4] – Frankfurt may serve as an example with the building of ten new museums between 1980 and 1990 to secure its European banking position alongside London. More recently, however, urban cultural policies have increasingly come to emphasise the employment potential of the cultural industries (O'Connor 1996 and 1999). In the meantime urban culture has taken on industrial proportions similar to tourism that became an industry because of its sheer size and mass character – tourism has, for example, become Manhattan's main source of income before banking and financial trading. Increasingly, tourism can no longer be separated from the culture industries. Art and culture are a 'megaindustry' in New York City, with an annual economy of 8 billion dollars. Art and tourism combined constitute one of the largest generators of tax revenues (Zukin 1995: 110).

[4] Andy Lovat notes as one of thefeatures of cities adapting their cultural policies: "... the emergence of city to city competitiveness at a national and supranational level where the management of the local image was deemed to be crucial in an increasingly globalised marketplace. This image was tied to the cultural facilities and 'vibrancy' of the city centre." (Lovat 1996: 145)

The traditional culture industries consist of the performing arts, music and the visual arts, as well as film, TV and publishing. Urban cultural industries increasingly include design activities, digital imaging and multimedia oriented Internet based activities[5]. Despite their importance for creating new employment and regenerating abandoned industrial areas or neglected districts such as Manchester's Northern Quarter, the means to effectively support an innovative milieu for these 'new' cultural industries are generally not understood by the authorities. In describing this experienced difficulty, O'Connor states how the critical infrastructure worked independently partly even in opposition to the developers' cultural model (O'Connor 1999).

[5] In Manchester these are noticed as the fast-moving media, popular music, leisure and communication sectors. (Taylor et al. 1996).

> *The resultant development, whilst based on images of leisure and consumption and aestheticisation taken up by urban boosterists, had limited cultural resonance, and especially amongst those whose labour would be crucial to the transformation of the centre into cultural landscape – the cultural intermediaties. They were deeply cynical.*
> — O'CONNOR 1999

Cultural intermediaries that could mediate between the world of the authorities with their technocratic and deterministic planning models and the needs of an innovative and creative milieu that is attractive to the new cultural industries need a close knowledge of the inner dynamics of the cultural field.

> *This implies a knowledge of the local, but also a deep understanding for these specific forms of consumption. It is this knowledge that allows cultural industries to both innovate in the local sphere and extend their operations beyond the local. ... Local economic development increasingly depends on the mobilisation of this knowledge, but the ability to do this depends on a range of historically specific social, economic, cultural and political factors. As a particular kind of knowledge intensive industry, and as one especially dependent on a negotiation and articulation of a local place-based cultural milieu within a 'global space of flows', the cultural industries sector represents an important indicator of the ability of particular cities to respond to the challenge of global restructuring.*
> — O'CONNOR 1999

For a city to be able to effectively use the employment potential of new cultural industries, a set of interactive and participative tools[6] will have to be developed that will most likely start to replace existing planning practice.

Flows

The driving forces of an innovative milieu for the cities are at once cultural and technological – cultural through its content, technological because this cultural content flows increasingly via new information and communication infrastructures. The capacity of the new information and communication infrastructure alongside the improvement of existing rail, road and air travel is creating an economy of another and new type. It is dominated and characterised by flows – flows of information, of images, of money, of goods and of people that are increasingly connected and that circulate ever faster. There is also less and less difference between the nature of these flows: from those of objects (goods) to those of subjects (people). Hence taxis, originally meant for people, now transport meals as pizza-taxi, and companies such as Federal Express or United Parcel Service each have over 500 aeroplanes just for shipping packages and letters – more than the largest European airlines, Lufthansa,

[6] Experiments indicate that these tools will be Web-based and database driven. A current research project at the University of Art and Design Helsinki operates with a system of database-driven Web pages that allow a redirection of the flow of information towards end-users in urban decision-making related to planning procedures for housing.

British Airways or Air France, have for passengers. These modes of transport are complemented – but are also in competition with – global telecommunications: the flows of transportation and those of information reinforce each other. Movement of information is, of course, a substitute for the movement of people (Hall 1991).

The flows of capital, money, commodities, labour, information and images create a series of impacts with different consequences. Firstly, the flows are responsible for constituting a network economy and networks become the dominant social morphology in society. Because these networks are used for communication their content is increasingly involved with cultural signs. Secondly, as it becomes necessary for people to evaluate and judge these signs and be involved in the increased production of culture, an aesthetic and reflexive movement captures society. People critically reflect upon their social condition and can in a different form find new meaning in the various spheres of social life. Thirdly, a space of flows threatens to disconnect people and places. Finally, because of all this, urban development increasingly comes under the influence of a new field condition, and evolutionary and participatory forms of decision-making become more plausible.

The Network Society

The flows themselves are only comprehensible if networks are taken into account, because it is through networks that people and objects are able to gain mobility. By 1992 the fastest-growing segment of the computer industry was network technology. This reflects the rate at which every sector of business is electronically organising

itself in networks. Networking is revolutionising almost every business. It alters what we make, how we make it, how we decide what to make and the nature of the economy we make it in (Kelly 1994). Networks are made up of a few basic elements: of 'bridges' or 'links', which connect points or nodes. These links stand out in lesser or greater relief from a background or 'support structure' and transmit or transport 'traffic' (Lash and Urry 1994). Networks are open structures able to expand without limits and integrate new nodes as long as they are able to communicate within the network. A network-based social structure is a highly dynamic, open system[7], susceptible to innovating without threatening its balance (Kelly 1994, Castells 1996). In his fundamental work, *The Rise of the Network Society*, Castells notes how networks constitute the new social morphology of our societies.

> *While the networking form of social organisation has existed in other times and spaces, the new information technology paradigm[8] provides the material basis for its pervasive expansion throughout the entire social structure. Furthermore, I would argue that this networking logic induces a social determination of a higher level than that of the specific social interests expressed through the networks: the power of flows takes precedence over the flows of power.*
> — CASTELLS 1996: 469

In other words the fact that networks exist and tend to function bottom-up becomes more powerful and important than the existing modes of top-down decision-making. The debate about controlling the Internet is, of course, a typical expression of the struggle for power over a network that in fact can no longer be controlled by traditional power structures.

The network morphology reorganises the power relationships, and presence or absence in the network becomes a critical source of change in our society. This is true for firms, so-called network enterprises, not just in their internal organisation, but particularly in their relationship to other firms, as well as for institutions such as universities or hospitals and, of course, cities. Switches connecting networks are the privileged instruments of power – they become the power holders (Castells 1996). We may take as an example the French TGV high-speed train network that was developed ten

---

[7] Particularly Kelly in *Out of Control, The New Biology of Machines* (1994) stresses the cybernetic aspects of networks as self-organising systems. According to him a pure network has the following traits: *distributed, decentralised, collaborative,* and *adaptive.* For a company it would mean: there is no single location – it dwells among many places; it outsources as many activities as possible to subcontractors; it looks for symbiotic partners in strategic alliances; it shifts its attention from products to services (customer support). A network is a factory for information. (Kelly 1994, 189–194)

[8] Information's critical rearrangement is the widespread, relentless act of connecting everything to everything else – communicating between all beings and all objects. All the most promising technologies making their debut now are chiefly due to communication between computers – that is to connections rather than computations. All the major consequences of stand-alone computers have already taken place. (Kelly 1997: 140)

years before the German ICE (Inter-City Express) as an attempt to make Paris the main hub or switch of the Trans-European HST network, which otherwise might have been in Frankfurt. This complies with the fact that Paris fears being bypassed, because geographically it lies outside the mainstream of Europe – the European urbanised corridor that stretches from the English Midlands along the river Rhine to Milan, and along which the main flow of goods and capital moves in Europe.

There is daily evidence for the fact that the new economy is organised around global networks of capital – it has become part of our experience in news headlines of mergers or bankruptcies. But more important is that beyond the networking of capital, firms and localities the convergence of social evolution and information technologies in particular has started to create a new basis for the social structure in society. At the core of the social structure is the process of work. If we follow Castells, the impact of the transformation of work and employment by new information technologies is twofold: the individualisation of work and the fragmentation of societies.

> *The new social and economic organisation based on information technologies aims at decentralising management, individualising work, and customising markets, thereby segmenting work and fragmenting societies. New information technologies allow at the same time for the decentralisation of work tasks and for their coordination in an interactive network of communication in real time, be it between continents or between floors of the same building.*
> — CASTELLS 1996: 265

At the same time we realise that culture becomes the main content of these new information and communication structures:

> *Cultures are made up of communication processes. And all forms of communication, as Roland Barthes and Jean Baudrillard taught us many years ago, are based on the production and consumption of signs. ...In all societies humankind has existed in and acted through a symbolic environment*
> — CASTELLS 1996: 372

In this respect he also states:

> *In a broader historical perspective the network society represents a qualitative change in the human experience. ...Because of the convergence of historical evolution and technological change we have entered a purely cultural pattern of social interaction and social organisation. This is why information is the key ingredient of our social organisation and why flows of messages and images between networks constitute the basic thread of our social structure.*
> — CASTELLS 1996: 477

Thus what is specific to the new communication system, organised around the electronic integration of all communication modes from the typographic to the multimedia, is that its content is increasingly culture and that it particularly consists of images and signs.

Aesthetic Reflexivity

In this context an interesting aspect of contemporary societies becomes the fact that people are increasingly able to monitor and evaluate these images as well as place themselves within the world, both historically and geographically. The more that societies modernise, the greater the ability of knowledgeable subjects to reflect upon their social conditions of existence. Lash (1994) characterises this as 'reflexive modernisation'. In a world of ever-faster change and growing abstraction the process of reflexivity opens up possibilities for the recasting of meaning in work and leisure and for the heterogenisation and complexity of space and everyday life. Confronted with the increasing cultural content of flows, reflexivity becomes aesthetic – a notion for which Lash and Urry argue in their book *Economies of Signs and Space* (1994). They state that the majority of people in the advanced countries produce 'semiotic' rather than industrial goods. The mobility of these objects or goods in flows changes their nature – they are progressively emptied of both symbolic and material content and thus of their traditional local meaning. Culture in pre-modern societies was exercised through symbols, which were full of meanings, contents, peopled with gods and demons. In contemporary society the production of culture and ordinary manufacturing industry

are becoming more and more alike. What increasingly is being produced are no longer material objects but signs. Even non-material goods such as pop music, cinema or video have a substantial aesthetic component. (Lash and Urry 1994)

Because of the component of sign value or aesthetic image in material objects, design becomes a more important aspect in producing goods.

> *This aestheticisation of material objects can take place either in the production or in the circulation and consumption of such goods. In production the design component comprises an increasing component of the value of goods. The specific labour process is becoming less important in its contribution to value added, and the design process is progressively more central. This can be seen in the increased research-and-development or 'design intensity' of even industrial production. This increased R&D intensity is often importantly aesthetic in nature, as in the case of clothes, shoes, furniture, car design, electronic goods and so on. Further, goods often take on the properties of sign value through the process of 'branding', in which marketers and advertisers attach images to goods.*
> — LASH AND URRY 1994: 15

Thus, apart from the component of knowledge or information intensity, increasing design intensity becomes apparent in industrial production and, with the decline in importance of the labour process in production the design process starts to grow in importance. Economic life itself becomes cultural.

But even though objects are being progressively emptied of meaning and people are bombarded by an overload of signs, the contemporary condition of society produces not just a flattening, but also a deepening of the self – people become, as we have seen, more reflexive, more critical. Through this growing reflexivity, which causes a gradual freeing of individuals from traditional social structures, people reflect upon their condition, and in a changed form, once more, find meaning in the various spheres of social life. In terms of consumption, aesthetic reflexivity can be seen in several senses. First there is the increased choice element in consumption. For example in fashion, dress styles involve a very important set of identity choices: an aesthetic-expressive dimension of the modern self.

[9] An account of Sharon Zukin's, *Loft Living* (1982), is given in Justin O'Connor's contribution, 'Popular Culture, Reflexivity and Urban Change', later in this publication.

Finally this increased aesthetic reflexivity of subjects in the consumption of, for example, travel and of the objects of the culture industries creates a vast real economy. It produces a complex network, which Zukin begins to capture in "Loft Living" [9], *of hotels and restaurants, of art galleries, theatres, cinemas and pop concerts, of culture producers and culture 'brokers', of architects and designers etc.*
— LASH AND URRY 1994: 59

The importance of aesthetic reflexivity lies in its contribution to people's ability to judge and distinguish images and symbols operating at the level of feeling. Travel becomes an increasingly important experience for this ability. Many of the signs or symbols that advertise commodities or goods, for example in TV commercials, are connected with place and travel and a sense of 'cosmopolitanism'. Understanding aesthetic reflexivity as part of a critical historical movement connected to the increasing mobility of people Lash and Urry state:

We have therefore argued: first, that in the 'West' over the course of the nineteenth and twentieth centuries a reflexivity about the value of different physical and social environments has been established; second, that this reflexivity is partly based on aesthetic judgements and stems from the proliferation of many forms of real and simulated mobility; third that this mobility has served to authorise an increased stance of cosmopolitanism – an ability to experience, to discriminate and to risk different natures and societies, historically and geographically; and fourth, that the social organisation of travel and tourism has facilitated and structured such a cosmopolitanism.
— LASH AND URRY 1994: 256

Thus aesthetic reflexivity raises the critical awareness and concern of people for their own environment.

The Space of Flows

The economy of flows does not leave urban space untouched – it has a significant impact on its character. In the case of Lille, due to the new rail connection between

London and Paris through the Channel Tunnel, one stop of the high-speed train Eurostar creates a new urban centre: Euralille (Koolhaas 1996). Rem Koolhaas calls this change in position of the city a 'quantum leap'. Lille, once a significant mining and textile town, is part of a depressed industrial region in Northern France. Although it lies in the geometric centre of the heavily trafficked business triangle between London, Paris and Cologne, air traffic simply flew over the city.

> *But two new givens – the tunnel between England and the continent and the TGV network – will transform Lille as if by magic and make it important in a completely synthetic way. Not only will it become the intersection of major north-south and east-west axes, but reduced travel times, through train and tunnel combined, will minimise the importance of distance and suddenly give Lille a strategic position: it will become the centre of gravity for the virtual community of 50 million Western Europeans who will live within a 1 1/2 -hour travelling distance.*
> — KOOLHAAS 1995: 1158

Only through a change in the mode of transportation – the new high-speed rail link between Paris, London and Brussels competes with air-traffic as total travel times from city centre to city centre are about the same – is Lille able to connect to the inter-metropolitan business network and become a node in this network. Thus as Castells (1996) points out, a business centre does not exist by itself, but by its connection to the other locales organised in a network that forms the actual unit of management, innovation and work. Typically, the programmes of such urban spaces are clustered around information, communications and advanced producer services as well as being dependent on telecommunications, airlines (or in this case high-speed rail) and important parts of tourism and leisure (Lash and Urry 1994). At Euralille we find exactly over the new TGV station a series of office towers housing a World Trade Centre, a bank and a hotel, and a short distance away a huge new conference centre has been built.

As we have seen, a place such as Euralille can only exist by being connected to other business centres, as part of a network. With the increased presence of flows in our economy Castells (1996) makes a case for the space of flows, in which he refers to *the city as a process*[10] rather than as a place that has a history and an identity. Because

[10] The space of flows is an abstract space of creating opportunities for the flows of business information. It becomes concrete in the way offices spatially organise their global transactions and the way in which services are offered to businessmen and women, such as airport lounges, etc

function and economic power in society are increasingly organised in such a space of flows, the structural domination of its logic essentially alters the meaning and dynamic of a place as we know it – the space of place.

> *Dominant functions are organised in networks pertaining to a space of flows that links them up around the world, while fragmenting subordinate functions, and people, in the multiple space of places, made of locales increasingly segregated and disconnected from each other ... Throughout the global networks ... capital and labour increasingly tend to exist in different spaces and times: the space of flows and the space of places, the instant time of computerised networks versus the clock time of everyday life. Thus they live by each other, but do not relate to each other...*
> — CASTELLS 1996: 475–476

He further states that unless cultural and physical bridges are deliberately built between these two forms of space, we may be heading for a life in parallel universes whose times cannot meet, because they are warped into different dimensions of a social hyperspace. On the one hand we are projected and connected throughout the world, while on the other our lives and experiences are rooted in places, in their culture and in their history. My point is that exactly the 'new' cultural industries and their actors are building these cultural and physical bridges.

Field Conditions

On a more general level the flows that have changed the character of the economy, created the networks that we now communicate through and increasingly started to influence our private activities also reinforce the 'field condition' of cities. Allen (1997) introduces the term 'field conditions' in relation to recent movements in art and technology as:

> *an intuition of a shift from* object *to* field *in recent theoretical and visual practices. In its most complex manifestation, this concept refers to mathematical field theory, non-linear dynamics and computer simulations of evolutionary change. It parallels a shift in recent technologies from analogue object to digital field. ...The infrastructural*

elements of the modern city, by their nature linked together in open-ended networks, offer another example of field conditions in the urban context.
— ALLEN 1997: 24

The field condition is characterised by forces and effects perhaps comparable to those of a magnetic field, where metal particles start to align themselves according to an invisible force field. Understanding the city as a field means accepting it being in a state of continual flux and continuous change like a sea or an ocean in which tides, streams and waves are the movements induced by forces of gravity from the moon, the spinning of the earth, the wind, or a combination of these. But not only the water or its surface moves; in the water of the sea many different objects such as fish also move using the water as a medium. In a similar fashion the city and its architectural objects change and grow under the influence of different large-scale forces such as the new economy of flows, whereas within the city and its buildings people move and networks are becoming the main form of exchange between them. For example, aesthetic reflexivity is a force that flows through the urban field and is carried by bodies of people in the form of fashion, but it also influences the form of urban space, where these people meet – the cafés, squares, etc. Such a field phenomenon is defined by simple local conditions and is in fact relatively indifferent to the overall form and extent of the city[11]. Global movements such as de-industrialisation or new information and communication structures determine the forces in a local field, but the actors on the spot behave according to local conditions, including habits, tradition and consensus. The question lies in how far can these actors that have, as we have seen, become very critical about their environment be directly involved in planning urban development.

Under field conditions architecture and planning have to shift their attention from the traditional top-down forms of control and begin to investigate more fluid bottom-up[12] approaches (Allen 1997). Although it is evident that urban planning and particularly architecture have had great difficulties in adequately addressing the complexities of urban life, there is little evidence that the discipline is adapting itself to the new field condition. Similarily Lynn (1997) points to a different architecture that must be concep-

[11] Field conditions are bottom-up phenomena: defined not by overarching geometrical schemas, but by intricate local connections. The overall shape and extent of the parts are highly fluid. Form matters, but not so much the forms of things as the forms between things (Allen 1997: 24). Similar to the structuralistic principle that in complex matters the relationship between things becomes more important than the things themselves, field conditions lend themselves very well to a definition of urban space as the space 'between the buildings'.

[12] When everything is connected to everything else in a distributed network, things happen at once. When everything happens at once, wide and fast-moving problems simply route around any central authority. Therefore overall governance must arise from interdependent acts performed locally, and not from central command. (Kelly 1994: 469)

tualised and modelled within an urban field. The urban field is understood as dynamic and characterised by forces rather than forms. To an architect, urban questions have up to now usually simply been questions of large-scale form or fabric. Instead of form, patterns of organisation should be addressed on the urban scale. In this context Lynn (1997: 55) finds it necessary that architects begin to design using dynamic simulation systems of urban forces and fields. Also Allen asks:

> *How to engage all the complexity and indeterminacy of the city through the methods of a discipline so committed to control, separation and unitary thinking? We thrive in cities exactly because they are places of the unexpected, products of a complex order emerging over time*
> — ALLEN 1997: 30

He suggests that architecture and planning need to recognise the limits of their ability to order the city, and that they learn from complex self-regulating orders[13] already present in the field of the city. Attention has to be shifted to systems of service. With growing recognition of the urban field architectural objects tend to loose their power – we move from the one toward the many, from objects to fields.

The field forces that are gaining power in urban development align themselves around problems such as rising unemployment, aesthetic reflexivity, the urban periphery as location for contemporary programmes, and the Europe of competing metropolitan regions. In the case of planning that has to look ten to twenty years ahead these forces increase the degree of uncertainty on top of the already existing process of rapid changes in the global economy with which cities are increasingly confronted. The possible development of the urban field becomes unpredictable and master planning as a long-term predictive tool is questioned. Instead the multiple scenario technique[14] becomes a possible new tool for urbanism. Its advantage is that it lends itself well to a strategic conversation with all actors in the city. Scenario planning is connected to the principle of learning organisations, which means that once a strategic conversation between the different members of a community is set in motion it can learn from mistakes and evolve.

---

13 Self-organised order in evolutionary systems occurs if the rules of the game are composed from the bottom up. Interacting forces at the bottom level will change the rules as the game progresses. Systems balance themselves by learning and adapting.

14 The technique of scenario planning was developed in the business world of large companies such as Shell in order to deal with uncertainty. Scenario development comes from the observation that, given the impossibility of knowing precisely how the future will play out, a good decision or strategy to adopt is one that plays well across several possible futures or scenarios.

To be able to make a more robust long-term plan, scenarios are created in plural, in such a way that each scenario diverges markedly from the others. These sets of scenarios are essentially specially constructed stories about the future, each modelling a distinct, plausible world where we might someday have to live and work. The purpose of scenario planning is to highlight the large-scale forces that push the future in different directions, and allow plans or projects to react to them. In practice, scenario thinking basically allows people to tell each other stories about how the future might work, to understand the imagination and forces behind each of them and to evaluate their credibility (Schwartz 1991). This leads to a narrative process of participation and will allow a community to find the most pleasing future scenario.

Evolutionary Decision-Making Systems

All this means an increasing demand for a notion of potential and open-ended solutions, which architecture in a traditional sense cannot provide. Buildings that can readily adapt to different and changing programmes and scenarios become necessary. Furthermore, the architectural design process will have to connect itself to an urban development process that is becoming increasingly interactive and networked. At the same time the traditional deterministic path can no longer be the method of decision-making within the architectural design process or within urban development. Existing bureaucratic and technocratic tools only allow disordered, discontinuous change, instead of ordered, continuous change – incremental change over time. Kelly points to the character of tools that continually pump in bits of change – they have an adaptive evolutionary spirit; they need a heart of change at the core of the system (Kelly 1994: 354). He defines evolutionary change that will gradually replace existing structures as follows:

> *Evolution is a structure of organised change. But it is more. Evolution is a structure of organised change which is itself undergoing change and reorganisation.*
> — KELLY 1994: 362

The genius of an evolutionary system is that it is a mechanism for generating perpetual change. Evolution is a conglomeration of many processes which form a society of evolutions. *Change changes itself.* Because new technological tools have to fit within an existing system, the process of their introduction becomes by its very nature evolutionary. New innovations even grow in a biological fashion – sprouting slowly from earlier technologies. Most evolutionary changes are biological in nature.

> *The only way for a system to evolve into something is to have a flexible structure. ... A decentralised redundant organisation can flex without distorting its function, and thus it can adapt. It can manage change. We call that growth. ... But we cannot import evolution and learning without exporting control. ... There is no control outside a self-making system.*
> — Kelly 1994: 448

Thus, urban decision making may have to abandon its linear, mechanical, and unworkable notion of control. Consequently, the icon of the Network Society, the Net, has no centre – it is a bunch of nodes or dots connected to other dots.

> *The Net is the archetype – always the same picture – displayed to represent all circuits, all intelligence, all interdependence, all things economic and social and ecological, all communications, all democracy, all groups, all large systems.*
> — Kelly 1994: 25

In this sense the Net becomes an emblem of multiples – out of it emerges 'distributed being'[15]. As a banner the Net is hard to live with, because it is a banner of non-control. A network is the least structured organisation that can be said to have any structure at all. This means decentralised control – no central planning. Control such as distributed control cannot just be implemented; it has to be grown from simple local control. Complexity must be grown from simple systems that already work. To complexity belongs divergence, but divergence needs to be kept together. A plurality of truly divergent components can only remain coherent in a network. No other arrangement – chain, pyramid, tree, circle, or hub – can contain true diversity working as a whole. This is why the network is nearly synonymous with democracy or the market.

> *A distributed, decentralised network is more a process than a thing. In the logic of the Net there is a shift from nouns to verbs. Economists now reckon that commercial*

[15] When the sum of the parts can add up to more than the parts, then the extra being (that something from nothing) is distributed among the parts. The spirit of a beehive decides as a whole when and where to move – it possesses intelligence that none of its parts does. A single honeybee brain operates with a memory of six days; the hive as a whole operates with a memory of three months, twice as long as the average bee lives. Likewise the behaviour of an economy, the thinking of a supercomputer, and the life in us are distributed over a multitude of smaller units (which themselves may be distributed). Whenever we find something from nothing, we find it arising from a field of many interacting smaller pieces. (Kelly 1994: 469)

products are best treated as though they were services. It's not what you sell a customer, it's what you do for them. It's not what something is, it's what it is connected to, what it does. Flows become more important than resources.
— Kelly 1994: 25

In the Net there are no chains of linear causality – there is only circular causality. In the realm of recursive reflections, an event is not triggered by a chain of being, but by a field of causes. Rather than cause and control being dispersed in a straight line from their origin, they spread horizontally. Control is not only distributed in space, but is blurred in time as well. In this context the development of distributed text or hypertext such as HTML (HyperText Mark-up Language) in the World Wide Web is an interesting example. Hypertext is a texture of signs that point to other signs.

The total summation of what we call knowledge or science[16] is a web of ideas pointing to, and reciprocally educating, each other. Hypertext and electronic writing accelerate that reciprocity. Networks rearrange the writing space of the printed book into a writing space many orders larger and many ways more complex than that of ink on paper ... At the same time the very shape of this network space shapes us. It is no coincidence that the postmodernists arose in tandem as the space of the network formed.
— Kelly 1994: 465–466

He then explains that in the last half-century a uniform mass market – the result of the Industrial Age – has collapsed into a network of small niches caused by the present information tide. What remains is an 'aggregation of fragments' – the only kind of whole we have. Our society has become a working pandemonium of fragments – in fact a distributed network much like the Internet itself. People in a highly connected yet deeply fragmented society can no longer rely on a central canon for guidance. In the process of connecting everything to everything else, computers elevate the power of the small player – they make room for the different. In this sense Kelly quotes Bolter[17]:

---

16 Kelly (1994, 454) makes a case for scientific knowledge as a parallel distributed system. "It has no centre, no one in control. A million heads and dispersed books hold parts of it. It too is a web, a co-evolutionary system of fact and theory interacting and influencing other facts and theories." Science can be pictured as a network of agents searching in parallel over a rugged landscape of mysteries.

17 Bolter, Jay David (1991). *Writing Space: The Computer, Hypertext, and the History of Writing.* Lawrence Erlbaum

Just as our culture is moving from the printed book to the computer, it is also in the final stages of the transition from a hierarchical social order to what we might call a 'network culture'.
— KELLY 1994: 450

In a broader historical perspective, the Network Society represents a qualitative change in the human experience (Castells 1996: 477). At the end of his *The Rise of the Network Society* Castells draws as conclusion that beyond the Modern Age and the Industrial Revolution, which saw the domination of Nature by Culture, we are entering a new stage in which Culture refers to Culture. It means that we can consider culture as its own self-organising, self-evolving system – a system setting its own agenda. Learning plus evolution is basically the recipe for culture. We clearly live in an era in which the economic has become thoroughly 'culturalised' – culture is a global business. Culture is doing business in the corporate world: global entertainment corporations such as Sony, Time Warner, Disney, Bertelsmann, whose business is the production and distribution of 'cultural' hardware and software[18] have become amongst the most powerful economic actors in the world (du Gay 1997). Further, more and more goods and services across an even wider range of sectors than entertainment can be conceived of as 'cultural' goods[19]. It has led, as we have seen, to an aestheticisation of everyday life. This process has been accompanied by the increased influence of cultural intermediaries which create identification between production and consumption by signifying cultural meaning in advertising, design and marketing. Finally, the internal life of organisations, companies or processes becomes the subject of cultural reconstruction. Culture is seen to structure the way people think, feel and act in organisations – it is a means of changing the way people conceive of and relate to the work they perform, the way they identify themselves with their organisation or environment. The production of culture cannot be divorced from the processes of work and forms of organisation – the processes of cultural production are themselves cultural phenomena as meaningful practices for people to conduct themselves by (du Gay 1997). In other words the *production of culture* is defined by specific *cultures of production*.

[18] Sony, for example, deals in consumer electronics from PCs to Walkmans, music, film, television, computer games, Time Warner and Bertelsmann additionally in print media and satellite broadcasting, but not in consumer products.

[19] Cultural goods are inscribed with particular meanings and associations and are produced and circulated to generate desire for them by consumers.

If in the Network Society the production of culture has become pervasive and its main content will be produced by new cultural industries, then the actors of these industries will define the climate or culture of production – they will have to be in control of their environment. Urban development that in future wants to attract these industries, or in other words to become a 'creative city', will have to have a distributed decision making system, it will have to operate as a complex adaptive system. Complex systems survive because they anticipate, and a transparent medium such as a wired network helps them anticipate.

BIBLIOGRAPHY

Allen, Stan (1997). From Object to Field. In *Architecture after Geometry*, Architectural Design, Vol 67, No 5/6 May-June 1997. London: Academy Editions.
Castells, Manuel (1996). *The Information Age. Economy, Society and Culture. Volume I: The Rise of the Network Society*. Oxford: Blackwell.
Du Gay, Paul (ed.) (1997) *Production of Culture / Cultures of Production*. The Open University. London: Sage.
Hall, Peter (1991). Moving Information: A Tale of Four Technologies. In Brotchie et al. (eds.) *Cities of the 21st Century: New Technologies and Spatial Systems*. London: Longman Cheshire.
Hall, Peter (1998). The Creative City in the Third Millennium. In Verwijnen, Jan and Panu Lehtovuori (eds.), *The Creative City: Cultural Industries, Urban Development and the Information Society*. Helsinki: University of Art and Design.
Kelly, Kevin (1994). *Out of Control: The New Biology of Machines*. London: Fourth Estate.
Kelly, Kevin (1997). New Roles for the New Economy, Twelve dependable principles for thriving in a turbulent world. *Wired* 5.09, September 1997.
Koolhaas, Rem (1995). *S, M, L, XL*. Rotterdam: 010 Publishers.
Koolhaas, Rem (1996). Architecture against Urbanism. In Verwijnen, Jan and Panu Lehtovuori (eds.), *Managing Urban Change*. Helsinki: University of Art and Design.
Landry, Charles, **Lesley Greene**, **François Matarasso** and **Franco Bianchini** (1996). *The Art of Regeneration: Urban Renewal through Cultural Activity*. The Round, Bournes Green, Stroud: Comedia.
Lash, Scott (1994). Reflexivity and its Doubles: Structure, Aesthetics, Community. In Beck, Ulrich, Anthony Giddens and Scott Lash, *Reflexive Modernisation*. Cambridge: Polity.
Lash, Scott and **John Urry** (1994). *Economies of Signs and Space*. London: Sage.
Lovat, Andy (1996). The Ecstasy of Urban Regeneration: Regulation of the Night-Time Economy in the Transition to a Post-Fordist City. In O'Connor Justin and Derek Wynne (eds) (1996). *From the Margins to the Centre: Cultural Production and Consumption in the Post-industrial City*. Aldershot: Arena.
Lynn, Greg (1997). An Advanced Form of Movement. In *Architecture after Geometry*, Architectural Design, Vol 67, No 5/6 May–June 1997. London: Academy Editions.
O'Connor, Justin and **Derek Wynne** (eds) (1996). *From the Margins to the Centre: Cultural Production and Consumption in the Post-industrial City*. Aldershot: Arena.
O'Connor, Justin (1999). Popular Culture, Reflexivity and Urban Change. In Verwijnen, Jan and Panu Lehtovuori (eds.), *The Creative City: Cultural Industries, Urban Development and the Information Society*. Helsinki: University of Art and Design.
Schwartz, Peter (1991). *The Art of the Long View: Planning for the Future in an Uncertain World*. New York: Doubleday.
Taylor, Ian, **Karen Evans** and **Penny Fraser** (1996). *A Tale of Two Cities: Global change, local feeling and everyday life in the North of England. A Study in Manchester and Sheffield*. London: Routledge.
Zukin, Sharon (1991). *Landscapes of Power: From Detroit to Disney World*. Berkeley: University of California Press.
Zukin, Sharon (1995). *The Cultures of Cities*. Oxford: Blackwell.

The Creative City in the Third Millennium

Peter Hall
Professor, University College London

Introduction

Throughout history, cities have been the source of innovation. They have been the places where human creativity flourished; from them came the world's great art, the fundamental advances in human thought, the great technological breakthroughs that created new industries and even entire new modes of production. And, ever since cities became large enough and complex enough to present problems of urban management, they also became urban laboratories, places that developed the solutions – technological, organizational, legal, social – to their own problems of growth.

Thus, three main kinds of urban innovation can be distinguished: cultural/intellectual; technological-productive; and technological-organizational ("urban innovation"). Since the first industrial revolution at the end of the eighteenth century, the second and third categories have become progressively more important; with the development of mega-cities, the third type assumes even greater importance. And, during the twentieth century, the first and second types of innovation have tended to fuse together. During the twenty-first, we can expect that all three kinds of innovation will do so.

This paper presents some findings from a study of urban innovation in history, now nearing conclusion. It is based on a series of urban case studies, illustrating each of the three types of innovation, extending over two millennia, but with a special stress on the last two centuries. From those findings, it concludes by speculating on the likely nature and location of urban innovation in the 21st century.[1]

[1] This paper is based on my forthcoming book *Cities in Civilisation* (London: HarperCollins 1997), a study of urban creativity in world history, where detailed evidence is presented.

The Culturally Creative City

Cities became culturally creative long before they proved very adept either at technological advance or in managing themselves effectively. From ancient Athens through Renaissance Florence to the great capital cities of modern Europe – London, Vienna, Paris, Berlin – cities enjoyed golden ages even while the majority of their citizens laboured in abject poverty, and even while most people lived in conditions of abject squalor – at least, by the standards of the late twentieth century. One question is why diverse urban societies should have set themselves this apparently odd order of priority. Another, closely related, question is whether this has anything to do with the kinds of urban societies they were.

There are some general lessons; but none that comfortably fits all the facts. All these cities were undergoing rapid and radical economic and social transformation. Athens was the first global trading emporium with a complex system of exchange arrangements; the others were all capitalist cities with strong precapitalist features: Florence and London were still guild craft cities, while Vienna and Paris had strong atelier traditions; only Berlin was a fully-fledged capitalist manufacturing city, but – just like the other two – it industrialized through state action on the continental European model. All then were cities in transition, out of the known and into new and still unknown modes of organization. All were great trading cities, and trade produced new ways of economic organization, and thus new forms of production. Economically they were aspiring world leaders (Athens, Florence, London, Berlin), or laggards (Vienna, Paris); there is no clear pattern, but all were at any rate the most advanced locations in their territories, which made them magnets for talented people to move to, and generators of wealth to use that talent.

The excess wealth was clearly crucial. Even Athens, far from rich by modern standards, had wealth to spare; the other European cases were by far the richest places in their areas, and the wealth was highly concentrated. Wealth brought individual

38 · Peter Hall

patronage, but also community patronage at the level of the city or state. It seems that the community always played a critical role in commissioning works that were too expensive, or too controversial, for the individual to afford.

All these were cities of high culture, and – after Athens – minority culture. Unequal distribution of wealth produced an aristocratic or bourgeois public with the means to support and enjoy it. But wealth did not guarantee cultural creativity; talent may have been more important. Strikingly often, recent in-migrants – sometimes from the nearby countryside, often from distant areas – provided both audience and artists. These cities were invariably cosmopolitan; they renewed themselves through new waves of immigration, bringing new cultural strains.

Because these cities were in economic transition, they were in course of transformation in social relationships, in values and in world outlook. Invariably, they were wracked by tension between conservative and radical forces. The transition to capitalism describes some of it, but it was more complex: by the nineteenth century, the richer bourgeoisie might actually become a brake on new artistic forms, and it might take a near revolutionary situation to generate the creative spark. The dissonance must be experienced and expressed by a creative group who feel themselves to some degree outside the system; because young or provincial or foreign, or because outside the established order. A creative city, one might say, needs such outsiders. They must be sufficiently connected to the mainstream that they communicate their notions to part of that wider society; that presupposes a certain fundamental schism in ideas and values. Creative cities are not likely to be stable or comfortable places; but they must not have surrendered to total disorder either. Rather, almost invariably they are places in which the established order is under prolonged challenge by the new creative groups, whether or not that challenge takes an explicitly political form.

Creative cities, as the critic Hippolyte Taine argued a century ago, thus share a certain milieu. The question is whether a Marxist explanation will work, or not: is the milieu purely a reflection of broad socio-economic forces in a particular place at a particular time, or does it spring from cultural traits that develop almost independently of the economic substructure? This is the most difficult question, not easy to resolve from the evidence. It is almost as if there is such a socio-economic explanation, but it is hardly enough to bear the weight of explaining why an Athens, a Florence, should have developed so uniquely.

Interestingly, culturally innovative cities and technologically innovative cities share some key traits: they are dynamic, wealth-generating places. But cultural cities are invariably older and more mature than technological cities; it is almost as if talents transform themselves from the hard business of life to the art of the good life.

The Technologically Innovative City

The technologically innovative cities were in every sense different. They were not generally established cities, 20th-century Tokyo excepted; they were cities somewhat on the periphery of the established world, neither right at the centre (as the culturally innovative cities were) nor right at their periphery. They were middling cities, plugged into what was happening in the world, but keeping their distance: they were emerging, upstart places, places like Manchester at the end of the eighteenth century, Glasgow in the mid-nineteenth, Berlin at the end of that century and Detroit at the beginning of the next, the San Francisco Bay Area in the mid-20th century and Tokyo towards its end.

The Japanese example apart, these case studies seem to show the continuing strength of bottom-up, individualistic innovation. The innovators were outsiders living in outsider cities. Most were middle class; though some of the early ones had little education, most were at least well grounded in basic technical skills. A surprising number were self-taught. All followed careers that taught them what they needed to know, in a related industry or field; they were well-grounded, so that their success was no accident. They all relied on strong local networks, supplying specialized skilled labour and services, and creating a climate of innovation among small firms sharing knowledge but also competing. Even when firms grew bigger, networks remained surprisingly important.

More closely analyzed, as a number of commentators have recently emphasized, in the late twentieth century there seem to be at least two, perhaps three, models of capitalism, with different attendant models of innovation: the American model of bottom-up innovation in a laissez-faire environment, and the German-Japanese model of state-guided capitalism. Following the lead of Schumpeter half a century ago, English-speaking commentators have favoured the American model. But this is unfounded, and the success of the Eastern Asian economies may well indicate the opposite. The evidence is contradictory: while the integrated model falters in the west, it proves successful so far in the east; but some Japanese observers doubt that their system can really compete on fundamental innovation. So the verdict is not in; but provisionally one might conclude that there is a general tendency toward scale, bureaucratization and state-industry relationships, which is interrupted by bursts of networking, synergy and spin-off.

The innovative places could all be called edge cities: more accurately, they were not at the centre but neither were they off the edge of the world altogether. All had some strong previous tradition that proved critical. They were not trammelled by old traditions or ways of doing things. Most had egalitarian social structures: they lacked old wealth and were not hide-bound by class; they were open societies in which careers were open to talents. They shared an ethos of self-reliance and self-achievement; they tended to have open educational systems, or at least apprenticeship systems, with a stress on the practical uses of scientific knowledge. They might well have recently acquired wealth, in the hands of adventurous people who will willing to take another risk. Many of the infant firms in these places seem to have started by catering for a local market whose characteristics they understood. It might be a consumer market, but often it was a market of related producers; in this case, there might be a chain of interactions in which the demand spurred producers to innovative solutions to overcome problems.

However much these cities had elements in common, they were also very different places: Berlin in 1870 does not have many obvious similarities to Detroit in 1900. And some are more difficult to interpret than others. Los Angeles seemed to have little going for it in 1905; yet once the process took over, for whatever proximate cause, the agglomeration economies were irresistible. Tokyo was not at all an edge city, though perhaps in 1868 it seemed so in relation to Kyoto, the old capital, and to the west.

Further, in common with Berlin down to 1918, it certainly lacked a fluid social structure. But both, like the others, seem to have offered educational pathways to people of ambition and ability.

Primary innovation does not seem to have been crucial, indeed of decreasing importance: what was important was the downstream innovation, tuned to the market. New entrants like Ford could achieve this; so could established Tokyo corporations. Local demand helped here, but it does not provide a satisfactory total explication. One can say that there was something else: continuing ability to innovate, to ally technical knowledge to the changing demands of the marketplace. Tokyo has proved outstanding in this regard, and is thus one of the outstanding innovative milieux of all time. Though external venture capital was important, some places could do without it: Tokyo, with its integrated banking-industrial system, is again the example.

Geography relates to industrial organization. Theoretically, as examples like GE and IBM show, the giant bureaucratized corporations can exist on a self-contained basis far distant from the city. Yet the Japanese corporations continue to lock into Tokyo and its surrounds, apparently fearing the consequences if they move R&D too far from the city.

The Creative-Innovative City

Finally, the twentieth century offers two and very interesting examples of a new development: the development of a commercial mass popular culture through the injection of new technology, allowing it to be simultaneously distributed and sold worldwide. Both examples are American. The first was the creation of the motion picture industry in Los Angeles around 1920. The second was the birth of rock music in Memphis, Tennessee, in the mid-1950s.

Both these places were quite unlike any previous centre of cultural creativity. They were very distant, upstart places: Los Angeles was an underdeveloped city in an underdeveloped state, far distant from all previous centres of wealth and culture; Memphis was a regional capital serving an impoverished rural area that preserved the strongest precapitalist traits in all the United States. Both generated a new commercial art, buoyed by the consumer power of a new mass market: essentially, they commodified and mass-produced art, just as Ford mass-produced cars or, earlier, other American companies had pioneered the mass production of guns and sewing machines and typewriters. It could probably only have happened in America, where these earlier models existed. And both illustrated the importance of bottom-up generation of innovation through new entrepreneurs who were quintessential outsiders: the Jewish movie moguls of Hollywood and the local southern recording studio and radio station proprietors of Memphis. There was one crucial difference: Hollywood represented an immigrant culture in every sense, derived from New York which remained the financial basis of the studio system, whereas Memphis represented true local folk cultures which finally triumphed over the New York Tin Pan Alley system.

The marriage of popular culture and technology has continued apace in the late twentieth century, with network television, the compact disc and the promise of multimedia. It has interestingly been accompanied by conflicting tendencies in the organization of the media industries: on the one hand the collapse of the old integrated studios and the rise of the independent producers, on the other the development, through takeovers, of integrated electronics and communications companies in the 1980s. It is too early to see clearly the impact of multimedia on the entire system. In any case, the cultural industries remain unique because they continue to combine mass production and distribution with the continued importance of the live performance; their geography is thus a complex one, in which mass production continues to be concentrated in a few cities (Los Angeles, London) while live performances are distributed in major cities around the globe. I want to come back to this point in a little while.

Urban Innovation

Urban innovation, the third kind of major innovation, is subtly different in kind from the two varieties so far considered. It consists in cities attempting, generally through public administration but also through private enterprise, to solve the emerging problems caused by their own growth: water supply and waste disposal, traffic and transport, police and criminal justice, provision for the poor and destitute. None of these problems is unique to large cities. The point is that in such large cities, roughly

those with one million and more people, they attain a new dimension of complexity: local wells and cesspits no longer suffice, people have to move over long distances, crime can no longer be handled by informal means, destitution can no longer be managed within the extended family. In every case, cities have to respond through organizational innovation, and often through technological innovation as well. So the places that make urban innovations are usually the biggest and most complex places of their time: cities like ancient Rome, London or Paris in the nineteenth century, or New York in the early twentieth century and Los Angeles at the mid-century, or London again in the 1980s; though we can legitimately include a much smaller city like Stockholm or indeed Helsinki, which made important urban social innovations after World War Two.

Such cities make urban innovations because they have to (though not all cities that need to succeed in doing so, as twentieth-century history plainly shows). This means that they have reached a certain threshold of size and complexity. Rome, London, Paris and New York were among the three biggest cities of the world when they first made urban innovations; with the exception of Rome (estimated at 650 000 in 100 AD), London (861 000 in 1801) and Stockholm (889 000 people in 1950) all had one million or more people within their city boundaries. However, Los Angeles was the 27th city in 1925 and Stockholm the 80th in 1950, so rank or size in itself is no guarantee of innovative power.

What may matter more is the speed of growth. London had doubled in size in the century before 1800, Paris had grown by two and a half times in the century before 1850; New York had doubled in the quarter century before 1900 (albeit with a major boundary change); Los Angeles grew ten times in the first quarter of the twentieth century. Such cities had to cope quite suddenly with a drastic increase in the scale and complexity of urban organization. They had the capacity to do so, because all were in countries that were highly evolved economically and technically. Further, because they were well networked both nationally and internationally, there were only minor barriers to importing knowledge from other places. Knowledge of urban innovations like water aqueducts, collector sewers, streetcars, subways and motorways all diffused very rapidly, though there were significant differences in the rate of takeup from city to city; European cities, in particular, were relatively slow in absorbing transport improvements like the telephone, the electric streetcar and the urban motorway.

Demographic growth often went hand in hand with economic growth, if only because aggregate growth was almost bound to increase in line with population. That meant buoyant demand for new services and a supply of surplus capital to fund infrastructure, whether out of municipal coffers or out of private pockets. There seems to be a relationship between urban innovation and long waves of economic growth: London was highly innovative at the start of the second Kondratieff long wave (1842–97), New York and Los Angeles at the start of the third (1897–1954), Stockholm at the start of the fourth (1954–); Paris fits less well, though its major urban investments were all made before the crash of 1873, which ushered in the end of the growth phase of the Second Kondratieff. Further, such periods of growth by definition brought the immigration of talented and energetic individuals, some of whom at least were major agents: Edwin Chadwick, architect of so many of the London reforms, was a Mancunian by birth, Harry Chandler in Los Angeles was an easterner, though other key players – Haussmann in Paris, Veiller in New York – were native-born sons of their cities.

There is however a basic distinction: Rome, London and Paris were unambiguously at the centres of their respective worlds, New York was the emerging commercial centre of the most dynamic part of the world of 1900. But Los Angeles in 1925, as already remarked in discussing Hollywood, was by any measure at the edge of the American urban system; and Stockholm was a relatively small city on the periphery of the European system. Los Angeles, a city that combined political conservatism with maverick capitalism and eccentric philosophies, seems to have been a very special case, a frontier city that had thrown off most of the trammels of older cultures; Stockholm may have been an equally special case, a Protestant society in course of secularization, in which particular ideas of social responsibility developed in response to the depression of the 1930s.

Finally, London represents an equally specific development: its regeneration in the 1980s represented the quintessence of the Thatcherite vision in an urban context, and that vision represented a kind of cultural counter-revolution, a systematic attempt

to demolish the established institutions of British life and to replace them by a return to unfettered entrepreneurial capitalism. But equally, the Docklands enterprise represented the idea that property development in itself could equate with substantive economic regeneration, as if the one would axiomatically produce the other: an assumption that many were to question, especially after the great crash at the end of the 1980s. Wrong or right or partially right, this view is consistent with the Thatcherite notion that Britain as a manufacturing economy was largely finished and that the aim was to rebuild a new service economy on the ruins of the old. And this belief, never as consistently expressed as in Britain, nevertheless formed a belief underlying much radical-right rethinking, worldwide, in the 1980s.

One can conclude that, while earlier urban innovations were directly driven by hard physical problems and had an element of the inevitable, more recently innovation has come from a variety of more specific conditions. Nevertheless it remains a fact that, once made, innovations tend to provide some kind of model to the rest of the world. Stockholm in the 1950s became the model of the socially-conscious city, whose urban design solutions were imitated in every city; Los Angeles in the 1960s came to be seen as model of a new kind of urban society, one based on style and mobility and hedonistic conspicuous consumption; London in the 1980s, even while it repelled some observers, became almost a television soap opera parody of itself, the city driven by creation of new forms of wealth and power against a background of a new high-tech urban landscape. All these urban images have powerfully persisted even while the attempts at imitation have often collapsed in failure and recrimination; perhaps urban archetypes do not lend themselves so easily to imitation.

The Next Innovative Wave

The next time round the driver, as so many times before, will be technology. But not in any simple or determinist way: new technology shapes new opportunities, to create new industries and transform old ones, to present new ways of organising firms or entire societies, to transform the potential for living; but it does not compel these changes, and indeed in some societies and in some places the resulting opportunities may never be seized. There will always be leaders and laggards. Just as Manchester led the way at the end of the eighteenth century, Detroit at the end of the nineteenth, Los Angeles and the San Francisco Bay Area in the middle of the twentieth, so surely will new cities blaze a trail in the coming century.

We can be reasonably certain that there is now a very fundamental burst of technological innovation, which will precipitate a new economic upswing, the start of the fifth Kondratieff[2]; but it may be more even than that. The essence of the present change is that, as Manuel Castells has put it, we are moving from an industrial era to a informational era, from an era in which most people worked to make or handle goods, to one in which most of us will make and manipulate and transmit and exchange information.[3] This has been cumulative: but at the end of the twentieth century the process has reached a new and distinctive stage.

2 Hall and Preston 1988

3 Castells 1989

In the mid-1990s, however, almost every observer is agreed that something really new is in train: the question must be whether it represents the basis of a fifth Kondratieff long wave, or a fundamental evolution of capitalism itself from an industrial to an informational era, or – as seems likely – both at once. Most identify it as the advent of the so-called information superhighway, which – in Bill Gates's words – will transform our culture as dramatically as Gutenberg's press did the Middle Ages.[4] But, as Gates himself argues, underlying this is something even more fundamental: the fact that almost all information will be digital.[5] This means that there will soon be a critical mass of pervasive digital communications, available to most offices and homes around the world, coupled with the ability to store and manipulate many different forms of information in a common digital form, and with very small yet very powerful devices for processing, display and communications.[6]

4 Gates 1995: 9

5 Gates 1995: 21

6 Taylor 1995: 42

The creation of this system will be one of the great pieces of infrastructural construction in history, paralleling the railways of the 1830s and 1840s, the metros and subways of the 1890s and 1900s, and the motorways and freeways of the 1950s and 1960s; and its effects will be equally momentous. Yet what will be crucial, as before in history, is not the basic infrastructure, but the structure of services that the infrastructure generates[7]: information businesses such as tele-medicine and tele-health care, tele-education and tele-learning, online information services, electronic publishing, financial services, trading and brokering, tele-shopping, entertainment of

7 Goddard 1992: 179

all kinds (film, video, theatre, music, multimedia pop, animation, virtual reality, games), electronic sports and competitions and virtual reality expressions, security and surveillance, earth resources information, environmental monitoring and control, digital imaging and photography, data mining and processing.[8]

8 GB Office of Science and Technology 1995b: 31; Taylor 1995: 48–49

Education is perhaps the most obvious of these applications: information technology will not destroy the teaching profession, as some fear, but will change it beyond recognition, by allowing teachers to produce high-quality lessons to suit the needs of individual pupils, as multi-media presentations allow students to pace their own learning. Teachers will thus find themselves performing new roles: as "guides" or tutors; as "communicator/interpreters" on TV; as "scholar/interpreters", turning research into teaching material, and as "assemblers", packaging this material into products; all working in teams, on the model set in the 1960s by the UK's Open University.[9]

9 Hague 1994: 12–13; Gates 1995: 185

Healthcare will be similarly transformed, as physicians and consultants and nurses learn new roles.[10] Similarly with other professions: information and communications technology could take over routine functions in law and accountancy and medicine, leaving specialists for the higher-level tasks; higher-level consultancy, which has a training element, will operate very like education.[11]

10 Harrison 1993

11 Hague 1994: 13–14

The Multimedia Revolution

The biggest single group of applications will arise in the media, where the digital-fibre optic revolution will generate virtually unlimited capacity to send moving images into a computerized box in the home, whether TV or PC: multichannel digital television almost immediately, interactive broadcasting in the future. Nicholas Negroponte forecasts that "broadcasting" will be replaced by "broadwatching": each individual will pick what he or she wants from cables full of digital information. But Nick Colchester questions whether there really will be enough good-quality information to carry all this: more than ever, customers will trust good-quality brand names.[12]

12 Colchester 1995; Negroponte 1995

New firms will result: already, some key companies are "a motley collection of young companies, university students and entrepreneurs. Netscape Communications, started in 1994, rules the Internet software market; Cisco Systems (1987) and

Sun Microsystems (1982) sell the most hardware ... Almost anything that made a difference on the Internet was produced by people whom the corporate world might consider nobodies."[13]

[13 Anderson 1995: 5]

And this will continue: as The Economist has put it:

> ... "killer applications" will probably not come from boffins. Instead, they will come from a new breed of high-tech bohemians – call them techno-bohos – who combine computer skills with story-telling and/or artistic flair.
> — ANON 1993

They are straddling a fundamental human divide long thought unstraddlable: between what Liam Hudson christened Contrary Imaginations, the divergent imagination of the artist and the convergent imagination of the scientist-technician; digital film production, one of the fastest-growing of the new applications, is a prime example. Significantly, it is clustering both in Los Angeles, in an arc between the old Hollywood studios and the ocean, and in the San Francisco Bay Area, both in Silicon Valley – hence Siliwood – and in San Francisco[14]; but New York's Silicon Alley is likewise a new phenomenon, arising from the fact that "the city has always attracted arty types"[15], and the city is the home of media conglomerates like Sony, Hearst, Bertelsmann and Time Warner, who lack the expertise themselves. Advertising houses provide a pool of graphic designers, while New York University is winning a reputation for turning out multimedia talent.

[14 Scott 1995]
[15 Tran 1995]

There are two critical and difficult questions here. The first is whether it is even possible to create a single global media and advertising market. It is not even certain that it could be done for Europe, where global marketing would involve the dissolution of old cultures and identities and their replacement by a standard "European consumer": it is unclear that such a European audience exists for every kind of programming. The second is the nature of the new "killer applications": as with the first tentative experiments with movies a century ago, no one knows what these might be.

The Death of Distance

The question for urbanists is the effect of all this on the geography of production and collective consumption. The promise is of a new world of information, available to order at the touch of a button. Currently, the diffusion is highly uneven: a system, that in theory could be available in the far reaches of Wyoming or New Mexico, is almost uniquely available in midtown Manhattan.[16] But that will not last: what is in prospect, in consequence of this multiple technical revolution, is the process described by Frances Cairncross:

> *The death of distance will mean that any activity that relies on a screen or a telephone can be carried out anywhere in the world. Services as diverse as designing an engine, monitoring a security camera, selling insurance or running a secretarial paging service will become as easily exportable as car parts or refrigerators.*
> — CAIRNCROSS 1995: 39

Or, as Bill Gates puts it:

> *There will be a day, not far distant, when you will be able to conduct business, study, explore the world and its cultures, call up any great entertainment, make friends, attend neighbourhood markets, and show pictures to distant relatives – without leaving your desk or armchair. You won't leave your network connection behind at the office or in the classroom. It will be more than an object you carry or an appliance you purchase. It will be your passport to a new, mediated way of life.*
> — GATES 1995: 4–5

Theoretically, then, it should become as easy to produce or consume services in any place as in any other place: the world becomes a uniform accessibility surface. The experts think so[17], and it is the experience of previous technological breakthroughs, like the telephone and the car; the information superhighway will simply take the trend to its logical conclusion. Some kinds of activity – routine clerical work, higher education, shopping – could be conducted remotely, in the home or in local workstations, via teleworking or distance learning or teleshopping. But the critical question is whether this will finally produce the long-predicted death of the city; as William Mitchell puts it:

> *The Net negates geometry ... it is fundamentally and profoundly aspatial. It is nothing like the Piazza Navona or Copley Square ... The Net is ambient – nowhere in particular but everywhere at once.*
> — MITCHELL 1995: 8

This "City of Bits" has no geographical roots; it exists purely in cyberspace.[18]

[18] Mitchell 1995: 94, 160

But the question remains: will this mean the end of the traditional city? The answer is that it almost certainly will not: as in the past, technological change will bring about not a general dispersal, but a resorting of the map. Those activities capable of being performed efficiently from decentralized locations will move out to back offices, as already seen for the past three decades; some may even move to homes or local workstations, where they may also be semi-casualized. But other activities will remain concentrated in face-to-face activity centres, though not always in their present locations: growth and decentralization within large metropolitan areas will produce a polycentric pattern of regional dispersion and local reconcentration, already observable in the "Edge Cities" developing around London, New York, San Francisco and Tokyo.

A critical element in this pattern is the nature of the dynamic leading-edge activities and their resulting locational needs. The almost certain growth drivers are of course all informational: they combine artistic and intellectual creativity with technological innovativeness, on the model first created in Hollywood between 1915 and 1940, but now replicated on an immeasurably larger scale through the digital revolution. They include multimedia and broadband telecommunications as the basic platform; arts, culture and entertainment, in both live and broadcast versions; the media, both print and electronic; educational and health services; tourism and personal services; management generally, especially command and control functions; high-level financial services, involving judgement and information and the capacity to innovate; and associated specialized business services ranging from law, accountancy, advertising and public relations to architecture, engineering, management and design. It is significant that these are precisely the functions peculiarly associated with the highest-level global cities, London, New York, Tokyo and their immediate competitors; and, just as manufacturing and routine information processing diffuses both nationally and globally, so do these high-order functions appear to concentrate ever more fiercely, in what has been called a new division of labour by process.[19]

19 Castells 1989; Sassen 1991; Hall 1995 GB Government Office for London 1996

These economic drivers are closely related and even overlapping: museums and concert halls and theatres are both cultural and part of tourism; conferences are educational, often include entertainment and are part of tourism. Traditionally, they have all involved face-to-face contact, and so enjoy what the economists call agglomeration economies, both in production and in consumption (which may be in one and the same place, as with the live performing arts, or tourism); and these economies tend to cause them to cluster in cities, generally in their centres. This may seem contradictory, because – as repeatedly emphasized in this paper – all or most of them are about to be transformed through electronic information technology. Multimedia will make all forms of entertainment and information instantly available; distance learning and remote medical diagnosis should reduce the need for agglomeration; theoretically, shares can now be traded anywhere. But this simplistic logic ignores two considerable complications.

First, the genesis and manufacture of the basic electronic product will involve agglomeration – and often, if previous high-technology industry provides any guide, quite extreme agglomeration, because of the importance of networking in the development of innovative products: witness the recent histories of Silicon Valley and Tokyo. Multimedia follow the same pattern: as already observed, they seem to be locating in the centres of established cities like New York, San Francisco and London as well as in newer (but also well-established) high-technology enclaves like Silicon Valley or the old "Aerospace Alley" of Los Angeles. This suggests that the new products may be born in more than one kind of innovative milieu: both in traditional city centres, because they are and will be the centres of artistic creativity (London, Paris, New York, San Francisco, Tokyo); and in specialized technopoles, often university-based (Cambridge, England; Cambridge, Massachusetts; Berkeley and Stanford, California; Kyoto), sometimes artificially created (Sophia Antipolis, Tsukuba); and entertainment centres (Hollywood).

Second, as observed in all human experience since the invention of the telephone, the increasing use of electronic media may paradoxically increase the need and the incentive for face-to-face contact, as when distance learning is followed by live seminars, or video viewing by visits to live concerts or theatres. And the relationship can paradoxically be the other way round, as where urban tourists visit museums of virtual reality. Consider the fact that during the third and fourth Kondratieffs, when information technology was first developed and then diffused throughout the world, no reduction in travel or face-to-face contact was ever observed; on the contrary, innovations in telecommunications were always parallelled by innovations in transport technology: thus, between 1880 and 1910, the telephone by the commuter railway and the metropolitan subway; between 1920 and 1940, the radio by the automobile and the aeroplane; between 1950 and 1970, television and the transistor radio by the motorway and the jet aeroplane. The traffic graphs – local telephone and urban rail traffic in the 1900s, broadcasting and car travel in the 1920s, long-distance telephone traffic and international air traffic in the 1960s – always marched together.[20] Further, the urban impacts were contrary, almost contradictory: homes and local services diffused, but central nodes were if anything strengthened. Los Angeles from the 1920s provides the exception; but, even there, the city retained a unique magnetism: the change was only that, instead of one primary downtown node, there were several.

20 Graham and Marvin 1996: 262

And the same will surely be true this time: places with a unique buzz, a unique fizz, a special kind of energy, will prove more magnetic than ever for the production of products and above all the performance of services. Even William Mitchell, in his argument for the existence of a new kind of cybercity, agrees:

> *Does development of national and international information infrastructures, and the consequent shift of social and economic activity to cyberspace, mean that existing cities will simply fragment and collapse? Or does Paris have something that telepresence cannot match? Does Rome have an answer to Neuromancer? Most of us would bet our bottom bits that the reserves of resilience and adaptability that have*

> *allowed great cities to survive* (in changed form) *the challenges of industrialization and the automobile will similarly enable them to adapt to the bitsphere.*
> — MITCHELL 1995: 169

These traditional places are also invariably the preferred residences of the high-consuming wealthy populations who set trends and guide tastes; thus they become the logical centres of conspicuous consumption and of the high-touch production that caters to it – the fashion and design industries of London, Paris, or Milan, which increasingly attract an international clientele. They also tend to have concentrations of historic buildings, significant museums and galleries, and charming ancient residential quarters, making them attractive to well-heeled cosmopolitan residents and tourists. These advantages are cumulative and mutually reinforcing, subject only to the rule that mass tourism brings crowding and pollution, eroding the very qualities that made these cities attractive in the first place.

Therefore, the rule seems to be that even if the total volume or value of electronic product increases faster than that of direct-experience product, the latter may nevertheless grow impressively: witness for instance the explosive growth of the worldwide conference business[21]. The strong probability is that even in an age when cultural renaissance comes out of electronic technology, cities and their cores will retain their unique attraction for a wide range of activities that require face-to-face contact for production or consumption, or both. The risk is that, side by side with this, there will be continued decentralization of other activities from the middle and outer city, leaving acute problems of polarization: affluent islands may find themselves surrounded by seas of persistent poverty and social malaise. This surely is one of the critical questions now needing to be addressed in strategic urban thinking.

21 Summers 1995

REFERENCES

Anderson, C. (1995). The Internet: The Accidental Superhighway. *The Economist*, 1 July.
Anon (1993). The Tangled Webs they Weave. *The Economist*, 16 October.
Cairncross, F. (1995) Telecommunications: The Death of Distance. *The Economist*, 30 September.
Castells, M. (1989). *The Informational City: Information Technology, Economic Restructuring and the Urban-Regional Process*. Oxford: Basil Blackwell.
Colchester, N. (1995). Great Medium, Shame about the Message. *The Independent*, 29 May.
Gates, W. (1995). *The Road Ahead*. London: Viking.
GB Government Office for London (1996). *Four World Cities: A Comparative Analysis of London, Paris, New York and Tokyo*. London: Llewelyn Davies Planning.
GB Office of Science and Technology (1995). *Progress through Partnership: Technology Report Foresight Report 8: IT and Electronics*. London: HMSO.
Goddard, J.B. (1992). New Technology and the Geography of the UK Information Economy. In: Robins, K. (ed.) *Understanding Information Business, Technology and Geography*, 178–201. London: Belhaven.
Graham, S., Marvin, S. (1996). *Telecommunications and the City: Electronic Spaces, Urban Places*. London: Routledge.
Hague, D. (1994). *Push Button Professionals*. Demos, 4/94, 12–15.
Hall, P. (1995). Towards a General Urban Theory. In: Brotchie, J., Batty, M., Blakely, E., Hall, P., Newton, P. (eds.) *Cities in Competition: Productive and Sustainable Cities for the 21st Century*, 3–31. Melbourne: Longman Australia.
Hall, P., Preston, P. (1988). *The Carrier Wave: New Information Technology and the Geography of Innovation, 1846–2003*. London: Unwin Hyman.
Harrison, B. (1993). Is there a Doctor on the Screen? *Financial Times*, 29 June.
Jackson, T. (1995). Public Libraries RIP. *Financial Times*, 1 May.
Mitchell, W.J. (1995). *City of Bits: Space, Place, and the Infobahn*. Cambridge, Mass.: MIT Press.
Negroponte, N. (1995). *Being Digital*. London: Hodder & Stoughton.
Sassen, S. (1991). *The Global City: London, New York, Tokyo*. Princeton: Princeton U.P.
Scott, A.J. (1995). *From Silicon Valley to Hollywood: Growth and Development of the Multimedia Industry in California*. Los Angeles: University of California, Los Angeles, Lewis Center for Regional Policy Studies. [Working Paper 13].
Summers, D. (1995). International Conferences and Exhibitions: Showing Signs of Recovery. *Financial Times*, 22 February.
Taylor, J. (1995). The Networked Home: Domestication of Information. *Journal of the Royal Society of Arts*, April, 41–53.
Tran, M. (1995). Big Apple Gains Electronic Core. *The Guardian*, 19 June.

ASPECTS OF THE CREATIVE CITY

The Creative City or Redesigning Society

BERT MULDER

Information Advisor, Dutch Parliament

The cities are the heartland of our civilisation – the centres of a society that is in a process of transformation. This means that at the end of the 20th century the centres for social and cultural change are the cities and their metropolitan regions. My hypothesis is that the 'creative city' serves as a metaphor for the shaping of these changes. First of all the city becomes the source of change in society, and in this sense the creative city will manifest the power with which people transform themselves. But the notion of the creative city also embodies the process of the changing city itself – the search for new policies, interventions and programmes to co-ordinate the developments that are starting to replace the current forms of government and control[1].

In both cases there is a threat of becoming overtaken by these new activities – thus the dynamics of the situation need to be identified. Further, the tools and methods to unlock the potential of these dynamics also need to be developed. This article will attempt to outline the larger context of these different developments, examine them from the perspective of the Information Society, and introduce the 'domains of creativity' in the city. It will show that each of these domains is changing, and attempt to identify ways of using information and technology to structure the processes of ongoing change in a creative way. It will further attempt to explain the 'creative city' as a city on the brink of the Information Age and understand the city as a way for people to organise themselves. The article will particularly try to outline the patterns of

[1] See also Peter Hall's contribution in this publication: *The Creative City in the Third Millennium* (p. 36)

development that can help the different actors in the city to be creative within this process of ongoing change.

Domains of Change in the Creative City

First I will suggest how to understand 'creativity' in relationship to change. Creativity is clearly different from ordinary change. It may result in change, but is not synonymous with it. Creativity differs in the sense that it includes a constructive element. For the sake of clarity, I propose to define creativity as *'inspired' change that increases the quality of life* – creativity is only useful if a new quality embodying added value is the outcome of the process of change. Further, I propose to understand the city as a way for people to organise themselves – as a society in which people coexist through networking, developing their skills and co-ordinating their activities in different spheres of life. Change in the creative city will challenge the following domains:

- business & education
- government
- culture
- education
- the citizen

At the end of the 20th century, because of the increasing complexity of society, a transformation of each of these domains is taking place. If, following our definition of creativity, the 'creative city' seeks inspired change to enhance the quality of life, a synergy between all these domains will become necessary. Attending solely to an isolated, independent domain will not help. We need to create a context in which we can deal with the combined effect of these domains.

Complexity of Context

Since the 1990s, complexity has increasingly become a part of our existence. Not only in the sense of ever-faster technological development – the power of computers is growing exponentially, doubling in less than 18 months[2]. If we think what this means, we realise that the process of change has not even really started yet – we will have to completely transform ourselves, because as we shall see later, these exponen-

2 Moore's Law states that the power of computers doubles every 12–18 months. This means that in 5–7 years the computers will be 32 times faster and since we are concerned with cities, we have a much longer time frame to consider. So counting onward the pace becomes 64, 128, 256, 512 and 1024 times faster after 10–15 years. This means that the simple computing power of a PC and its networking possibilities will then be a thousand times faster than today.

THE END OF THE 20TH CENTURY

COMPLEXITY

PEOPLE
TECHNOLOGY
INFORMATION
TRANSPORTATION
COMMUNICATION

tial developments will cause all parts of life to converge and bring people into networks. But also social, political, intellectual and psychological developments show increasing speed, creating at once risks and opportunities. Co-ordinating this multiplicity of developments is becoming an increasingly daunting task. Sociologists such as Ulrich Beck (1992) describe these developments as aspects of the 'risk society' – we are sidetracked by outer appearances and seem unable to integrate the many different factors into a meaningful whole. The traditional infrastructures are crumbling and the bureaucratic organisations seem rather to hinder development than facilitate it. The creative city will have to search for patterns, models and modes of organisation that provide a renewed vigour and a strong basis for the future. In order to develop this theme I shall introduce the following notions as structural components for change:

- population growth
- the phases of change
- information
- networks
- heterarchy
- reflection

These notions will be first be described and then later applied to the domains of change in the city that I mentioned earlier: government, business, culture, education and the citizen.

Population Growth as a Source of Change

In general the definition of a problem is determined by its context. In what context then do we place the multiplicity of new developments to enable us to understand their meaning and judge their value? How did the changes that we face today come about? In their book *World Population and Human Values* Jonas and Jonathan Salk (1981) comment on the development of the world's population. They show that during the last few centuries we have experienced a worldwide growth of population from millions to billions. This sudden growth, following at least 8 000 years of population stability, is the context of the current changes we are experiencing. An exploding population leads to increased interaction between people and thus to more development, leaving us every day with a world more complex than the day before. The authors continue to explain that, historically, human civilisation has experienced a whole series of restructuring attempts, in which it has tried to adjust itself to a new situation. These processes of restructuring are characterised by a phase of disintegration, when older structures are no longer effective, and later reintegration as we find new patterns to organise ourselves. At the end of the 20th century we find ourselves in such a phase of reintegration. Salk and Salk see this happening to both developed and developing nations, in the arts as well as the sciences, and in both large-scale and small-scale issues. In other words, all of the experiences of disintegration over the past 500 years are now being reintegrated. If we talk about the 'creative city', we have to realise that the force for these almost autonomous changes originates from a larger context of societal transformation.

The Phases of Change

What happens when society lives through a transformation of this kind? The Dutch professor van Praag has identified the following sequence of five phases or revolutions that generally seem to characterise the process of large-scale developments:

- a methodological phase, 17th century
- a scientific phase, 18th century
- a technical phase, 19th century
- a social phase and, finally,
- a cultural phase, 20th century

Applying this to history allows us to understand the forces that are responsible for the changes of the Information Age that we witness today. In other words, we can trace the origins of information back to the 17th century, to Newton and Leibniz, who introduced a methodological revolution. Thus we come to the following sequence: a methodological revolution in the 17th century is followed by a scientific one in the 18th, a technical one in the 19th, a social one in the 20th, and finally by a cultural revolution in the coming 21st century.

After the change in thinking, for which Newton and Leibniz were responsible, their initial ideas were developed into a body of consistent knowledge – science. This science formed the basis for the technical development that created the Industrial Age. The agricultural society was transformed by industrial technology. Social change followed and established our Welfare Society. Today we see the development of material and social changes creating new modes of expression and perception towards a cultural revolution. The sequence of these revolutions seems self-evident – it points out today's situation as a highly cultural one. Thus culture will play a central role in coming developments. In urban development the first signs of that role are becoming visible in the importance that cultural programmes and urban culture have recently gained for the growth of cities (Bianchini 1996).

Seen in such a large context it becomes evident that the pace of development is surprisingly autonomous in character and thus cannot really be influenced by money, local politics or technology. On the contrary, money, politics and technology will be forced to adjust to the development and transform themselves. The following chapters – information, networks, heterarchy and reflection – may be understood as ingredients of the transformation that is taking place. Together they determine the dynamics of the situation and affect different domains of the city.

Information

INFORMATION
COMMUNICATION
COORDINATION
COOPERATION

In fact all developments are characterised by the same underlying structure: they are affected by changes in information. The word 'information' is often used as if it refers to something real and solid, something that can be collected, stored, worked with, moved around and even digested. It can be sold and owned, stolen and retrieved. But that view of information is somewhat one-sided and deprives us of its real meaning. We need to look at information more in terms of *what it does* than what it is. In this sense the most important influence of information is that it creates patterns of interdependence. Furthermore, all information is meant for communication. And when two parties communicate, they influence each other, co-ordinating their actions. As this co-ordination increases, its action it starts to create a set pattern, which basically means that it evolves into co-operation. Consequently, this leads us to accept the fact that information is not a neutral tool, but that it will rather lead people towards increasing interdependence. In other words, information implies communication, which leads to co-ordination and thus to co-operation.

Referring to the increasing sense of complexity of society at the end of the 20th century as described earlier, the growing use of information technology can be explained as society organising itself increasingly through patterns of co-operation. Therefore, in the field of information technology 'communities of trust' are increasingly becoming an issue (Fukuyama 1996). For example, payment systems on the Internet are likely to not only benefit the present economy, but beyond that will provide local communities with a tool to organise themselves better through creating a local economy. Thus the consequences of the use of information technology are effectively creating a new and vibrant infrastructure of the 'creative city' that will organise and support its community.

Networks as the Structure of Organisations

Today's organisational structure is characterised by networking. The patterns of co-operation that we met before operate via networks. Although the term 'network' is often used in a narrow technological sense, it has almost universal applicability. Networks might be called the 'architecture of information'. Simply put, networks consist of nodes and the relations between them. Weak networks have simple nodes with a small amount of communication between them, while strong networks have developed nodes and intensive communication. When networks grow in strength, as we see happening in the information society, we meet two seemingly opposite developments: an increasing autonomy of the nodes and therefore a disintegration of the whole, while on the other hand a growing interdependency between the nodes, which causes an integration of certain groups of nodes. In this sense the 'network' becomes a general organisational model that can be recognised in all domains of society, be it technology, politics, business or education. The creative city will therefore be characterised by a decomposition and later recomposition of the existing ways of organising itself.

INDIVIDUALIZATION AND INTEGRATION
AUTONOMY INTERDEPENDENCY
SELF-SUFFICIENCY SYMBIOSIS

HIERARCHY

EXPLICIT ORDER
COERCIVE LEADERSHIP
SHARED ORDERS

HETERARCHY

IMPLICIT ORDER
LEADING BY SERVING
SHARED VISION
STABILITY THROUGH
FLEXIBILITY

From Hierarchy to Heterarchy

Networks have different forms. Stable networks usually become hierarchies: the communication is predictable and fixed and nodes become specialised in doing more of the same thing. Specialised nodes agglomerate in layers and groups and develop their own communications. Power is concentrated in a few nodes at the top – other nodes will have less power or none at all. What must be done can be communicated clearly and explicitly. The activities and their results are predictable and can be planned in advance. More flexibly organised networks have nodes that are more equal and their relationships tend to be more diverse. Any of the nodes may co-ordinate the others, thereby pooling the resources of the whole network. We call these flexible networks 'heterarchies'. In constantly shifting configurations they co-ordinate their activities and adjust to new needs. Power is distributed between the nodes; order is unfolding and implicit. But a shared vision needs to be developed. All nodes must be able to sustain the vision as partners and constantly review it. In order to deal with the increasing complexity of today's world, networks have to become more flexible. Consequently, organisations and their activities increasingly show signs of heterarchy.

Thus the creative city of the future will be a city of heterarchical networks, where development is maintained in constant dialogue between partners whose responsibility and position shift according to the problem at hand. Next to the well-known relationships between the city, business, the citizen and the financial world there will be new partners, new ways of organising, and therefore new futures.

Reflexivity

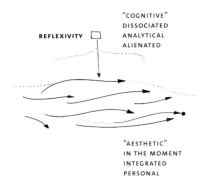

REFLEXIVITY

"COGNITIVE"
DISSOCIATED
ANALYTICAL
ALIENATED

"AESTHETIC"
IN THE MOMENT
INTEGRATED
PERSONAL

Reflection is a reaction to change, which tends to break up existing structures. We deal with that change and its disturbance by reflecting on it. As change destroys older patterns we try to look for a new meaning and create new contexts. In their book *Economies of Signs and Space*, Lash and Urry (1994) describe what happens in a world of increasing change and introduce the notion of 'reflexivity'. According to Lash and Urry we deal with change in two different ways: either in a distanced, analysing, theoretical and judging way or in a participating, synthesising, personal and integrating, and according to them aesthetic, way. Lash and Urry identify these two different

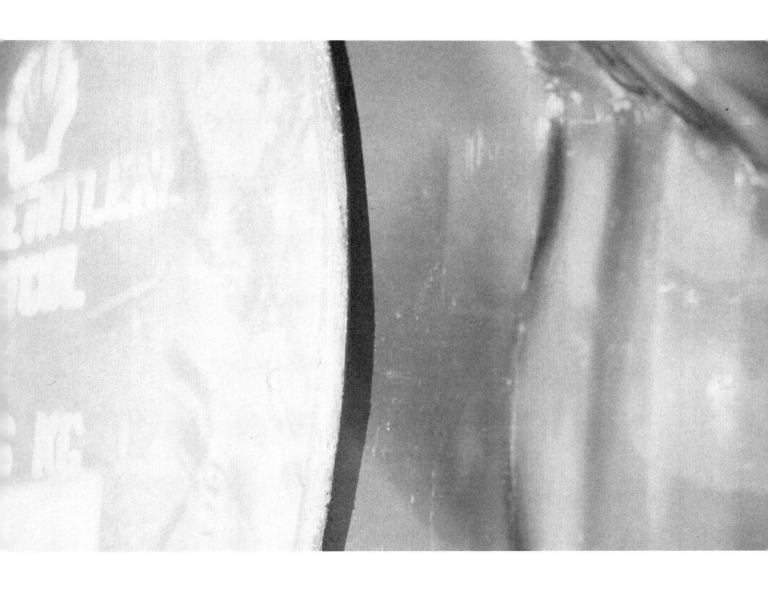

ways as cognitive reflexivity and aesthetic reflexivity. We may think of this as an analogy to the two different ways of dealing with the world: analysis and synthesis. While we are generally good at analysis, we do not excel in synthesis. We may be good at analysing problems, but not very good at synthesising a solution. In other words we seem to be better prepared for a world of stability than for one of change. In this sense we find yet another meaning of the 'creative city' – a city that will continuously create itself not by planning and explicit notions but in a process that might be called 'aesthetic' in its localised, participative, personal and integrated manner. This increasing necessity of synthesis is why design and designers will play a more important role in shaping the future. They are educated to think in terms of solutions.

My assumption is that these structural patterns characterise many of the changes taking place in different domains, particularly the domains of creativity defined at the beginning of this article. They allow us to order the otherwise incomparable changes into ordered patterns. In the following paragraphs I will describe each of the domains in detail.

CITY

CITIZEN
PSYCHOLOGY

BUSINESS
ECONOMY

CULTURE
LEARNING
ENTERTAINING

DEMOCRACY
GOVERNMENT

DOMAINS OF CREATIVITY

Business & Economy

The changes that information and communication technology bring to society are most clearly seen in the world of business. We see organisations changing from hierarchies to more networked structures, and 'virtual organisations' maintained through electronic communications that have no strong central authority. But national economies also show the same trend, becoming more and more dependent on global markets and thus other nations. All major companies use global production infrastructures that allow them to move productions easily between international centres, thus becoming increasingly networked.

Even the relationship between producers and consumers begins to change when customisation becomes possible. Production comes more and more under the control of the customer – without the customer's order production does not take place, and the final product will only be realised to his or her specifications. The consumer is the producer, composing his product. This new flexible economy even changes the role of work. Whereas before we would work for a single company for many years, now the

NEW ECONOMIES
REVALUING MONEY
"FACTOR 20"

NETWORKED COMPANIES
INTERACTIVE
CO-OPTATION

CONSUMERS — PRODUCERS

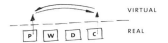

flexible economy based on knowledge will make us change jobs more often – sometimes holding even more than one job. It makes the worker more independent and requires a larger amount of creativity and assertiveness. Furthermore, our current notions about 'the economy' will change as we actually begin to operate in different economies, each with their own dynamics in terms of production, consumption or labour – Storper and Salais (1997) introduced the concept of 'multiple economies' with independent 'action frameworks'. Consequently, the creative city will be a city of multiple economies, each with their own action frameworks.

Government

The somewhat hierarchical relationship between government and people (on both national as well as local levels) will develop into a more dialogic one. In what is currently identified as interactive policymaking or open planning procedures the citizen increasingly takes part in the development of strategic policy. Often this has been the result of an effort to achieve a better understanding and control of complex developments. Some people even talk about the 'virtual state' as a network of concerned parties that co-ordinate their collective decision-making among themselves.

Some of these developments already show forms of local government that contribute more to society than the current top-down centralised way of governance. The use of information technology by government organisations for their own internal processes of 'shuffling paper' will create more 'transparent' government, where it becomes possible for citizens to freely access the information of the organisation and assess the status of the process they are involved in. Government in the creative city will be like an infrastructure that facilitates people to organise their own existence.

Culture

At the onset of the Information Age the immaterial character of things becomes more important than their material side – the cultural content becomes the focus of attention. As a result, the understanding of culture shifts to a different and wider interpretation than the traditional notion of 'high culture'. As artistic expression, cultural variety increases manifold and whole new industries start up as new tools become

CENTRALIZATION & DECENTRALIZATION
LOCAL SELF SUFFICIENCY
INTERACTIVE POLICY MAKING

available. House music developed with the availability of inexpensive computers that allowed sampling and mixing. The subsequent thriving industry has had such a grassroots character that it never really became part of the main music industry. The same will become true in publishing. Now that the tools for production and distribution have become more or less freely available everyone is able to publish. Thus cultural industries will become stronger than today. This changes the structure of culture, demands a different notion of quality and creates a new dynamics in cultural development.

A further consequence is that the narrative content becomes more important than the product itself. In other words providing meaning is what counts. In urban regeneration culture, the arts and artists are already playing an increasingly important role. In urban planning, cultural programmes become a new feature. The intensity of an urban society seems rather to be determined by the power of its culture than by the amount of its money[3]. The current dominance of the economy as a structuring force in society will diminish in favour of another, more balanced appraisal of forces. Globalisation has already started to make societies multicultural. But in more general terms one can say that in a society where actors are so strongly interdependent the quality of co-existence becomes a major factor in the resilience of those societies. The creative city will be a city of cultures. It has to re-invent itself continuously, feeding on diversity and creating an ongoing dialogue between all the actors involved.

DESIGN DRIVES DEVELOPMENT
CULTURAL EXPRESSION
SHAPES IDENTITY

[3] See Sharon Zukin's notion of the symbolic economy in Jan Verwijnen's contribution *The Creative City's New Field Condition* (pp. 10–33).

Education

The information society is also known as the 'knowledge society'. Current developments are leading to a situation where 90% of knowledge will be obsolete after only seven years. This means that learning and knowledge are central to society. 'Learning to learn' and 'lifelong learning' are new pedagogical developments currently under construction. New forms of certification throughout society and the integration of school, business and organisations will make these new forms of learning possible. Society will increasingly create learning communities and learning networks to deal with these new needs for knowledge. The current forms of education can no longer be effectively based on cognitive functions and role learning. New forms of education

INDEPENDENT THINKING
AESTHETIC REFLEXIVITY
INTEGRATED PERSON
LIFELONG LEARNING

will be more student driven – as a 'consumer' composing his product. Furthermore, aesthetics and discovery will play a more central role. The didactics of the Information Age will be adjusted to a life in constant change. The creative city will be a city of learning, where learning is distributed. The quality of the city will depend on its learning infrastructure and the ability of its citizens to develop themselves whenever the need arises.

The Citizen

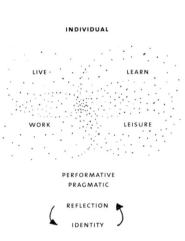

But all this has concerned abstract 'systems'. What happens to the citizens, the people? If we once more go back to the notion that complexity will increase at the end of the 20th century, we have so far only identified complexity from the outside. But human existence is basically characterised by its inside – the capacity for mental and spiritual development. In shaping life there is a constant balancing between the outside and the inside of human existence, and one's perceptions and ideas shape the world inside oneself while living in the world surrounding the self. When, as we noticed, the outside complexity increases, this will logically be reflected by an inside complexity. When the world changes, one's identity changes with it. A new world causes a new psychology. Thus, when we talk about the 'creative city' as a place where life takes on a new dynamic shape, we actually talk about 'creative citizens' that will be at the centre of these developments, shaping and developing life in their daily actions. The new infrastructures for the exchange of ideas and communications will provide them with a new platform to do this. They will be in contact with the constant changes and use these to shape their own lives. Lifelong learning, living in multiple economies and greater cultural diversity will make the inhabitants into 'creative citizens'.

Generic Infrastructure

When we are building the information society, what structure will it have, what will be the architecture of the information society? Several new generic infrastructures – networks, information technology, data, information and services – will form its foundation. 'Generic' in this sense means the available tools, methods and material will be widespread and used by everybody. These infrastructures need to be developed

INFORMATION ENVIRONMENT

GENERIC INFRASTRUCTURE
UBIQUITOUS COMPUTING
ACCESS TO DATA
EASY TOOLS FOR INFORMATION

NETWORKED
COMMUNITIES OF TRUST

PROCESS, NOT PRODUCTS
CATALYSING EXAMPLES
DIVERSITY & DIVERGENCE
VISION
GROWTH
EVOLUTION
RE-USE OF KNOWLEDGE
VALUES

in the next 5 to 10 years. For this to happen, the creative city needs to perceive its activities from the point of view of 'information' rather than from a perspective based on its existing material infrastructure. This new paradigm will be basic to the infrastructure of the creative city in the information age.

But at the heart of the matter there also lies a new central value. A networked society of increasing interdependency and co-operation has only one feasible way to sustain its existence – through *caring*. The driving force for all the developments that were discussed earlier will need, not just as an ideal or hope, but as a necessary systemic characteristic, the central value of 'caring'. Interdependence and co-operation will only function when 'the other' exists in a healthy and stimulating way. We need to sustain the other in order to sustain ourselves. In the years ahead 'caring' will become a more and more explicit notion for all the different fields of the creative city.

The Way How

How do we operate in a time of pervasive change, when we cannot predict developments, let alone plan them as we used to? We need a new paradigm for development, one in which large-scale, top-down and strictly defined plans no longer work and projects grow through a series of incremental developments following a programme. In describing successful companies, Waterman (1994) identified as a criterion for success not only the ability to once create a long-term vision, but to be able to repeat this again and again for every project. In this sense the image of the future acts as a context for the process of development. Without an image of the future we are constantly at the mercy of changes, always trying to catch up. But without the drive to catalyse such a vision and create solutions that express it, we will not be able to develop the necessary creative environment. At the same time the persistent fluctuations and quick changes require very flexible designs and adaptable development structures. They also require a good vision of the possibilities. As a result, new developments are increasingly being directed by examples that catalyse through their strength. These new developments stimulate and sustain diversity and divergence. Consequently, the creative city needs to permanently redevelop a vision of the future to sustain its ongoing change and therefore be truly creative.

REFERENCES

Beck, Ulrich (1992). *Risk Society: Towards a New Modernity*. London: Sage.
Bianchini, Franco (1996). 'Cultural Planning: An Innovative Approach'. In Verwijnen, Jan and Lehtovuori, Panu (eds.) (1996). *Managing Urban Change*. Helsinki: University of Art and Design.
Frissen, Paul (1996). *De virtuele Staat, politiek, bestuur, technologie: een postmodenr verhaal*. Schoonhoven: Academic Service.
Fukuyama, Francis (1996). *Trust: the Social Virtues and the Creation of Prosperity*. New York: Free Press Paperbacks.
Lash, Scott and **Urry ,John** (1994). *Economies of Signs and Space*. London: Sage
Salk, Jonathan and **Salk, Jonas** (1981). *World Population and Human Values: A New Reality*. New York: Harper and Row.
Storper, Michael and **Salais, Robert** (1997). *Worlds of Production: the Action Frameworks of the Economy*. Cambridge, Mass.: Harvard University Press.
Tapscott, Don (1996). *The Digital Economy: Promise and Peril in the Age of Networked Intelligence*. New York: McGraw-Hill.
Verwijnen, Jan & **Lehtovuori, Panu** (eds.) (1996). *Managing Urban Change*. Helsinki: University of Art and Design.
Waterman, Robert (1994). *The Frontiers of Excellence*. London: Nicholas Brealy Publishing.

Popular Culture, Reflexivity and Urban Change

JUSTIN O'CONNOR
Director, Manchester Institute for Popular Culture,
Manchester Metropolitan University

Introduction

The cultural industries have been increasingly seen by policy-makers and academics as a source of new employment opportunities, especially for older industrial cities[1]. More generally, they have been characterised as the leading edge of structural change associated with the shift from Fordist to Post-Fordist economies, where design-led, information-rich companies work within a new 'flexible' organisation of production[2]. Cities are now beginning to address the problems of promoting such knowledge-intensive industrial growth in conjunction with cultural policies aimed at providing a creative milieu conducive to the attraction and retention of such knowledge or 'symbolic' specialists[3]. The encouragement of the 'creative city' is thus beginning to bring together cultural and economic policy at an ever more strategic level[4].

However, whilst the cultural industries are being approached as part of a wider repositioning by many cities, there has been very little research as to how these industries actually operate. Existing research has tended to focus on the larger, more established sectors and on those that operate in ways accessible to standard economic analysis. There exists a serious lack of research amongst those micro and small enterprises (MSE's) which make up a large proportion of the cultural industries sector – its seedbed and innovative end.

It is this MSE sector which is a major driver for innovation and creativity in the cultural industries sector, operating in complex interaction with the big cultural

---

[1] Wynne, 1991; Bianchini & Parkinson, 1993; Lewis, 1992; Crewe & Haines, 1996

[2] Lash & Urry, 1994; Crooke, 1992; Hall & Jacques, 1989; Harvey, 1989; Kumar, 1995; Amin, 1995

[3] Handy, 1994

[4] Landry, 1995; Knights, 1992; Businaro, 1994; Mommaas, 1995; O'Connor & Wynne, 1996; Bianchini, 1993

industry production and distribution companies[5]. It is this sector which is most responsive to local milieu as an attractor[6] and which provides the real source of a locally vibrant culture.

The sector has frequently been invisible to research, either because it does not register on established indicators[7] or because researchers have misrecognised its character – not 'real' jobs or simply niche employment for certain ('trendy', 'yuppie') groups[8]. Moreover, this sector is notoriously difficult to investigate[9].

This situation has been mirrored in the lack of support for the sector by economic development and training agencies. There is a persistent tendency for these agencies to see the cultural industries sector as 'soft', 'volatile' and 'unbusiness-like'. Historically, this relates to a deep-seated divide between art and industry which has hampered the emergence of a design culture in traditional manufacture; but it also relates to a serious gap between orthodox models of business practice which underpin standard business education, training and support services and the way in which these small cultural businesses actually operate.

This paper will thus look at the cultural industries sector from the point of view of those actively engaged within it. However, we begin with a brief overview of the role of the cultural sector in some recent approaches to urban regeneration and some of the issues thrown up by the increasingly close connection between cultural producers and urban regeneration agencies. As such we will examine the role of 'cultural intermediaries' in the work of Sharon Zukin and, to a lesser extent, Bourdieu. We will conclude with some brief remarks concerned with 'reflexivity'.

A New Model for Urban Regeneration

In the mid-1970s, whilst the language of urban decline was reaching a peak in North American and European cities, there emerged a new discourse on the city – that of urban regeneration. A new valuation of city living, drawing on the lifestyles of artistic-bohemian counter-cultures and a rediscovery of the heritage of late 19th and early 20th century buildings and vernacular, gave rise to a new approach on behalf of urban developers. Rather than tear the old city centre down they began to see value in its preservation and 're-packaging'. The old working class areas adjacent to the Central

5 Lash & Urry, 1994
6 Clarke, 1996
7 Mole, 1996; Clarke, 1996
8 Taylor, et al, 1996; Zukin, 1994; 1995
9 Purvis, 1996

Business District (CBD), once the home of localised productive communities, are now transformed into centres of consumption.

This transformation of the urban downtown vernacular is the focus of a famous book by Sharon Zukin, *Loft Living* (1982). The argument is well known, though its complexities are not often spelled out. SoHo was a downtown vernacular juxtaposed to a financial district intent on expansion in alliance with political forces that saw no future for manufacturing on Manhattan. The future lay with finance. The attempt at a classic 1960s-style development was successfully resisted by the artist and ancillary community that had moved into the old 19th century lofts, attracted by the cheapness and space in a New York now at the centre of the world art market. The victory, through an alliance with the growing communitarian and anti-development movement of the 1970s, led to the designation of SoHo as an artists' zone. But the end result was that manufacturing and 'down market' retail was pushed out by this zoning, and the old vernacular became prime real estate as 'loft living' became a desirable commodity. Ultimately, many artists found it impossible to buy or rent, and any indigenous bohemian artist quality now became totally packaged, landscaped, for wealthy residents.

The narrative in *Loft Living* is complex. Zukin wants to show how those dealing in cultural knowledge were responsible for the transformation of SoHo, creating a new value that could be recouped by development capital. Two forces are prominent. Firstly, the historic buildings groups began to see the cast iron frontages as aesthetic objects that should be protected rather than torn down. This represented an aestheticisation of past use which immediately devalued current industrial usage. Legitimate usage of these buildings was increasingly restricted to those who could appreciate this historical aesthetic. Secondly, the artists' community claimed for itself the central role in the revitalisation of a 'derelict' district. The economic importance of the artists to New York was stressed, but it was their cultural impact on the area that was primary. The Loft was a metonym for an artistic lifestyle which, drawing on the bohemian and counter-cultural elements of the 1960s, would bring back a new vibrancy to the downtown area. However, although this vibrancy drew on the qualities of downtown vernacular, it was now based on a 'lifestyle' no longer linked to a productive commu-

nity. It was a lifestyle that could be consumed, whether in the form of the newly fashionable lofts, or the bohemian ambience of the restaurants, bars, galleries and shops.

Thus the aestheticisation of the vernacular achieved by cultural specialists mediated its emergence as an object of consumption. Once this cultural work had been done and the vernacular re-absorbed into the cultural landscape, the cultural specialists lost ground to those wielding economic power. In *Loft Living* the outcome is paradoxical, the victors ending up as losers. The developers quickly appreciated the importance of cultural consumption in the revalorisation of undervalued downtown areas. After SoHo they became proactive. But, as we shall see, the transposition of this model to other areas was not without its problems.

The logic of standardisation and repetition meant the rapid elaboration of regeneration models that could be sold to different city governments. By the late 1970s a number of large cities in North America, especially those with historic centres, began to invest in these regeneration models[10]. It was clear that whilst the 'artistic community' was often brought in to these local growth coalitions, it was the developer who held the upper hand. The transformation of historical and/or waterfront areas into retail/leisure and residential developments was based around 'up-market' consumption coupled with a high cultural input. This could include cultural animation programmes, artists' residences, subsidised workshops and a public art that fitted well with a new 'postmodern' aesthetic. Such cultural input was encouraged by city governments employing 'percentage for art' programmes, and 'planning gain' initiatives. These areas had an 'up-market' ambience of speciality shopping and 'designer' restaurants and bars. They also aimed at establishing the sense of vibrancy that once attached to downtown areas, but a vibrancy now mediated by a bohemian image represented by the presence of artists and 'artisans'. The vibrancy was one of an aestheticised 19th century, where the image of the downtown areas was reappropriated via the image of the artist-bohemian in the guise of flaneur. The new-old spaces of urbanity were not those of productive communities, but of the middle class stroller who had the time and the cultural knowledge with which to stroll through the landscape and absorb the vernacular as aesthetic.

10 Bianchini, 1993; Wynne, 1992

For Zukin this aestheticisation of both the buildings and the vernacular associations of downtown areas is a cultural work of landscaping. It is an imposition based on the cultural labour of a certain social group, though these may not be the main beneficiaries of this labour. This group Zukin calls the 'critical infrastructure', the cultural specialists who both promote and have expertise in the production and consumption of cultural goods. Zukin's work thus represents a severe indictment of the project of culturally based urban renewal, and of the role of cultural specialists as both mediators of the new consumption and as destructive of the values of place.

In *Landscapes of Power* (1992), building on her *Loft Living* (1982), Sharon Zukin attempts to analyse more closely this shift from production to consumption. For Zukin this restructuration of the city centre is one not of the 'creative-destruction'[11] of the built environment but of the imposition of a new perspective on the city, a perspective based on cultural power. This cultural power emerges in a context of mass cultural consumption, giving rise to new mechanisms of inclusion and exclusion, and in a context where cultural consumption is increasingly abstracted from place-based production and consumption, and driven by globalised flows of information, capital and cultural goods[12]. This is crucial because it is precisely along these lines – the promotion of cultural production and consumption – of, and in, the city – and the attraction of cultural specialists, the creation of a critical infrastructure – that cities in Britain and Western Europe have attempted to engage with the problems of the 'post-Fordist' city.

It is this new ersatz urban realm which was initially characterised as 'postmodern', in a way that confused the debate. Both admirers and critics seemed to see this as an incarnation of the postmodern zeitgeist, without inquiring as to how people used these places and to what extent, and on what basis, they were successful[13]. However, the transposition of the model of regeneration by developers is fraught with problems. If the imposition of a landscape of cultural power is to have any chance of success, even defined in narrowly economic terms, a 'critical infrastructure' is necessary. Despite Zukin's occasional functionalisms, this critical infrastructure cannot just be created as required. As specialists and insiders they have a relative autonomy and a close knowledge of, and relationship to, place. It is in this context that a specific

[11] Harvey, 1986

[12] Harvey, 1992

[13] Chambers, 1990; Cooke, 1988; Harvey, 1992

localisation involves a series of negotiations around the new emergent landscape which can be laden with meanings very different to the standardised 'postmodernity' of the development models.

Economic and Cultural Capital in the New Urban Regeneration

I have discussed some of the specifics of this attempted transposition elsewhere, with reference to the Manchester case[14]. Here I simply want to flag up certain local specific problems and broaden these out into some larger theoretical questions concerning the role of cultural intermediaries.

[14 O'Connor & Wynne, 1996a & 1996c]

This model of urban regeneration development around historical-cultural urban centres was directly imported into Britain in the early 1980s. In this transposition the specificities of the local context were crucial.

Firstly, there was the political context. The Thatcher government, having won a resounding second term in 1983, made 'inner cities' its target, especially after the riots in 1981 had underlined these inner cities as symbols of the 'British disease'[15]. The major British industrial cities were mainly held by the opposition Labour Party. Central government was loath to give them credit for any possible success in these programmes; moreover, they blamed these councils for the socialist-bureaucratic failures of the 1960s and 1970s. Urban regeneration was to be a symbol of Thatcherite Britain's escape from the cycle of post-war failure. The government wanted to use a free enterprise approach which demanded deregulation and a more flexible planning system. To this end a whole series of legislative changes were enacted restricting local government, freeing private capital's access to public land and development contracts, and creating new semi-autonomous bodies outside the control of local government. This in itself caused tremendous political opposition amongst local city elites, many of whom had looked towards the GLC model of democratic access and the redefinition of (multicultural) citizenship.

[15 Robson, 1987]

Secondly, this was a time of massive and catastrophic deindustrialisation. Apart from the social and economic consequences this was also a cultural dislocation, especially in the northern industrial towns where identity, much more than in the south, was centred on work, on manual and industrial labour[16]. Urban regeneration

[16 Shields, 1991; Mole, 1996; Taylor, 1996]

was based on a conscious and explicit shift of the economic base from manufacturing to service industries, symbolised by the redrawing of the old historical industrial areas in terms of leisure and consumption. This generated widespread opposition and/or cynicism, which included 'cultural intermediaries'. But it also introduced a tension within the political elites in cities, whose conversion to 'arts and culture' led regeneration was never straightforward (we cannot deal with this here). Thus the work of urban regeneration was seen by many on the Left as a symbol of Thatcherism, and despised as such. The debate around yuppification, gentrification and 'postmodernity' in 1980s Britain cannot be divorced from this political context. This had a direct impact upon the functioning of 'cultural landscaping' and the role of the 'critical infrastructure'.

Thirdly, though culture was increasingly promoted to the forefront of policy debates, the model of urban regeneration imported from North America was to be primarily driven through as an economic programme and 'arts & culture' justified in this context. This prioritisation of the economic was to set the agenda for debate around the arts throughout the 1980s, exemplified by John Meyerscough's studies. This was an explicitly hegemonic attempt to redraw the territories of economic and cultural capital in Bourdieu's sense. Thus 'arts & culture' were being promoted at a time when Thatcherism was engaged in an onslaught on the 'chattering classes', the liberal, intellectual, 'pinko' elites who had organised the 'culture of consensus' around a series of closely intertwined cultural institutions[17]. Culture-led urban regeneration was thus frequently pursued in opposition to this arts establishment who were held partly responsible for Britain's post-war social and moral decline (the sixties, permissiveness etc.).

Fourthly, this was part of a larger problem. Cultural policy within cities had largely centred on the maintenance of the established institutions of civic culture – the library, concert hall/opera house, theatre, meeting hall, civic squares, etc. Beyond these, 'arts & culture' usually fell under quite low level officers – often merged with 'leisure', giving rise to the unkind stereotype of the officer responsible for the arts being a former public baths attendant. The heightened profile of cultural policy did see a growth in the number and seniority of arts officers[18], but it was really a question of deep-seated cultural change. How did the city authorities begin to address the

17 Hewison, 1995

18 O'Connor, 1991

question of culture? The old 'city fathers', drawn from the industrial bourgeoisie, had a range of standard models to follow. The great town halls and warehouses of the northern cities had looked to well-codified architectural and cultural models[19]. The established canon of modernism, in both architecture and the arts generally, was under attack from Thatcherism, though it had never been fully accepted in English culture. This coincided with the emergence of 'postmodernism', which was not so much a new style as an attack on all established canons as such. Whether legitimating the popular opposition to modernism or undermining the legitimating authority of the University, 'postmodernism' opened up the field to the new culture-led urban regeneration models and allowed some insightful developers to act as guides through the alien minefield of culture.

[19] Briggs, 1961

What I want to bring out here is that the relationship between cultural and economic capital is more complex than Zukin suggests, and the local context is crucial in the way in which this relationship is negotiated.

> *Significantly, cultural value is now related to economic value. From demand for living lofts and gentrification, large property-owners, developers, and elected local officials realised they could enhance the economic value of the centre by supplying cultural consumption.*
> — ZUKIN 1992: 194

But the initiation of culture-based urban renewal by a quasi-political body dominated by a 'free enterprise' ethos with an anti-cultural bias, and one that worked primarily with a development capital using tried and trusted models for the formation of a cultural landscape, was damaging. It meant that the resultant development, whilst based on images of leisure and consumption and aestheticisation taken up by urban boosterists and sociologists alike (but with opposite intentions), had limited cultural resonance, and especially amongst those whose labour would be crucial to the transformation of the centre into cultural landscape – the cultural intermediaries. They were deeply cynical.

Zukin argues:

> *Gentrification received its greatest boost not from a specific subsidy, but from the state's substantive and symbolic legitimation of the cultural claim to urban space. This recognition marked cultural producers as a symbol of urban growth.*
> — ZUKIN 1992: 194

This legitimation on the part of the developers was in exclusively economic terms, where cultural production has direct economic consequences. In fact, the imposition of a model in these terms, which denied the autonomy of the cultural sphere, actually excluded cultural specialists – it refused their specific expertise. There are two points here.

Firstly, as Bourdieu (1984) makes clear, cultural capital, whilst related to economic capital, must also stress its distinction from it. Too close a connection undermines the claim of culture to be disinterested, to be 'more than' economics. Whilst we must ask the question as to what extent this is true in the context of any postmodern cultural field, and indeed whether Bourdieu's fields themselves are not tied to an older notion of aesthetic distinction, it is certainly true that cultural value can suffer from too close a connection to the economic.

Secondly, cultural intermediaries are precisely that – intermediaries. They are able to interpret, package, transmit and manipulate symbols and knowledge in a way that produces new value. As both producers and consumers they are able to claim an expertise, a close knowledge of the inner dynamics of the cultural field[21]. Thus in Manchester developers attempted to sell 'city centre living' in the absence of an image of city living, of a vibrant 24-hour city centre outside of working hours and of a 'European' city of sociability across a range of social groups – the absence, that is, of a highly valued centrality. When this workable image did emerge it was within a cultural sphere associated with a pop music scene which was only latterly picked up by the urban regeneration elites. The critical infrastructure thus worked independently of, or in opposition to, the developers' cultural model[22]. Thus, though the Rave and Gay scenes in Manchester, for example, were annexed by parts of the regeneration elite there were many problems as regards other regulatory and legitimising authori-

21 Martin, 1991

22 O'Connor & Wynne, 1996c

ties (police, magistrates, etc.). Thus the work of cultural producers emerged within a complex field in which the "state's substantive and symbolic legitimation of the cultural claim to urban space" was far from fixed, and was indeed a product of negotiation and conflict.

New Cultural Intermediaries

The term 'new cultural intermediaries' derives from Bourdieu. In *Distinction* (1984), he identifies a new middle class which breaks with the established field of the petty bourgeoisie and attempts a radical challenge to the existing hierarchies of cultural distinction. In this, their 'organic intellectuals' derive from the field of the new media and other new professions associated with lifestyle, leisure, self-exploration, etc. They articulate and guide this new middle class through the new landscape of consumer society with which they are so closely associated. This notion has been extensively adopted as an explanatory schema for 'postmodernity', most characteristically in the work of Mike Featherstone[23]. A crucial characterisation of those at the vanguard of cultural change, those new cultural intermediaries who (a mixture of Gramsci and Elias) would expand the values of the 'counter-culture' to a wider sphere, was 'the aestheticisation of everyday life'.

23 Featherstone, 1991

The growing popularisation of the artistic-bohemian lifestyle was part of a much more widespread shift in cultural hierarchies and an increasingly reflexive construction of lifestyle. Consequent on the expansion of higher education and the cultural radicalisms of the 1960s, knowledge of cultural goods expanded enormously. At the same time the transgressions of the artist, the experimentation with new experiences, the desire to create the self as a work of art – all these became absorbed into a wider culture. This fed into the growing incorporation of art and culture into the design of consumer goods, and into the techniques of advertising and marketing. In *Landscapes*, Zukin is much more explicit in linking the operations of the new groups of cultural specialists to both the promotion of consumption and the gentrification of the city.

> *Mediating the dialectic of power and centrality depends on a critical infrastructure for cultural production and consumption. Here I am thinking of men and women*

> *who produce and consume, and also evaluate, new market-based cultural products. Like artists, they both comment critically on, and constitute, a new kind of market culture. Their 'inside' view opens up new spaces for consumption. They enhance market values even when they desperately want to conserve values of place.*
> — Zukin: 1992: 201–2

This is the tragic function of the counter-culture. Ultimately, their concern with culture merely opened a new field of consumption, which, exposed to the forces of abstraction and internationalisation, destroys the object of their desire. For Zukin, the role of these cultural specialists is functional to social distinction in an age of 'mass-produced and mass-distributed culture'. In the absence of 'hierarchies based on personal networks and social position' cultural specialists, 'the critical infrastructure', emerge to promote and to guide us through the new landscape of consumption.

> *Today cultural consumption follows the lead of several mediators: the artist, the primary consumer, and the designer, who interpret desire and direct the consumer to equate awareness of consuming with awareness of life, and the line producer in new service industries, catering to a jaded consumer "who yearns for homespun to ease the chintz."*
> — Ibid: 204

The question this opens up is one Featherstone poses at the end of his book (1991) – is this merely the jockeying for position of a new postmodern class fraction or part of a wider series of cultural shifts? Our research would indicate the latter. In doing so we would also add that the elaborate hierarchies established by Bourdieu, as different social groups competed for cultural distinction, should perhaps be seen as applicable to the era of scarcity (in Beck's (1992) notion). In an era of post-scarcity the cultural hierarchies are much more fragmented and plural. This has enormous consequences for any attempt to account for cultural change in the contemporary city.

CULTURAL INTERMEDIARIES AND CULTURAL INDUSTRIES

I want to shift focus and look more closely at those concerned with the production of culture at the local city level. The following builds upon two research projects conducted at the Institute for Popular Culture – Metropolitan Lifestyles and the New Consumption and Cultural Production in the City (O'Connor & Wynne, 1996b).

Metropolitan Lifestyles and the New Consumption

[24 Featherstone, O'Connor & Wynne, 1994]

This was an ESRC research project[24] examining new forms of cultural consumption and the construction of lifestyle in the contemporary city. These new forms were associated with a range of developments which included:

1 the dramatic increase in the production and consumption of symbolic goods;
2 the shift of consumption from use value to sign value;
3 the destabilisation of established symbolic hierarchies through the articulation of alternative tastes and styles;
4 the rise of popular and commercial cultures as alternative forms challenging established 'high culture';
5 the emergence of new urban spaces creating 'play spaces' for new forms of sociability, leading to;
6 new forms of display and social mixing representing a movement away from rational goal-directed activity, permitting a more playful, carnivalesque exploration of emotions – a preoccupation with the æstheticisation and 'stylisation' of life as opposed to more fixed lifestyles.

This research represented a systematic examination of these processes in the context of cultural consumption in the city centre and the lifestyles of selected inhabitants. For our purposes here we can pick out three significant results:

1 the emergence of a 'mix and match' lifestyle amongst the 18–35 age group who are most prominent in the use of the cultural and leisure facilities of the city centre. The lifestyle emphasised 'anti-rationalist' values usually associated with artistic, bohemian or counter-cultural milieus – intuition, self-expression, creativity, the exploration of subjectivity and the body, pleasure and hedonism – but linked to a keen sense of the positional and distinction value of symbolic goods and services;

2   the extension of the notion of 'cultural intermediaries' from the new middle class to a much wider range of the population, through the increased involvement of popular culture in the creation of the new city centre sites of consumption;
3   these new and extended forms of cultural consumption, characterised by rapid turnover and complex distinctions, were seen to feed directly into cultural production in order to supply these new markets.

Cultural Production in the City

These findings formed the basis of a large-scale investigation into new forms of cultural production in the city. The research indicated that for those involved:

1   making money and making culture were often one and the same activity;
2   there was a frequent inability and even antipathy to making a distinction between work time and leisure time;
3   there was a heavy reliance on informal networks for information and ideas;
4   there was an emphasis on intuition, emotional involvement, immersion in the field and an 'insider's' or 'enthusiast's' knowledge of the market;
5   a realised ambition to 'work for themselves' and to 'break the 9–5'.

The findings of both these studies pointed towards theoretical work in the social sciences which attempted to ground some of the claims of the 'postmodernity' debate in more empirical research[25]. The research also linked in to the debates around 'reflexivity', which was the subject of a number of conferences, articles and books in 1993–94[26]. It was argued that large-scale social processes meant that the individual was decreasingly presented with objective social roles and had to construct her/his own identity in a situation of fluidity, anxiety, and risk. The individuation of consumption thus brings an increased reflexivity, which tends to move away from a predominantly cognitive to a more aesthetic reflexivity, increasingly mediated through aesthetic objects or symbolic goods.

In summary this research suggested:

- that if consumption is increasingly reflexive then so too is the production intended to satisfy that market;

25 O'Connor & Wynne, 1996c

26 Beck, 1992; Beck & al., 1994; Lash, 1993

- in targeting these forms of consumption the cultural industries sector uses different forms and circuits of knowledge, has a different conception and relationship to the consumer, and has a different approach to the very notion of 'running a business' – different, that is, from the conceptualisation of this business practice in mainstream business education and training.

Business Support and Training

Other Research at MIPC by O'Connor and Wynne conducted for Manchester City Council and North West Arts into the cultural industries in 1989[27] emphasised the divergence between the cultural industries and orthodox business models and highlighted the gap between this sector and the local business training and support services. It stressed: 1) the negative experience of this education and training expressed by these businesses and 2) the difficulties encountered by these businesses in being taken seriously by larger firms and the established business infrastructure (banks, Chamber of Commerce, TEC's, Enterprise Allowance, Business Link, etc.).

This was confirmed by ethnographic work amongst postgraduate researchers at MIPC: aside from certain technical knowledge (accountancy, grants, basic office computing), most of these small cultural businesses found the language and the theoretical models of business education disempowering, alienating and frequently useless. Enterprise Allowance (now New Business Support) and other business start-up schemes provided many of these businesses (very few with any formal business education) with free, compulsory (if benefits were to be received) business training courses. The language and models used were felt to have little relevance to both the way in which they worked and the motivations for setting up business in the first place. There were exceptions, where courses were created by individuals active in the cultural industries sector. This notion of 'soft' business education was however criticised and then dropped by the local TEC.[28]

This criticism derived from and reflected traditional models of business theory and education. However, our initial research suggests that these producers use distinct circuits of knowledge which allow them to access these markets, relying on knowledge derived more from 'cultural' discourses than 'business' discourses.

[27] Wynne, 1991; O'Connor, 1997a; 1997b

[28] O'Connor & Wynne, 1996c; O'Connor, 1997c; Lovatt et al, 1994; Mole, 1996; Purvis, 1996

Business Education and Business Practice

The work at MIPC has complemented independent work by the Economic Awareness Teacher Training Programme (ECATT) at the University of Manchester which has questioned the nature of economics education in the light of the continuing debates about 'postmodern' knowledge[29].

Business theory, especially as used within business education and training, has rarely been the object of debate – unlike economics education[30] and jurisprudence[31] – despite the fact that the knowledge produced by the modernist social sciences has been at the very centre of the poststructuralist and postmodernist debates[32]. Generally, the poststructuralist challenge to modernist social science is that the latter promotes a notion of a universal, 'totalising' truth dividing the 'essential' from the merely contingent; and, further, that this truth is a strategy of power whereby one 'master discourse' comes to dominate other discourses by representing those others as 'in error'[33]. Yet there is also evidence to suggest that a positivist methodology and associated search for a universal truth outside of a specific context may prevent businesses from acknowledging and/or responding to the profound changes in consumption patterns and circuits of knowledge associated with the condition of 'postmodernity' referred to above[34]. This has a number of consequences for business education:

1. Borrowing from the positivist methodology of the natural sciences, orthodox modernist social science promises an incremental model of theoretical business knowledge and business practice which can be universally applied to a variety of business settings. This tends to marginalise the local and contextual basis of business activity as secondary or contingent. The need to understand the embeddedness of economic activity in the specific local and historical context is now increasingly on the research agenda.

2. This approach to method is reflected in the representational epistemology which assumes *an unproblematic relationship between representations and the objectifications they supposedly represent*[35]. Following Knights we suggest that positivist business knowledge, with its roots in orthodox macro and micro economics and mainstream industrial and organisational sociology and psychology, *treats the representations of subject and object unproblematically, refusing to reflect deeply on the subject that makes these*

[29] Thomas & Hodkinson, 1988
[30] Thomas and Hodkinson, 1988
[31] Goodrich & Douzinas, 1993
[32] Hollway, 1989
[33] Usher & Edwards, 1994
[34] Knights and Odih, 1994
[35] Knights, 1995

representations possible[36]. This knowledge assumes a stable and objectified subject, such as rational 'economic man', and then develops complex systems on this narrow base.

3 This 'master discourse' excludes awareness of other ways of describing the situation. It may be used to reinforce business models that may in fact be entirely inappropriate. Indeed, it may be the case that representational business knowledge is not an innocent seeker of truth for the benefit of consumers and producers, but that it is instead frequently grounded in a desire for order and security in a changing world[37]. The pursuit of scientific status then may also be as much about personal and professional identity[38] as it is about describing a business situation. According to certain feminist critiques[39], business knowledge may be an 'ego ideal', an emotional investment in securing a (masculine) world of objective security and order. In this context the language of expertise may constrain rather than enhance flexible and creative thinking[40].

4 Similarly, the 'primacy of the consumer' in market discourses may often be largely rhetorical when it constructs a model of consumer 'need'. As pointed out above this is often a narrow and artificial model presented as an objective reality, in which consumers' lives are reconstituted as a problem (need) to be resolved (satisfied) by the product on offer. Research to identify 'needs' prior to consumption is then highly artificial since it is abstracted from the circumstances in which needs are created and sustained[41].

5 This inadequacy is compounded by the tendency of objectivist models to reinforce the distinction between hard and soft, cognitive and intuitive, science and emotion, economics and culture, male and female – a dualism running through much modernist discourse. This may have enormous consequences for the ability of business to operate in the cultural realm, and to understand the nature of the shift from economies of trade in material goods to the flow of signs and information. This is especially important in the context of the ability of cities to respond to long-term structural change.

These concerns indicate that formal business knowledge, generated through positivistic and representational epistemologies, is the foundation for most business education and training programmes. It is suggested that these programmes of study/

[36] ibid

[37] ibid

[38] Knights and Raffo, 1988

[39] Game, 1991; Clough, 1992

[40] Morgan, 1993

[41] Knights, Sturdy and Morgan, 1994: 43

The heuristic model on business practises

BUSINESS AREA	CULTURAL PRODUCERS POSTFORDIST / POSTMODERN	TRADITIONAL BUSINESS ORGANISATIONS FORDIST / MODERN
Market	The market is understood as subjective and volatile, linked to both mind and body, is defined by the ephemeral, the cultural and the symbolic. Cultural producers understand the market through informal networks, the 'story'. Marketing is adaptive, intuitive, reflexive, unstructured, informal and symbolic.	Market research methods. Marketing is strategic, objective and uses the tools of the marketing mix in a structured and formal way.
Product and production	Design intensive, aesthetic, cultural and symbolic. Individualistic and embedded in the market. Production strategies demonstrate flexible specialisation to accommodate volatile markets.	Formula design and linked to market research findings. Multiplicity of product linked to main design theme. Piloted and then developed. Uniformity of production strategies linked to regularised markets eg seasonal fashion industry.
Lifestyle and the work/leisure distinction	Cultural producers do not necessarily see the work/leisure distinction. They are often seen as cultural intermediaries who become a focus for those attempting to creating identity through lifestyle.	Business organisations market a leisure activity rather than an identity forming lifestyle option. Not a leader of change but responsive to change.
Business goals and business success	Linked to lifestyle and the cultural. Business success not primarily viewed as profit but as the cutting edge of change and development in the particular cultural sphere.	Profit and margins. Achievement of performance indicators. Growth and market share.
People and management styles	Recruitment – informal and from same cultural milieu. Contracts – informal and fragmented. Management style – participative, stakeholder, pluralistic, de-centred, empowering.	Recruitment – formal and from a variety of labour markets. Contracts – formal and often short-term. Management style – hierarchical, centralised, authority and power, a unitary perspective.
Business knowledge and business learning	Business knowledge acquired through experience and networks. The knowledge is subjective and contextual, cultural and embedded to the local. It is fluid and multi-disciplinary. Business learning of cultural producers demonstrates a constructivist perspective on learning.	Business knowledge acquired putting orthodox business theory into practice. Business knowledge is based on research and is objective and global. Business learning is viewed as competencies that need mastering.

training are unable to meet the requirements of SME and micro-business practitioners in the cultural industries. The business theories used are based on a language of 'expertise' that has little relevance to the everyday interaction that these practitioners have with their markets. Given the importance of the cultural industries in terms of the production strategies required to meet increasingly reflexive markets, we suggest that our research should act as a focus for a re-examination of business education generally.

Investigating Business Practice and Knowledge

It would seem from the above that cultural businesses operate in ways very different from the standard models of business practice which underpin orthodox business education, training and support services. Much of this could be described as modernist; in fact, our and others' research suggests that small cultural businesses operate more as 'postmodern' organisations.

Our on-going work intends to foreground these research findings and rigorously test them as a central hypothesis. In order to conduct this test we have developed an heuristic model designed to polarise the difference between cultural/traditional, modern/postmodern and fordist/postfordist.

Local Cultures and the Creative City

What does this imply for creative cities?

Academics have attempted to characterise the present structural change as a shift from Fordism to post-Fordism – involving the multiplication and fragmentation of markets, along with the acceleration of product turnover and volatility (or fickleness) of demand foregrounding the marketing and design functions of firms. Flexible specialisation[42] means margins of competitiveness depend on the generation and exploitation of new knowledge; successful firms are R&D and innovation intensive, constantly redesigning business organisation to create the flexibility required to accommodate this. In terms of marketing and design functions, this capacity can be defined as a cultural capacity – the ability to accumulate knowledge and manipulate symbols. This is clearest in those sectors which deal primarily with the production and

42 Lash & Urry, 1994

distribution of symbolic goods – the cultural industries. This sector can be seen as a cutting edge; *ordinary manufacturing industry is becoming more and more like the production of culture. It is not that commodity manufacture provides the template, and culture follows, but that cultural industries themselves provided the template.*[43]

43 Lash and Urry, 1994: 123

This has also been termed the 'informational economy', referring to a new form of economic production and management characterised by the fact that productivity and competitiveness are increasingly based on the generation of new knowledge and on the access to, and processing of, appropriate information[44]. Thus the transformational aspects of this information society include a new and important association between the productive elements of the economy (knowledge generation and information processing) and the cultural capacity of society – that is, its ability to accumulate knowledge and manipulate symbols[45].

44 Castells and Hall, 1994

45 Shearman, 1996; Castells, 1994a

Cities can be seen as nodes within a global economy[46] and the intersection of the global and the local becomes crucial in local economic development. Whilst control and distribution functions may remain in globalised (or centralised) hands, this can only be on the basis of a sophisticated understanding of consumption patterns in specific and often very localised markets[47]. It is a knowledge of the local mediation of the global circuits of 'signs and space' that frequently defines the success of cultural industries in the local city context[48]. This implies a knowledge of the local, but also a deep understanding for these specific forms of consumption. It is this knowledge that allows cultural industries to both innovate in the local sphere and extend their operations beyond the local.

46 Sassen, 1991

47 Sassen, 1994

48 Lash & Urry, 1994

The above points underline the new centrality of knowledge, with an increased emphasis on the cultural and symbolic aspects of this knowledge. Local economic development increasingly depends on the mobilisation of this knowledge, but the ability to do this depends on a range of historically specific social, economic, cultural and political factors[49]. As a particular kind of knowledge-intensive industry, and as one especially dependant on a negotiation and articulation of a local place-based cultural milieu within a 'global space of flows', the cultural industries sector represents an important indicator of the ability of particular cities to respond to the challenge of global restructuring. As a recent work on Manchester argued:

49 Mole, 1996;
O'Connor & Wynne, 1996;
Landry, 1995; Knights, 1992;
Businaro, 1994; Mommaas, 1995

...the youth culture industry in Manchester has a more general purchase on the whole social and economic formation: an expression of the very rapidly changing economic circumstances of the 1980s (the 'New Times' of 'disorganised global capitalism')... There is little question that this challenge is quite well understood amongst those employed in the local high-technology and 'cultural intermediary' professional classes in Manchester, particularly, we think, in the fast-moving media, popular music, leisure and communication sectors.

— TAYLOR & AL, 1996: 272, 303–304

However, whilst a thriving cultural industries sector may indicate a level of local creativity, it is the ability to nurture this sector and link its creativity (of business and milieu) to wider economic innovation and development which is a crucial test of the adaptability of cities to this global challenge. If this ability to develop and mobilise the knowledge base of the City is (amongst other things) a cultural capacity, then cultural policy is due to be more closely integrated with local economic strategies – as has been the case, with very mixed results[50].

As stated earlier, academic writing and policy is increasingly directed at this sector, yet there has been no detailed research as to how cultural industries actually operate. There is hardly any research into those creative urban milieus within which cultural businesses (especially at the pop-cultural end) tend to emerge. There is a need to look at how milieu, networks, districts/quarters and embeddedness may operate within this sector[51]. There is growing research into the city as a distinct economic generator – this is only now being linked to the question of local city cultures and the ability to change and adapt[52]. Cultural policy previously aimed at attracting 'knowledge specialists' must also begin to promote innovation and creativity – to become 'intentional'[53]. This depends on linkages, networks, communication and openness that themselves cannot be divorced from the particular history of the city, its particular 'structure of feeling'[54].

50 Bianchini, 1993; O'Connor & Wynne, 1992; 1996c; O'Connor, 1996; 1997a

51 Crewe, 1996; & al, 1996; Harrison, 1992; Kumar, 1995

52 Castells, 1994; 1994b

53 Businaro, 1994

54 cf. Taylor, 1996

BIBLIOGRAPHY

Amin, A. (ed.) *Post-Fordism: A Reader*, Oxford, Blackwell.
Beck, U. (1992). *Risk Society*, London, Sage.
Beck, U., Giddens, A. & Lash, S. (1994). *Reflexive Modernisation*, Polity, Cambridge
Belk, R. (1995) 'Studies in the New Consumer Behaviour' in Miller, D. (1995), *Acknowledging Consumption*, Routledge, London and New York
Bianchini, F. & Parkinson, M. (1993). (Eds) *Cultural Policy and Urban Regeneration*, Manchester University Press
Bourdieu, P. (1984). *Distinction*, Routledge, London.
Briggs, A. (1961). *Victorian Cities*, Penguin, Harmondsworth.
Brookes, K. (1992). 'Education for Economic and Industrial Understanding: An Economics Foundation' in Bloomer, G., Brookes, K, & Jephcote, M. (1992), *Putting the Economics into EIU: the choices and implications for teacher education programmes*, EATE Research Report No.4, Oct 92 , Employment Dept.
Businaro, U. (1994). *Technology and the Future of Cities: Responding to the Urban Malaise; an agenda for the EU*, European Commission, DG XII July, 1994.
Castells, M. & Hall, P. (1994). *Technopoles of the World: The Making of 21st Century Industrial Complexes*, Routledge, London and New York.
Castells, M. (1994b). 'European Cities, the Informational Society, and the Global Economy', in *New Left Review*, 204.
Chambers, I. (1990). *Border Dialogues*, Routledge, London.
Clarke, D. Owens, P. & Creasey, C. (1996). *Transaction Tracking – A Research Project in the EconomicLives of Practioners in the Cultural Sector*, DCA Limited, Cardiff.
Clough, P.T. (1992). *The End(s) of Ethnography: From Realism to Social Criticism*, Newbury Park, California: Sage
Cooke, P. (1988). 'Modernity, Postmodernity and the City' in *Theory, Culture and Society*, 5(2–3).
Crewe, L. & Haines, L. (1996). *Building a civilised and competitive city: The Lace Market as a Cultural Quarter*, Report to Nottingham City Council, Feb 1996.
Crook, S., Pakulski, J. & Waters, M. (1992). *Postmodernisation*, Sage, London.
Featherstone, M. (1991). *Consumer Culture and Postmodernism*, Sage, London.
Featherstone, O'Connor & Wynne (1994). *ESRC Final Report* ref: R000233075
Game, A. (1991). *Undoing the Social: Towards a Deconstruction of Sociology*, Milton Keynes: Open University
Goodrich, P., Douzinas, C.& Hachamovitch, Y. (1994). *Politics, Postmodernity and Critical Legal Studies - The Legality of the Contingent*, Routledge, London.
Hall, S & Jacques, M. (1989). *New Times*, Lawrence and Wishart, London.
Handy, C. (1994). *The Empty Raincoat*, Arrow Business, London.
Harrison, B. (1992). 'Industrial Districts: Old wine in new bottles?' *Regional Studies* Vol. 26.5 pp. 469-483.
Harvey, D. (1989). *The Condition of Postmodernity*, Blackwell, Oxford.
Harvey, D. (1992). 'Social Justice, Postmodernism and the City', *International Journal of Urban and Regional Research*, Vol. 16.
Hewison, R. (1995). *The Culture of Consensus*, Macmillan, London.
Hill, D. & O'Connor, J. (1996). 'Review of Tale of Two Cities', *City* No. 3 Oct. 1996 pp.109-119.
Hollway, W. (1989., *Work Pyschology and Organisational Behaviour*, Sage, London.
Jephcote, M. (1992). 'Understanding Economics or Economics Understanding? A Case Study for Developing Economics Understanding as a Pupil Entitlement', in Bloomer, G., Brookes, K, & Jephcote, M. (1992).
Knights, D. (1995). 'Organisation Theory in the Age of Deconstruction: Dualism, Gender, and Postmodernism re-visited' paper for Workshop on Action, Structure and Organisations, EESECIMD, Paris, May.
Knights, D. & Odih, P. (1995). 'It's about Time! The significance of gendered time for financial services consumption', *Time and Society*, vol.4 (2).
Knights, D., Sturdy, A. (1994). 'The Consumer Rules? An Examination of the Rhetoric and Morgan, G. "Reality" in Financial Services', *European Journal of Marketing*, 28, 3.
Knights, D. & Raffo, C. (1990). 'Milkround Professionalism in Personnel Recruitment: Myth or Reality' in *Personnel Review*, 19,1.
Knight, R . (1992). *The Future of European Cities Pt. 4 : Cities as loci of Knowledge-based Development*, Report for the FAST programme, European Commission, DG V.
Kumar, K. (1995). *From Post-Industrial to Post-Modern Society*, Blackwell, Oxford.
Landry, C. & Bianchini, F. (1995). *The Creative City*, Demos, London.
Lash, S. (1990). *The Sociology of Postmodernism*, Routledge, London.
Lash, S. and Urry, J. (1994). *Economies of Signs and Space*, London, Sage.
Lewis, J. (1992). *Art, Culture and Enterprise*, Routledge, London.
Lovatt, A. (ed) **(1994)**. *Towards the 24 hour City*, MIPC publication, Manchester
Lovatt, A. & O'Connor, J. (1995). 'Cities and the Night Time Economy', *Planning Practice and Research*, Vol. 10, No. 2 pp.
Lovatt, A. & Milestone, K. (1994). 'Culture and the Northern Quarter', *MIPC Working Papers* ,Series II.
Martin, B. (1991). 'Qualitative Market Research in Britain: A Profession on the Frontiers of Postmodernity', in Kellner, H & Heuberger, F (eds.) *Hidden Technocrats: the New Class and the New Capitalism*, Transaction Press, New York.
Milestone, K. (1996). 'Regional Variations: Northernness and the new urban economies of hedonism' in O'Connor, J & Wynne, D (eds) (1996)
Mole, P. (1996). 'Fordism, Post-Fordism and the Contemporary City', in O'Connor, J & Wynne, D (eds) (1996) pp. 15–48.

Mommaas, H. & Corjan, E. Urban (1995). *Cultural Policy in Europe*, Report to Cultural committee, Eurocities. Direct from authors.
Mommaas, H. (1996). 'Modernity, Postmodernity and the Crisis of Social Modernisation: A Case Study in Urban Fragmentation' in *International Journal of Urban and Regional Research* Vol.20 No. 2.
Morgan, G. (1993). *Imaginization: The Art of Creative Management*, Sage, London.
Mulgan, G. (1995). *Freedom's Children*, Demos, London.
O'Connor, J. (1997.a). *Research in the Cultural Industries Sector: A review*, Report for Manchester City Council. MIPC Working Paper.
O'Connor, J. (1997b). *Feasibility Study for Cultural Industries Development Service*, Report for Manchester City Council. MIPC Working Paper.
O'Connor, J. (1997c). *Qualifications and Business Support in the Cultural Industries Sector: A review*, Report for Manchester City Council. MIPC Working Paper.
O'Connor, J. (1996). *The Northern Quarter and Manchester's Textile Industry*, case study presented for the European Textile Network conference, British Council, March 1996.
O'Connor, J. (1995a). 'The Regeneration Business', *City*, Double Issue, Dec. 1995 No. 1 & 2 pp. 167–170.
O'Connor, J. (1995b). 'CultureNet', Telematics for Urban and Rural Development bid document, *On-Line publication Manchester Host*, February 1995.
O'Connor, J. (1993). 'Manchester and the Millenium: Whose City, Whose Culture', *Regenerating Cities*, 1993, No. 4 pp. 17–19.
O'Connor, J. (1991). 'Local Authorities and the Arts' in Wynne, D (1991).
O'Connor, J. & Wynne, D. (1996a). 'From The Margins To The Centre: Cultural Production and Consumption in the Post-industrial City' in Holmwood, J. Radner, H. Schulze, G. & Sulkunen, P. (eds) *Constructing The New Consumer Society*, Macmillan, Oxford pp. 152–172.
O'Connor, J. & Wynne, D. (Eds) (1996b). *From the Margins to the Centre: Cultural Production and Consumption in the Post-Industrial City*, Arena, Ashgate
O'Connor, J. & Wynne, D. (1996c). 'Left Loafing' in O'Connor, J & Wynne, D (1996) pp. 49–90.
O'Connor, J. & Wynne, D. (1992) 'The Uses and Abuses of Popular Culture: Cultural Policy and Popular Culture', *Loisir et Societe* Vol. 14, No. 2 1992: 465–483.
Purvis, S. (1996) 'The Interchangable Roles of the Producer, Consumer and Cultural Intermediary; The new Pop Fashion Designers' in O'Connor, J & Wynne, D (eds) (1996) pp. 117–140.
Quilley, S. (1996) 'Manchester's Gay Village', in *Transgressions*, Vol. 1
Robson, B. (ed.) (1987). *Managing the City: The Aims and Impacts of Urban Policy*, Croom Helm, London.
Sassen, S. (1991). *The Global City*, Princeton: Princeton University Press.
Sassen, S. (1994). *Cities in a World Economy*, Pine Forge Press, California.
Shearman, C. (1996). 'Communities, Networks, Creativity and Culture: Insights into Localisation within Globalisation', in Farrand, C., Falaley, T. & Toze, R. *Technology, Wealth & Power in the New Global Political Economy*, Routledge, London pp. 59–84.
Shields, R. (1991). *Places on the Margin*, Routledge, London.
Taylor, I., Evans, K & Fraser, P. (1996). *A Tale of Two Cities*, Routledge, London.
Thomas, L & Hodkinson, S. (1988). 'What is Economic Awareness?', *Journal for Economic Awarenes*, Sept. 1988.
Usher, R. & Edwards, R. (1994). *Postmodernism and Education*, Routledge, London.
Walker, S. (1994). *Hulme Telematics Strategy*, Report for Hulme Regeneration Agency, Manchester.
Whittle, S. (1994). *The Margins of the City: Gay Men's Urban Lives*, Arena, Ashgate.
Wynne, D. (ed) (1991). *The Culture Industry*, Avebury, Aldershot.
Zukin, S. (1995). *The Cultures of Cities*, Blackwell, Oxford.
Zukin, S. (1994). *Landscapes of Power; From Detroit to Disneyworld*, Berkley, UCLA Press.
Zukin, S. (1988). *Loft Living*, Radius, London (First Published 1982).

Programming Creativity:
Public Policy in an Information Age

GEOFF MULGAN
Director, Demos

Introduction

What can be done in public policy to promote rather than programme creativity? Over the last few decades it has become commonplace to hear of the second industrial revolution, the information revolution that will take economies and societies out of the industrial age, just as the steam engine took us out of the agrarian one. But we can go even further, and this is a reason to be interested in this. The Nomura Institute in Japan classifies four eras of economic activity: agriculture, industry, information – and a fourth – creativity. They argue that it is the natural evolution of rich information environments. The flows of creative interaction in groupware, inter- and intranets, makes something new, and once this interaction emerges information in itself ceases to be very interesting. It is only the unexpected, the unpredictable, the combinations that make something new that count.

We can understand this shift from information to creativity as a combination of three sets of laws:

1 **Moore's law** saying that the cost of computing power halves every 18 months;
2 **Metcalfe's law** stating that the value of a network rises exponentially relative to the numbers using it; and
3 **Kao's law**, by John Kao, stating that the power of creativity rises exponentially with the diversity and divergence of those users.

Out of these laws evolve quite new organisatorial principles, new approaches to work and life. This also means that even before many have caught up with the information revolution, others are already moving on. With that movement from the image of the world as a computer, a calculator, we shift into a new metaphorical zone: a new set of images of the firm, the government, the city.

We once thought in the terms of Machine. This was the legacy of the military bequeathed first to governments and then to manufacturing industry, the idea of the world as a potentially perfectly running closed system, well-oiled, efficient and measurable, the image Fritz Lang captured in *Metropolis* so well that the fact followed fiction. This image gave us the organisation man so feared in the 50s, and the source of many of the best sci-fi movies like *Invasion of the Body Snatchers*. The image perhaps reached its apotheosis in the ideas of cybernetics for running society like a smart machine.

When we are concerned with creativity today, it is at least in part because so many areas of human life are now open systems. Nations no longer have clear boundaries; nor do selves, art forms and academic disciplines spill over. Furthermore, all societies are all the time interacting with natural systems. Coming to terms with open systems, in ecology and culture, is one of the great challenges of the next century.

Most of our systems were designed for the Machine Age, and the application of it is bringing the apotheosis of the Machine Age, not its transcendence. Institutions live around the fixed hierarchies and structures it often strengthens and education systems concentrate on basic skills. In government there is the separation between representation and the citizen, the provider and the user, the planner and the planned. Yet the widespread interest in creativity is at least in part because so many of these systems are coming unstuck. Education, welfare systems, governments – all appear to lack the spark of creative adaptation.

At this point networking, the fact that there are always more interactions and possible combinations than in the past, combines with our understanding of the larger contexts of human existence. Therefore the emerging dominant images of our time are biological ones, operating in terms of DNA and evolution, self-organising systems, complexity and existence far from the equilibrium. These metaphors emphasise adaptation, change, the fit between things and their environment. Even intelligence is seen in these terms: the brain is modelled as a rain forest. It is always easier to change metaphors than the things themselves.

Institutions that seem more biological, adaptive and creative are thriving: firms like Microsoft create enormous value out of nothing. In cultural industries the least promising materials generate wealth. In politics, organisations like Greenpeace which control no governments and pass no laws have the power to make the multinational firms tremble. This message is understood even in economics, for example in the work of Paul Romer recognising that power grows from ideas and nothing else. It is a message understood in business, where the intriguing fact of the last 19 years is how Japan failed to create audio-visual industries, just as it was not Germany that created the competitors to IBM – but rather the US. This realisation takes us to a great search for the sources of prosperity and well-being in the next century, with a sense that somewhere in the heart of it will be creativity.

In what follows I want to talk about four different domains: education, enterprise, holism and symbols, which help us to think about creativity and how we can cultivate it, even programme it in the daily lives of modern cities.

Education

I am starting from the basics, the school and the formation of children. The essentially bureaucratic traditional schooling: uniform, standard attainments/outputs, easily measured/quantified is used to sort people for career selection and grade their progress. And attainment means jumping through hoops producing the right words at the right time on the right piece of paper. Once young people have jumped through enough hoops, they have got an education preparing them for a standard career in a 20th-century industrial bureaucratic organisation. The irony is that when I ask my nephews and nieces to tell a joke, sing a song, paint a painting they can all readily do so, whereas if I or most of my friends are asked, we shy away.

The problem is that this conception of education rests on two core intelligences, linguistical and logico-mathematical, of the seven articulated by Howard Gardner.

Therefore it seems to thin human potential rather than narrow it. There are ways to deliberately teach creativity, but I see the issue as broader than this. Programming creativity requires fuller, more imaginative use of the range of intelligences spatial, musical, interpersonal, intrapersonal or bodily-kinaesthetic intelligence. There are many ideas about how multiple intelligences could be cultivated in schools: early identification of promise in one or more; cultivation of learning and curiosity; curricula aimed for genuine understanding rather than repetition; return to apprenticeships mixing learning and doing; chances to learn in real environments by running your own projects, dealing with adults as partners and so forth. Often it turns out that the use of creative capacities is the route into getting the motivation to learn.

One intriguing experiment illustrating this is the University of First Age in Birmingham, piloted this year and experimenting with new approaches to teaching particularly for the less motivated at school. Each teenager is entitled to one vacation course a year, plus a range of other opportunities. Unconventional approaches are adopted, like using mime and dance to teach chaos theory and fractals and children are immersed in subjects for 25 hours at a time rather than for 45-minute lessons. As one schoolchild put it:

Normally in school things fall out of my mind,
but here I can remember everything I have done.

There is a marked difference in terms of motivation.

Another example is the Columbia School Mosaic – this school is a primary recognised for overcoming the disadvantages of its pupils, set in the East End. It wanted to do a local history project, children were interviewing local residents about histories, and came up with a mosaic for the outside wall of the school – 60 feet long, 7 feet high, depicting scenes from local history and culture, designed and made by every adult and child at the school. It was sponsored by local businesses, thus establishing new relationships and contributing to local infrastructure. The mosaic has not been vandalised in the seven years since its completion.

The third example is Children's Express, a UD model for taking children from relatively poor backgrounds and sending them out to write reports which get published in local newspapers. This project gives children a voice, confidence, a capacity to tell stories and to be empowered by their creativity.

What strikes me in these examples is that they are not adding creativity as another block in the curriculum, but rather building into learning a new kind of chemistry that brings out potentials otherwise crushed.

Enterprise

The second policy issue is enterprise. Enterprise is in some respects another way of talking about creativity – finding new solutions, putting together packages, brokering deals and making things happen. Unfortunately most of our machine systems are not very well designed for enterprise. In economics these systems have become very good at logistics, planning and long-term research, but on the other hand there are relatively few well developed venture capital industries in Europe willing to take a gamble on the idea and there is relatively little culture of personal risk-taking. This is probably why the US lead in many of the creative industries remains so strong.

There is still too little innovation and creativity in financing ideas for many reasons: our traditions of formal stock markets and bank finance are simply less appropriate when the key asset is no longer a building, a patent, a factory but rather a possibility. We may have to cultivate ideas like the expert corporation, where already successful entrepreneurs create funds to back new ones, spin-offs from existing multimedia or software firms, corporate venturing from big foreign ones and the provision of new forms of public and private organisational umbrellas to help start-ups through difficult phases.

We can also take the idea of the entrepreneur into other fields. In the social area there is an increasing interest in the idea of the social entrepreneur. In J.B. Syas' definition the social entrepreneur moves resources from less efficient uses to more efficient ones, economically, socially and culturally. You will find social entrepreneurs in communities, in arts, in housing, in health. They often mix things that are usually separate: art space, training, child-care, church space, coffee shop and health centre, where GP's pay rent to the patients. They often disrespect formal boundaries and work in ways that do not easily fit professional structures and systems. They are individuals, not institutions, and they often left school early.

The point about social entrepreneurs is very much that in practice they are often the keys to revivals. Yet the state is not well-suited for supporting them: either it provides grants which lock in dependence and upwards accountability, requiring compliance to bureaucratic details, or it requires creation of cumbersome organisatorial forms before becoming eligible for back-up. Much the same could be said about cultural entrepreneurs, and the need to find creative ways of supporting creative activities and especially learning from the experience of how generous state support can often actually destroy creativity – as has happened in German literature and film.

Holistic Thinking

The great trend of the machine age was to break things down. We have inherited firms disconnected from responsibility for actions, arts disconnected from any obligation – supreme and sovereign. Taxes are first pooled but then spent through separated departmental structures and agencies. The great challenge is to find new ways to put the pieces together again.

This is nowhere more important than in cities which are wholes – whole complex systems from waste to education, traffic to air, health to jobs. To get the cities to work creatively, we need new holistic tools.

Our example is very concrete – budgeting. There have been some limited innovations with integrated local budgets. It is still very hard in most countries for crime agencies to invest in job opportunities, or health bodies to tackle causes of ill-health which have more to do with lack of status and self esteem rather than curing. Yet I suspect that through holistic budgeting approaches, with general benchmarks and targets for the quality of life, the machine-like character of so many modern governments could be unstuck.

Another example is the use of monies as new integrators of city economies in a radically different way. There are some embryonic forms in Canada, where cities have created a parallel infrastructure to the orthodox market, using cards of one kind or another. People are encouraged in by offering discounts on retailing, they are offered newsletters for purchase of locally produced goods and services; the city can achieve 30-40% used creatively. Criteria for access, like environmental standards, can be created. Card networks can be used to raise awareness of cultural activities outside the centre or to use differential discounting to spread activity. They can tie in the voluntary organisations or trade unions to offer special arrangements for the use of all the cities' resources. At a later stage it is possible to offer points so that people can exchange services – child-care, driving, plumbing – making useful work for the unemployed in what ultimately becomes a kind of twin economy, more local, easier to access for many other people besides the dominant ones.

Symbols

Finally we need to symbolise creativity in the ways cities work. We need role models and leaders who live their lives in imaginative ways and juxtapose different activities. We need substantial gestures making it clear to the public that creativity is genuinely valued, not just a new rhetoric.

Paradoxically in an era of personal culture, the Walkman and cable TV, there is all the more need for spectacular events that populate the public spaces, taking us out of ourselves. There is all the more need for a bit of show, for the secular equivalents of religious festivals, carnivals that disrupt the normal pattern of things. There is now a chance to do these in radically new ways.

Conclusions

So what does this add up to, is it a programme, is it a fad, is it real? I think that we can be sure that the lines dividing creativity from economics are disappearing. Firms are using theatre and games to stimulate their creative juices. Symbolically, old factories like the Rote Fabrik in Zürich are being turned into arts centres. New creative sectors like multimedia recognise no distinctions. There may also be one final reason why creativity is becoming important in a way it has not been in the past.

I mentioned earlier the value of the childlike mentality, that instinctive creativity that so often gets smothered. We are living in an era when for the first time ever experience does not equal wisdom and age does not in itself warrant respect. Children understand the next generation technologies better than teachers or parents. Let me give you an example: earlier this year in the UK a 12-year-old developed a piece of musical software and sold it to a private company for around £70 000. The parents were delighted, but the educational authority decided to sue. This seems the worst possible response to me: if we want new solutions we should be celebrating. We should be showering such children with prizes and providing opportunities for those children who do not have PC's at home to get up to speed as well.

In this rather upside down world of creativity, everyone has to learn – the boss has to learn from a junior, the parents from their children. I enjoyed the way Nelson Mandela recently encouraged a delegation of school children to advise him on the First International Children's Conference on the Environment. I like the ways school children are being mobilised to change the behaviour of their parents on sustainability. A creative programme that does not involve children and give them some leeway to do things that may be uncomfortable for adults will probably not be at all creative.

I began saying that creativity cannot be programmed, but strangely enough there are now things called creativity audits, auditing systems for managing creativity and turning it into workable solutions in business. They look at the asset value of creative capabilities – people, equipment, architecture, at the value of products less than 1 or 5 years old, the productivity of creativity – how many ideas are turned into actions. Thus they see where they came from, what gave rise to them, how much benchmarking, responses to challenges or just free-floating imagination was needed. They aim towards understanding the people – who they are, what motivates them, how much you attract or lose.

It is possible to integrate creativity into management and into structures, but in the process structures become more open, less like machines and more like living organisms. The basis of government is consistency, reliability and a not too experimental approach, there is a part that has to remain like a machine. But we need to significantly widen the scope for the experimental and the future oriented and recapture the more childlike way of thinking, depending less on experts. Zen calls it the beginners mind, where there are many possibilities, whereas in the expert's mind

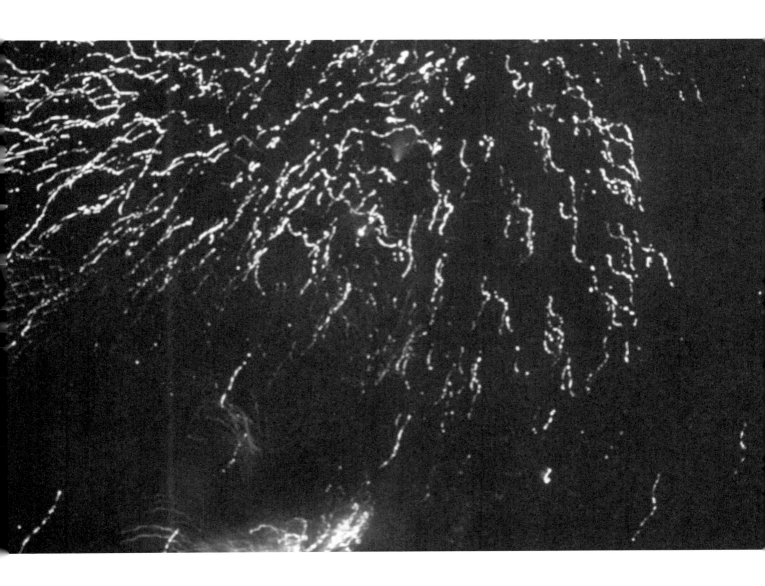

there are only a few. The point is to overcome the fear of the unknown, so vital to creativity, and then to have the strength of mind and discipline to match the chaos with clear discipline, clarity of purpose and targets, facing challenges and pressures.

This is a different balance from the past, a different way of thinking and, above all, it is the reminder that whereas in the machine age, even the computer age, consistency was everything, we are now in an age when, as Aldous Huxley wrote, consistency is against nature and the only people who are wholly consistent are the dead.

Urban Management in a Creative City
The Case of Rotterdam

L. VAN DEN BERG, I. BRAMEZZA, E. BRAUN AND J. VAN DE MEER

Introduction

The position of metropolitan regions in Europe is changing drastically. Owing to such fundamental developments as the globalisation of the economy, the transition to an information society and European integration, metropolitan regions are more and more becoming spatial economic entities. Recent research has confirmed that some "controlling capacity" on the regional level is indispensable[1]. Indeed the prosperity and continued success of a metropolitan region depend to a high degree on its organising capacity. The principal aspect of that capacity is to be able, adequately and on the proper spatio-economic scale, to anticipate, respond to and cope with changing intra- and intermetropolitan relations. Information technology may help to increase a city's organising capacity.

The city of Rotterdam has been very active and creative in increasing its organising capacity and, as a result, has been able to raise the quality of its urban management. To guide the big port city into the information society so that economic development is sustained demands great efforts, by the public as well as the private sector. The new ways of management Rotterdam has developed are illustrated through three case studies. First we elaborate the concept of organising capacity.

---

[1] van den Berg et al. 1993

Challenges for Cities and the Need for Organising Capacity

We can identify at least five challenges facing European cities.

1. In the competitive market cities have to offer attractive investment opportunities. They have to carefully look for what they can do or become, given their development potentials. Therefore, a precondition for a sustainable urban development is cities' capability to organise themselves so as to put their potentials to good use.
2. New market niches have to be identified and new activities developed to generate income, allow new investments, create new employment opportunities and increase the financial capacity of cities. Economic activities should produce positive externalities which increase the advantage for further activities to locate.
3. Moreover, cities have to look for a balance between economic development and the quality of the living environment, as this appears to be an essential precondition for economic growth.
4. As space has become scarce, cities have to find a balance between economic development and their spatial organisation. An excessive specialisation and functionalisation of urban space seems to be going on. Besides, the effects of the rapidly developing global networks increasingly impinge on the urban space.
5. Last but not least, cities have to look for balance between economic and social development. A favourable social environment is the precondition for the success of revitalisation projects and ensures sustainable development on the long term.

To be able to face the above challenges and develop harmoniously, cities must respond in an appropriate way. The key is the quality of urban management. High quality urban management can be defined as the development, execution and co-ordination of comprehensive strategies with the help of all relevant urban actors, in order to identify, create and exploit potentials for sustainable development of the city[2].

2 Bramezza and van Klin 1994

Improving the region's organising capacity has become an essential factor for sustainable development. Organising capacity should be coupled to a vision and strategy which integrate and direct all policy efforts at the metropolitan level. To formulate a vision and develop a strategy on this level requires a formally competent authority: the right administrative structure is important. Besides these two elements,

strategic networks are constituents of organising capacity. Administrative structure, strategic networks and their mutual interaction together form the governance structure: the patterns and the process of metropolitan governing. Organising capacity springs from the metropolitan governance structure.

Still other elements contribute to organising capacity. These are leadership (embodied in persons or organisations), political support (including the policy space that higher authorities leave to the local tiers) societal support (the strategies formulated have to be firmly based in society, among private citizens as well as market parties) and favourable spatial-economic conditions.

Vision and Strategy

Vision and strategy can be substantiated in many ways. An important element is support, a factor closely related to the variety of actors participating in the design of a vision and a strategy. The initiative, analysis and elaboration are usually reserved to the public sector: partnerships of metropolitan and local authorities. The immense effort required to create sufficient support can be relieved if private parties are also allowed to participate in the layout of a vision and strategies. Think of representatives from metropolitan enterprise (captains of industry), statutory trade corporations and housing societies, as well as scientists and prominent politicians. Another aspect to consider is the integrity of the vision and strategy. Developments in subareas that are not clearly integrated in an overall strategy are not satisfactory and may give rise to conflicts.

Strategic Networks

Strategic networks can assume many forms. A decisive element in the metropolitan context are the actors involved. The networks can logically be arranged in three classes.

1. Public networks: networks of public actors, including local or metropolitan authorities, in which different government levels and government bodies participate, such as the state, province, regional, metropolitan, local government and public companies.

2. Public-private networks in which, besides public representatives, there is also participation by entrepreneurs and other market parties, statutory trade corporations, organised interest groups, etc.
3. Private networks in which no authorities are represented: examples are bodies in which the business community in part or as a whole tries to evolve initiatives, or clusters of economically related enterprise.

Interaction between networks is another important feature of organising capacity. Public and private networks must be brought together: private networks can be "the meat on the bones" of the public ones. A situation where the public and private sector networks complement and reinforce each other best stimulates the creation of organising capacity.

Leadership

Leadership and the entrepreneurial spirit of key persons are qualities not restricted to governors. Others can also take initiatives and evolve ideas, for instance the president of the Chamber of Commerce, captains of industry or scientists. The main thing is that there is some kind of leadership; whether it emanates from the administrative structure or the networks, is of secondary importance. Nor is leadership inherent exclusively in individuals. It can also be exercised by specific organisation that has the formal competence or the right abilities, or power, to assume leadership.

Political Support

An obvious condition for metropolitan organising capacity is the degree of administrative autonomy. In some countries the national government distributes the financial means among the municipalities and also prescribes on what targets they must mostly be spent. In other countries the scope for developing a strategy at the metropolitan or local level is more generous. A national government may also formulate stringent rules for co-operation with private parties. Besides, European legislation can widen or narrow the margin for the metropolis or city to pursue its own policy. A relatively narrow margin limits the opportunities to develop a policy at the metropolitan or local level. For the successful undertaking of specific policies, support of the

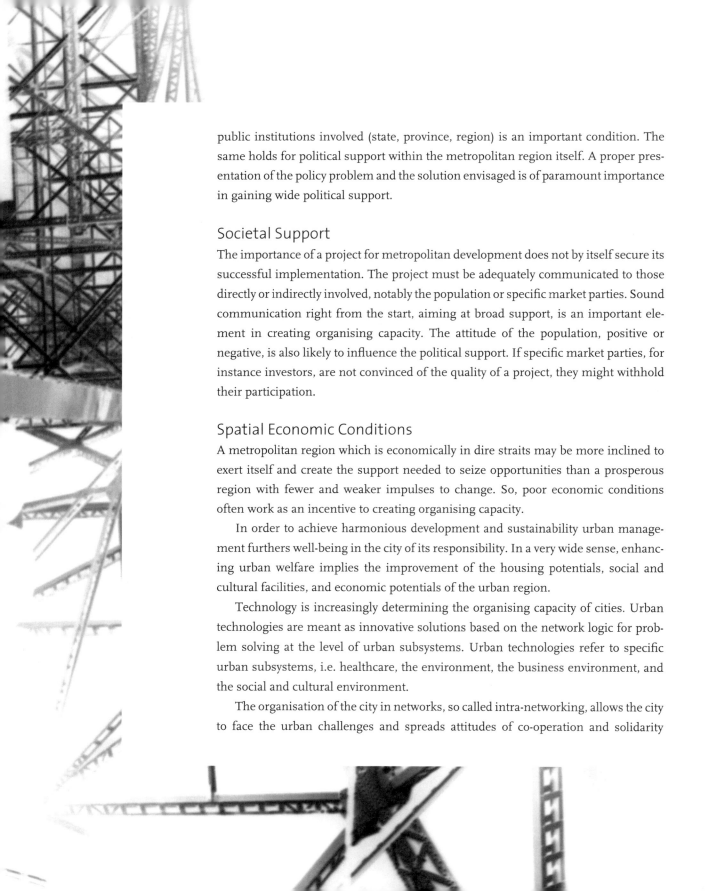

public institutions involved (state, province, region) is an important condition. The same holds for political support within the metropolitan region itself. A proper presentation of the policy problem and the solution envisaged is of paramount importance in gaining wide political support.

Societal Support

The importance of a project for metropolitan development does not by itself secure its successful implementation. The project must be adequately communicated to those directly or indirectly involved, notably the population or specific market parties. Sound communication right from the start, aiming at broad support, is an important element in creating organising capacity. The attitude of the population, positive or negative, is also likely to influence the political support. If specific market parties, for instance investors, are not convinced of the quality of a project, they might withhold their participation.

Spatial Economic Conditions

A metropolitan region which is economically in dire straits may be more inclined to exert itself and create the support needed to seize opportunities than a prosperous region with fewer and weaker impulses to change. So, poor economic conditions often work as an incentive to creating organising capacity.

In order to achieve harmonious development and sustainability urban management furthers well-being in the city of its responsibility. In a very wide sense, enhancing urban welfare implies the improvement of the housing potentials, social and cultural facilities, and economic potentials of the urban region.

Technology is increasingly determining the organising capacity of cities. Urban technologies are meant as innovative solutions based on the network logic for problem solving at the level of urban subsystems. Urban technologies refer to specific urban subsystems, i.e. healthcare, the environment, the business environment, and the social and cultural environment.

The organisation of the city in networks, so called intra-networking, allows the city to face the urban challenges and spreads attitudes of co-operation and solidarity among the urban actors, so increasing the organising capacity. The ideal situation would be a city with a "mega" networking system co-ordinating and including many other sub-networks.

SOME ILLUSTRATIVE PROJECTS

As an illustration of the way Rotterdam has tried to give substance to the notion of organising capacity, we discuss three cases.

Kop-van-Zuid

To cope with continuous social problems and the narrow economic basis of the city, the municipality of Rotterdam developed a new vision of and a new strategy for urban development. In this strategy a series of new projects was announced as the instrument for the revitalisation of the city. One of these is the "Kop-van-Zuid" project, a large-scale multifunctional urban renewal scheme. Deserted harbour grounds on the left bank of the Maas River, just opposite the city centre, are being transformed into a high quality waterfront with an attractive mixture of offices, housing, shops and cultural and recreational facilities.

The scheme was initiated by a small group of people from two municipal departments and the city council. Quality and accessibility were considered the key elements, and the scheme was to be realised in harmony with the surrounding town quarters and in co-operation with the private sector. An extensive communication strategy was developed to create administrative, societal and, at a later stage, political support. To secure support from the private sector and the national government, the municipality itself invested heavily in infrastructure, including a new bridge connection with the city centre, and the relocation of several municipal services to the development area.

The link between informal, non-committal networks and the official bodies has been cleverly accomplished by giving the project organisation the same status as the other municipal services, thus enabling better management through short communication lines. The strategic networks have served as a platform to generate sound support for the project. Finally, the flexibility of the Kop van Zuid concept has also proved its worth. The collapse of the office market was coped with by relocating several public offices and by increasing the amount of housing to be built.

ROM-Rijnmond

The Rijnmond area (the Metropolitan Region of Rotterdam) is one of the most densely populated and industrialised areas in the Netherlands. There is friction between further development of the main port and the quality of the living environment. At the initiative of the national Ministry of Housing, Physical Planning and the Environment, a dialogue was started between the region's municipalities, the Rotterdam port authority, the Province of Zuid-Holland and the regional business community. The aim was to develop a joint vision and strategy which would enable the simultaneous strengthening of the main port function and improvement of the living environment.

Initial difficulties in securing the commitment of various regional administrative entities have gradually been overcome by the shared desire to reduce the role of central government. The dialogue has resulted in the ROM-Rijnmond programme, which consists of 25 different sub-projects. These include for example the development of a new distribution estate (Distripark), a land-reclamation scheme at the mouth of the Nieuwe Waterweg, the reduction of traffic speeds and the planting of trees. The inclusion of several major infrastructure projects has secured the commitment of the business community to the realisation of the environmental projects.

Besides the flexibility of the network, a more formal structure is apparently needed. However, the establishment of a City Province (a new authority to be installed at the metropolitan level) with which the project was to be linked has not yet come to fruition.

The Health Service Network

Healthcare is a relevant sector in the Rotterdam economy, so it is an issue for the city government to help this sector to innovate. However, the healthcare sector is currently insufficiently organised, because of great competition between its main actors: hospitals, the regional health insurance company, general practitioners and specialists. The city of Rotterdam has taken the role of neutral and impartial broker. It has succeeded in bringing all the parties together around a table. A new solution, a network linking all relevant actors in the healthcare sector, has been created. The following actors take part in this electronic network for message transfer:

1. the local/regional insurance company (ZKZR), as supplier of a large share of the financial resources of the health sector;
2. the hospitals, as locations for the communication nodes and as places where electronic messages are sent to the general practitioners and insurers;
3. laboratories sending messages about the results of test to the general practitioners;
4. the specialists, who receive and send the messages to and from general practitioners about medical treatment and diagnoses of patients and send their declarations to the insurer; and
5. the pharmacists, who receive the prescriptions from the general practitioners and specialists directly through the network.

The process is one of slowly converging to the formulation of a common goal to improve the efficiency and quality of the healthcare system in the Rotterdam region. This process is being pushed by the municipality of Rotterdam. The initial costs for setting up the network have been sustained by the municipality. However, in the long run, the healthcare sector will be able to pay back the initial investment.

The advantages for citizens can be summarised as being a better, quicker and more efficient healthcare system in the region. Because of the better understanding of the partners in the healthcare sector, the citizen (the patient) is sure of getting a correct, quick and efficient transfer of information about his medical or clinical situation. The improved co-ordination between the partners in the medical sector will then improve the patient's situation.

Conclusions

The development of both the ROM-Rijnmond and the Kop van Zuid projects seems due to a unique combination of only a very few people. On the one hand this is an intriguing observation. On the other, there seems to be no blueprint on how to establish such a good combination. That many projects are less successful than the two discussed here might well have to do with the fact that unique combinations of key persons are far from common. Another fact to consider is that key people may change positions, thereby stripping a project of its "bearers".

That seems to be the case with the ROM-Rijnmond project. This long-term undertaking, which is now in its realisation phase, is having trouble in maintaining its momentum. Apart from key people having gone to other positions, there are other problems. One is that thus far ROM-Rijnmond has not produced any clearly visible results. Another problem is that the project management has not been given adequate competencies. The momentum may also be hampered by the fact that the citizens of the region are not actively involved. A stronger involvement could have provided wide support for such matters as the new land-reclamation scheme and the attempt to decrease the use of private cars. It might also have made it easier to secure financial commitment from the business community. For instance, the environmental projects might have got more funds because involvement of the public could have made businesses worried about their environmental image.

The cases show that a good communication strategy is a principal condition for creating societal support. If the population and market parties are not convinced that a project will contribute to their needs and wants, support will be minimal. Although explicit support by the population is not always needed to reach specific project objectives, it does tend to speed up project development, as the Kop van Zuid project shows. Besides, the Kop van Zuid project has been very well communicated by the media to the Rotterdam population, which is also reflected in the successful sales of many of the new houses even before they had been built. If a sound base in society is missing, the project runs the risk that the objectives will not be met in the end. That holds in particular for obtaining the interest of (commercial) market parties, such as private investors and end-users of offices. Especially the projects aiming at economic revitalisation (such as Kop van Zuid in Rotterdam) rely on the market to invest in the new business opportunities (office space, commercial housing, shopping) which the projects will create. In these projects marketing is highly important. We repeat what has been pointed out earlier: while good communication is a precondition for success, ultimate success will not be determined by communication alone. Other factors will be decisive in that respect. Nevertheless, a sound communication strategy, based on giving the right information to the right groups at the right moment, is an important means to convince the public and the market of the necessity of a project.

It is important to understand that projects like the ones just mentioned often stretch over a number of years. Given the duration, the number of actors, the number of variables and the complexity of renewal projects, one or more elements of organising capacity will inevitably change. The challenge is to prepare for change in order to keep the project on track. It is one thing to get the conditions right, it is another to keep them so. Sudden changes can occur, and organising capacity implies the ability to anticipate and be flexible enough to cope with them. Strategic networks provide the framework to realise that to some degree.

One of the instruments for sustaining the momentum is early and regular communication of the results so far achieved. Another instrument is flexibility. The experience from the Kop van Zuid project is that the vision must be flexible enough to cope with changing market conditions. At the start, the project gave much weight to the development of offices. However, when the market for office space fell into a recession, those responsible managed to switch to high-quality housing, for which demand had grown. Because of that flexibility the Kop van Zuid project is still on track.

Final Remarks

The Rotterdam case studies were carried out by EURICUR within a large scale international comparative study on organising capacity in eight European cities: Antwerp, Bilbao, Bologna, Eindhoven, Lisbon, Munich, Rotterdam and Turin.

The general outcome of this study, shortly to be published by Averbury, shows that indeed leadership, vision and strategy, strategic networks, spatial-economic problems, political support and adequate communication can all be regarded as critical factors of failure and success in terms of organising capacity; organising capacity comes in different disguises.

Organising capacity is really the key to urban innovation and the successful attack on problems and attainment of objectives. In view of the increasing integrality of urban issues, the road to success is almost always by the joint endeavours of various public and often also private parties. The challenge to the local and regional authorities is to mobilise the competency, knowledge and energy present in the metropolitan area, in order to achieve a creative city developing innovative strategies and structures. That calls for another type of urban manager to those prevailing until just a short time ago. An enterprising attitude putting the activation of networks and communicative abilities first will command the future.

LITERATURE

Berg, L. van den, E. Braun and J. van der Meer (1996). *Organising Capacity of Metropolitan Cities*, EURICUR, Rotterdam.
Berg, L. van den and I. Bramezza (1996). *The Development of Intra- and Trans-Urban Networks; 9 urban technologies as innovative solutions to urban problems*, European Commission, Brussels.
Berg, L. van den, H.A. van Klink and J. van der Meer (1993). *Governing Metropolitan Regions*, Averbury, Aldershot, UK.
Bramezza, I., and J. van der Meer (1994). *Urban Management, Backgounds and Concepts*, EURICUR, Rotterdam.

Making Space for Creativity
The Changing Responsibilities of Arts Organisations
and Artists in Contemporary Communities

JENNIFER WILLIAMS
Director; British American Arts Association

Introduction

The vision of the British American Arts Association I am representing revolves around the belief that the arts are central to human development, bringing insight to experience and value to community interaction. By giving us perspectives into the nature of human experience, the arts serve multiple functions in educational, social, political and economic settings and have extensive contributions to make. We believe there is something magic and vital about the existence of art and artists. But we also believe that the future of the arts as a sector and their ability to be able to apply some of that magic in contemporary communities, depends on them reshaping their relationship with the rest of society by encouraging access and consciously reaching out to new audiences and making new partnerships. Today I will explore some of the partnerships the arts have formed which have been shown to be most effective in terms of building sustainable communities: communities in which people feel valued and have a sense of security, identity, belonging and purpose.

If given a chance, the arts can play a crucial role in building communities. But the first point I want to make is that the commitment to allowing space for the arts and other cultural activity to have their effect is at a much deeper and more universal level than simply a commitment to the arts. The reality of living in cities, in communities, in the world is that you cannot build walls high enough to separate yourself from your neighbour. Survival and peaceful co-existence depend on subscribing to a value system that encourages the contribution of people with different experiences, different perspectives, and different ways of solving problems. We need this to ensure that we have the best mix in addressing the pressing issues of our time. We need this to make space for creativity.

In his *Reflections of a Foundation* President Franklin Thomas, recently retired from the Ford Foundation, urges us to focus on and value those who act, who affirm, who do things, who build things, instead on the critics of society, those who would tell us con-stantly what is wrong with this or that. He points out that a commitment to core values represents a commitment to the democratic process and provides the glue for society. If that is in place, the society can and should be as diverse as possible, because diversity adds to the richness of life.

In basing my introduction on the ideal of building communities and change on a shared sense of core values – with one of those shared values being the celebration of diversity – I want to set at least part of the context in which artists and arts organisations find themselves working in these years running up to the millennium. I want to look at how the arts and artists help communities and if they can help communities, how communities, in turn, can also help artists. And it is the people-centred part of urban regeneration that I am interested in today.

My focus is on some of the responses various arts groups and individuals are coming up with to acknowledge and facilitate what I hope is a groundswell of interest and action to expand their participation in building their communities.

Recently, I was privileged to join a panel discussion called Identity in Transition. Artists from South Africa, in London for a festival of South African music and dance, probed the changing realities for people of all backgrounds in the new South Africa. Everyone acknowledged that change could not be instantaneous but that everyone had to make adjustments and to learn to think and act in new ways now that at least the formal apartheid is at an end. In a parallel way, the arts are emerging from a kind of apartheid, where the established, elite single culture arts, having for many decades been separated from the broader cultures that spawned them, are having pressure put

upon them to reintegrate. This is a completely different topic, but the mechanisms for reintegration are most visible in the work of the arts in urban revitalisation and arts in education.

Today I will look at three groups including arts and cultural institutions, arts organisations based in the community and artists. Each of these groups takes as its entry point into the conversation some form of education, access or participation.

Arts and Cultural Institutions

In a succinct report called *Excellence and Equity* the American Association of Museums concluded that museums:

> *share the responsibility with other educational institutions to enrich the learning opportunities for all individuals and to nurture an enlightened, humane citizenry that appreciates knowing the value of its past, is resourcefully and sensitively engaged in the present and is determined to shape a future in which many experi-ences and many points of view are given voice.*

Current research by the British American Arts Association explores the interface between the artistic and education policies of cultural institutions. It is often through education policies that the clearest picture of contact with the community is found. The study is revealing a highly complex, fluid situation comprising a range of dynamic tensions. The education work can be highly professional and interpretative, supporting and developing the art form. It can be designed as a marketing tool, it can be used as a way to raise money. It can serve as a catalyst to help old-style organisations, like orchestras, to evolve into more modern structures, say as a group of ensembles and teachers coming together in full orchestra strength only occasionally.

For some institutions, education is a small part of their work. For the Royal Shakespeare Company, though they have a superb education department, the central emphasis of the theatre as a whole is around how to produce better plays. A number of arts institutions maintain that the art is intrinsically educational and doesn't need a special programme. On the other hand some newer concept organisations, like

Moviola in Liverpool, founded in recent years, have integrated education into every aspect of their planning and programming, with participation from all parts of the community in making, showing and appreciating film and other forms of the moving image.

From our perspective here today, what is interesting is that the traditional cultural institutions, always prominent in their communities, but sometimes quite exclusive, are being asked by those same communities to make their facilities, programmes, and whole ethos more accessible. The State Museum in Mexico City had a problem with homeless children sitting around the steps of the museum. Now they have initiated an education programme for those same children, in connection with the social services.

Institutions or projects which incorporate public art into their remit have the opportunity to bring a different sort of benefit to a community. With public art attention is often focused on the process as well as the final product; in many projects, engagement with the public in gathering content or context for a piece is widespread and accepted. The Glasgow European City of Culture Festival 1990, described so ably by the Comedia report *Helsinki – A Living Work of Art*, is a treasure-trove of examples of how a modern festival can orchestrate hundreds of successful public arts projects. Glasgow Lit Up, a massive lantern procession starting in all parts of the city and converging on the centre, and Glasgow is Stitches, an equally ambitious banner project, were cited as being among the most successful collaborations between the artists and the communities. The organisers recognised that a cultural celebration could not solve the historical economic problems and injustices that pervaded Glasgow's communities. Yet they believed that:

Creativity feeds on itself and leads to self-esteem for those who live in a city, and increased enjoyment for those who visit.

Another Glasgow example is the Garnethill project, a collaboration between the Goethe Institute, the Festival Office, the Department of Parks and Recreation, local planning groups and Dieter Magnus, a German artist. The end result is a park of first rate quality in a derelict site in an urban residential area with a lively multicultural community. Magnus believes that:

The survival of big cities will be decisively determined by the extent to which we succeed in expanding the scope of space for people, promoting their participation and their opportunity for development.

Theatre Royal Stratford East, in London, has led the way for years in combining quality professional theatre productions, which have a good record of transferring to commercial houses, with exciting community involvement through young playwrights' schemes and music hall evenings featuring local performers often alongside television personalities.

What I am trying to show with this set of examples is that many if not most cultural institutions are changing their traditional position in their communities. They are finding that they have much to offer and much to gain by being interactive citizens, creating new partnerships and new configurations of their arts "product". And increasingly they are finding it is not acceptable to be an elitist enclave. Indeed these institutions, though of a classic mainstream nature, are in varying stages of evolution towards full integration or reintegration with the communities in which they are situated. And because of all of these factors and more, cultural institutions can be strong partners in the wider urban revitalisation efforts in cities. Someone needs to initiate those conversations.

Schools and Community Based Arts Organisations

There are other arts organisations which have been conceived as community-linked in some basic way. The format varies from organisations which produce arts with people from the community to ones which work in educational or other alternative arts settings in an interactive way with their audiences. Perhaps the chief differences from their arts and cultural institution cousins is that they are designed to be of a scale that can easily be more local and perhaps more spontaneous; they are also different to the extent that their work often falls between the lines of funding categories, not quite "real" art, not quite "real" social services, not quite real urban design. At the same time the results can be superb as artistic experimentation, standards can be high, and often their social drive is high.

Last week I was taken by an arts group in Glasgow called Arts is Magic to visit a project of theirs in the Easterhouse estate in the east of the city. It has endless rows of tenement blocks, with a population of 40 000 people. There is nothing to do for children or adults. There are housing associations scattered throughout the estate and one is working on rebuilding and replacing housing. Through a partnership with Arts is Magic they are also redesigning the layout of the housing to make public park spaces. In order to build positive uses for the parks and a sense of local ownership, they have invited local children to help design everything from the furniture to the sculptures which will adorn the park.

When I visited, 12 children under ten were on their fifth of eight 4-hour working days in which, together with the artists, they were looking at the overall design challenge, learning in astonishing detail about positive and negative space, about working co-operatively and individually, and about the processes needed to make a sculpture. Other children hung about the edges of the activity, watching, wondering, almost asking to be included. Here the arts organisation is acting as a mediator-negotiator, a translator for the housing association to be able to locate artists, co-ordinate the whole activity, and eventually work to make sure that the follow-up is sound and sensible.

Another kind of participation can be found in Washington DC. Liz Lerman's Dance Exchange features a professional dance company with dancers between 18 and 80 years of age. The discipline is rigorous, the product splendid and the ethos of company and performance extraordinary and, for me, emotional. They work in a variety of alternative settings, performing in hospitals and old people's homes as well as at schools and universities. Connected to the performance are workshops for the audiences – workshops in movement and much more. The words that come to mind are dignity, celebration, humour, and quality.

A third example from the States is the Manchester Craftsman's Guild and Bidwell Training Centre located in Pittsburgh. Here, in a tough inner-city area, a miracle happens every day. The centre is a creatively thought out, mixed-use development consisting of a gallery, a high-tech performance theatre, an array of professional classes in photography, ceramics, music, furniture making, and more. It also houses

私は安全運転をしています。
永山 博

まかせてあんしん

D1331

training courses in literacy, cooking, and hotel management, fibre optics, and many other fields. All of these activities work side by side, each participant taking creative steps towards becoming a more well-rounded, trained person, each supporting the others by their presence. All are housed in a beautifully designed building with space to interact and space to think individually, the governing concept being respect for human ability and the right to discover and develop it. Each of these examples is driven by the vision of people who have chosen to invent new systems in which to work. The results can be called "educational" but they also focus on high quality artistic output through hard work and discipline, with a high regard for and measure of the processes involved.

I think that educationalists – teachers, parents, school governors – ought to be brought into the discussion about the creative revitalisation of cities, and the arts are a valid route for them to enter through. Most of these arts organisations, both classical cultural institutions and community arts organisations, work with schools; some also work with learning organisations outside the formal education systems. Many educationalists consider the arts a strong and valid route to learning. This having been said there is surprisingly little regular planning or policy contact between learning establishments and the arts world. A project we are working on at the moment, called Common Threads – the Arts for Life looks at connections between the arts and education located outside the formal education systems – in adult learning places, in opportunities for older people, in youth networks. These collaborations are not always easy to make successful. Often breaking down after first contacts, owing to the lack of a common language with which to negotiate a way to meld the learning aims with the learning aims. The common ground, if found, is usually located in a shares concern for strong communities, good environment and personal insight and interest. It is at the moment of finding that common ground that arts and learning organisa-tions alike are most likely to be open to participating together in urban revitalisation efforts.

Much arts contact with the community is of course done directly with schools. Cultural institutions and artists-in-residence programmes exist and as they mature come close to creating significant real partnerships. Terry O'Farrell, an Irish ceramics artist, worked in a school in North London as an artist-in-residence. The head teacher, concerned about a growing apathy, decided if she chose a theme and asked every curriculum subject to address it in some way, she could build something useful. The theme was gardens. Terry was invited to design an appropriate arts response. With nearly no resources, all teachers and all students and quite a few parents had designed and made a porcelain tile depicting some aspect of the history of the city. The tiles were then built into a permanent garden wall in the playground. Attendance records were shattered, teacher morale rose significantly, and the climate for learning was much improved.

Some interesting research which looks at some of the factors operating in this example is being conducted; it looks at arts and education in light of how a person acquires his or her personal attitudes, values and interests, how a person builds a talent for discernment. It is in this area that I've been thinking recently that there must be some strong work to be done which links schools and the arts and sustainable urban environments.

So I was delighted to meet Kiri Bjorka Hodneland from Oslo who had a wonderful story to tell about a drama unfolding in her country and in her city. Beginning in the autumn of 1997, Norway will be, I think, the first country to include architecture in the compulsory curriculum. This requirement, as I understand it, is part of the "arts and crafts" subject in the curriculum, a subject which includes industrial design, history of art, woodwork and needlework, among other things. Aesthetics is meant to form the overall base in this new field which comprises both theory and practice. According to the guidelines issued by the Ministry of Education, Research and Church Affairs:

- The local neighbourhood should be used as a reference area for the children's work.
- Teachers are encouraged to make the subject form an important part of the cross-disciplinary project work.

A fascinating pilot project in response to the new curriculum challenge has been designed for Oslo by Ms Hondeland and her colleagues. The project called The Small Ugly Looking Places Project is meant to form part of the larger Safe City Project which the city has launched challenging many departments to address the problem together. Through the "ugly" programme, school children are encouraged to define a part of the city, an environment, close to their school to engage with, adopt and understand. The pupils are encouraged to co-operate with the departments within the municipality such as the Planning and Building Department, the Parks and Sports Department and the Cleansing Department. The challenge is how these ugly places can become and remain pleasant outdoor areas which make you feel welcome and therefore encourage the desire for civic maintenance and responsibility.

The places and secrets are taught by older children to younger children, ensuring a continuity of caring. Children learn architecture, local history, local art, street furniture. And perhaps even more important, the lessons learned from the experience add to each participant's own identity and sense of place.

This pilot project and this commitment of a central government to the primacy of design and aesthetics in the nation's priorities are an inspiration to our discussions here.

Artists

Many if not most of the projects above involve artists in either planning or the execution of the interaction with the community or school settings in which the work takes place. But which artists are interested in this work, which are most suited? Why do some artists work in it and others keep well away? Can training help develop artists for this kind of work?

Artist John Fox in the UK was trained as a visual artist, but he had a strong sense of how his own work would be enriched by taking as his inspiration the changes that were happening in various communities, and working with the people being affected by those changes to produce arts pieces containing visual, musical and theatrical elements. When the Dockland area of East London called the Isle of Dogs was being changed beyond recognition from an outmoded, now out-of-work shipping community to a high-tech corporate headquarters with new fast rail systems and high-rise buildings displacing an old community, Welfare State Theatre went in and did an art piece, called "Raising the Titanic". The process, many months in the preparation, involved hundreds of local citizens, including crane operators, ship-makers, and a host of "ordinary citizens" in an all-singing, all-dancing, theatre celebration piece about change and adaptation. The whole operation drew a great deal of public attention to the plight of the soon to be disrupted citizenry of that part of London, and the event was credited with having at least helped to formulate a better new housing situation for the area.

In North Philadelphia, a tough city neighbourhood by any standards, Chinese artist Lily Yeh spotted a vacant lot outside her studio. She decided to work out there on building a sculpture garden. Without a grand plan in mind she simply started, people were curious, she allowed them closer, she "let them" help, they began to assume ownership and a pride began to develop. Today there is a wonderful, safe, respected park in the space. Her calm receptiveness and creativity and her ability to let others express their creativity worked magic in a small corner of the world.

I think that Mr Fox and Ms Yeh were naturally attracted to interacting with "real" people to fulfil their urges to make art, but many artists, especially after their training, are not so inclined. Traditionally, many artists have resisted any thought that their art might be "used" as a social tool. An interesting experiment at the Guildhall School of Music and Drama in London is showing that at least some artists, those inclined to want to, can be taught new concepts about what their jobs as artists will be – ones which allow them to apply and explore their artistic talents in a number of settings with many different collaborators. A group of graduate students have worked two years on a programme which is set in the crypt of a church in Tower Hamlets in East London. They work with Bangladeshi young people, they teach music, they learn music, they create various performances together. Everyone benefits. Just before leaving London this week I heard of an orchestra who put experience of work "in the community" high on the list of positive features to look for in prospective orchestra members. Some artists are finding that a broader application of their talents is quite acceptable, quite satisfying.

It is interesting to think of redefining what an artist's job is and to also look at what kinds of creative abilities any number of people might have when it comes to animating communities.

Before I close, I would like to read a short quote from the novel *Beloved* by Toni Morrison, the wonderful black American writer. I was privileged to hear her speak in

Washington recently where she was drawing our attention to the rather disconcerting observation that although the past is getting much longer – we know more and more about the formation of the universe – it seems that less and less is known or planned for in the future. Meetings like this looking at what can be developed and improved by the millennium and beyond are rare, and a twenty-year plan is very hard to locate. At the same time we are rushing into the newest life-extending, modern medical applications, we should all probably last until we are 90 or 100. "Live longer for what?" she asked an uncomfortable number of times

Instead, if I am optimistic, and in general I am, it is because I have become aware of a group of people who are driven to stimulate participation by other people in socially, environmentally or culturally sound projects. They have considered the reality that if they offer more opportunity to more people in order that those people can gain self confidence and a sense of their own effectiveness as individuals and as citizens, the community benefits, even shines.

In *Beloved*, the grandmother, Baby Suggs, acts as a sort of community animator, of a special sort that we need and rely on for success in the work we all take on. She is a sort of local hero, a priestess with powers to help people know themselves.

Ms Morrison says:

> *After situating herself on a huge flat-sided rock, Baby Suggs bowed her head and prayed silently. The company watched her from the trees. They knew she was ready when she put her stick down. Then she shouted, "Let the children come!" They ran from the trees toward her.*
>
> *"Let your mothers hear you laugh," she told them and the woods rang. The adults looked on and could not help smiling.*
>
> *Then, "Let the grown men come," she shouted. They stepped one by one from among the ringing trees.*
>
> *"Let your wives and children see you dance," she told them, and ground-life shuddered under their feet.*
>
> *Finally she called the women to her. "Cry," she told them. "For the living and the dead. Just cry" And without covering their faces the women let loose.*

It started that way: laughing children, dancing men, crying women and then it all got mixed up. Women stopped crying and danced; men sat down and cried; children danced, women laughed, children cried until exhausted and riven, all and each lay about the Clearing damp and gasping for breath. In the silence that followed, Baby Suggs, holy, offered up to them her great big heart.

She did not tell them to clean up their lives or to go and sin no more. She did not tell them they were the blessed of the earth, its inheriting meek, or its glorybound pure. She told them that the only grace they could have was the grace they could imagine. That if they could not see it, they would not have it.

I would say to you in closing, it is our right and our responsibility to think and act creatively in our cities. Sort out what you as an individual believe about sustainability, human dignity and self-esteem and about the value of diversity, work toward coming to a collective response with your colleagues.

The City Furnished

Jean Schneider
Professor, University of Art and Design Helsinki

English translation by Tim Pike, from the original paper published in DIZAJN, Feb. 1997. Reproduced by permission of DPI/Ministère de la Culture

Take the map of a city, and with an eraser, remove smoothly all the buildings, take away the street edges and wipe out the green blurs of the surrounding trees. At this stage, imagine that, as if in a Borgesian tale, these changes have actually taken place. All that remains now, in this bleak area, to help you find your way around are benches, road signs, bus stops, lamp posts and bygone images: a whole range of heterogeneous archaeological artefacts which, despite being so varied, describe accurately the way a city functions.

At this point, I would like to introduce the following idea: these accessories might make up the very basics of modern cities – as we know them –, and somehow much more than the architecture surrounding them. They are the very heart of a cities' existence, rendering it fit to live in. As much as the destiny of the skyscraper is tied to the one of the elevator, the structuring of various networks in a given space – and its visibility – is the basic condition of modern urban planning. Therefore, these technical objects are both the perceptible imprints and the silent witnesses of everything that flows through any city. It is increasingly easy to appreciate that the amount of street furniture is directly proportionate to the habitability – and the level of civilisation[1] – of the modern metropolis. Any African town epitomises this situation. If the township can be distinguished from any white district, it is definitely through the lack of lamp posts, water outlets, telephones boxes etc.

[1] The relation between civilisation and cities stems from the etymology itself.

But it is by no means sufficient to limit the analysis to this single observation, as it provides us with no means of backing up the design of these objects. If urban accessories enable us to live in cities, it might be because they are dialectically opposed to the rooted and static nature of buildings. The movement they embed originates sometimes from metonymy: though a bus stop does not move, it is still a threshold between two different velocities, and therefore two different patterns of a given territory. How about lamp posts, though? Firstly, they extend the day-time hustle and bustle through the night, as night becomes an abstract notion in cities, and ultimately a form of life of its own. Secondly, the movement might also come from the void that separates objects: this void generates visual tension and an appealing motion. When set up in networks, movement implies repetition within a given space and, as a consequence, this visual rhythm makes us aware of urban fluidity. Look at the way our painters portrayed our capital cities at the turn of the century, as they attempted to depict the aforementioned tension and the energy of rhythm. I can picture Janson's painting *Hornsgatan by night*, in which a snow covered town is shown only by a yellow pattern of glowing lamp posts. Look at *Metropolis*, a painting in which Grosz symbolically splits down a crowd, the people grimacing as they wait impatiently for a tram to come, shops and street signs flickering all around.

In order to get a sharper understanding, I would like to explore the cinematographic world. Serge Daney said once that films and cities share on common destiny, and it might be so because they owe their existence to motion: while one generates it, the other demonstrates it. In G.W. Pabst *Joyless Street*, an expressionist film of the 1920s, architecture is broken down to straightforward elements of darkness and light, the idea of space being amplified by the spherical beams generated by the arc lamps, as Lotte Eisner wrote, adding that streets and roads symbolise the call of Destiny, particularly at night with the dazzling traffic, the street lamps alight, the illuminated signs, the head lamps and the shiny asphalt wet with rain.

These urban signs might be the milestones of another geometry that we could call mobile-spaces.

One thing is already clear: due to their repetition, these urban accessories set the city in motion. But by going off at a tangent into cinema, we might discover even

more. Wim Wenders, upon a return from the United States, wrote that each and every city which could claim to the title looked alike. Everywhere, you saw the same wide streets and the same neon-lit petrol stations, the same neon-lit motels, the same neon-lit supermarket. Nothing else. Nothing beyond the surface. No genuine city identity, no genuine city life.

What I am mainly suggesting is that if the heart of the metropolis beats at a constant and unchanging pace – the rhythm, in the above example, being that of cars –, then the city dies away, and becomes nothing more than a built-up area. It might be Dziga Vertov – based on his constant research to capture motion – who gives us the sharpest definition:

> *The City is a cross-section of the present, where people, trams, motorbikes and trains come and go, each and every bus follows its itinerary, and each and every car goes about its business.*

To summarise it, one might be able to define the city by the fact that different scales of time mingle in the same given space. Metaphorically speaking, each and any network runs using its own internal clock which implies synchronicity, namely a certain homogeneous rate of movement. Thus, in Paris, the suburban rail network, the underground system and the bus routes are three independent webs, independent in time and space, but sharing the same territory. To take things further, we could approach a group of signs as the visible – and therefore noticeable – outlets of an associated mobile-space. If the idea of fitting into a city is more a case of feeling its pulses that visualising its lay-out, then we can understand the genuine purpose of urban accessories.

But a lurking danger threatens the city. Increasingly sophisticated and "urbanised" furniture organises the city so that it becomes identified and understood by a tiny minority: the one that has the power is the one that sets the order. These accessories are being used to keep check on all that is going on. Benches are replaced by single seats to prevent the homeless from lying down and have a rest. Phone card call-boxes or meters oblige customers to pay in advance a service they might use. Video cameras watch over the streets and public squares. In a softer manner, street maps are situated on the least visible side of the panels showing glossy TV images, and by doing this, cities are choosing to be more an object of desire than a place to live, more a product to be bought than something to be discovered. They believe themselves to be generating feelings of love when in fact they are selling their souls. Go and visit Budapest, Prague, Abidjan...The new street furniture – often from a unique manufacturer – is very much present, and believe it or not, the signs read Marlboro, Coca-Cola and McDonald's to a point where it almost seems grotesque. The mercenary metropolis is becoming more and more like the nostalgia-fuelled scenery of a television studio.

That is unless a shift takes place, leading to the fragmentation of the bonds of subordination linking cities to their suburbs. Suburban towns don't have a history to hide behind, and therefore need the aforementioned poly-rhythmic patterns all the more, since, as I have already emphasised, these patterns go hand in hand with the desire – and even the possibility – to live somewhere. Street furniture – in the broadest sense – must move away from ready-made solutions and emanate from a Genius Loci, the poetic interpretation of places. But this has to be but one aspect of a wider general policy. Converting a village square into a car park is a way of sacrificing old people and childhood; public benches, however attractive they may be, will never detract from that fact. The whole idea of creating pedestrian streets without the sort of public facilities that might allow you to stop or change a baby, or that demonstrate no link whatsoever with what sustains the town (its Hinterland) or what expresses its existence (the culture it produces), makes such pedestrian streets as false and artificial as open-air shopping malls. Does this fear seem to you to be vain? Well, any commercial centre often seems to proudly name itself as the Centre (East, West, 2 etc.). If these remakes are to be seen as mediocre and effortless attempts to mimic the original version, let us hope that the authentic city centres don't set about producing the number threes.

Inform(ing) City

DOINA PETRESCU
Architect, Radical Design Studio-Paris

The pictures of this article, by the courtesy of the author, show examples of kiosks and other post-socialist commercial hybrids in Bucharest, Romania.

Informe

Informe is a term and concept by which I have chosen to interpret and deform the title of this publication and the preceding conference, The Creative City. The French and Latin word *informe* plays with two opposite meanings: the Latin prefix *in* signifies a privation, a negation but also in, inside. *Informe* is without-form-in-the-form, the without form which, at the same time, nourishes and subverts the form in and from its very interior. It is always the without-form which is the origin of form. It is the *informe*, which informs. This term associated with the term "city" helps us to highlight certain matters connected to the condition of creation and creativity in the city.

For the sake of the following discussion, I wish to invoke the article Informe (translated into English as formless) by Georges Bataille. The operational force of the Bataillian term can be imported straight into the heart of our debate by operating with an analogic replacement of terms and mutation within the original text.

> ... *Informe (formless) is not only an adjective having such and such meaning, but a term serving to declassify, requiring in general that every thing should have a form. What it designates does not, in any sense whatever, possess rights and everywhere gets crushed like a spider or earthworm. For academics* [urbanists] *to be satisfied, it would be necessary, in effect, for the universe* [city] *to take a form. The whole philosophy* [urban thinking] *has no other aim; it is a question of fitting what exists*

into a frock-coat. To affirm on the contrary that the universe [city] resembles nothing at all and is only formless, amounts to saying that the universe [city] is something akin to a spider or a gob of spittle.

In this transcription of the Bataille's text, "city" replaces "universe" and works at the universal level: an enlargement, displacement and deformation of the notion city, and not only in the text. In the contemporary society, the city has become global universal condition as a specific form of social and economical organisational entity. Urban culture has definitely become universal and dominant with the contribution of new technologies and the physical city is supplemented, spread and generalised through the Cybercity. When this city as big as the universe is "something akin to a spider or a gob of spittle", the hyper collapses into micro and our whole urban thinking is turned upside down as the city becomes associated with the *informe*.

I suggest we keep this operation of logical inversion and investigate its effects in the elaboration of new strategies in urban planning, and that we keep also the metonymic figure of spider and gob of spittle which gets the Universal City out of its "mathematical frock-coat" and thus exposes it to "getting crushed everywhere", subjecting it to the possibility of unmediated and subjective decisions: after enlargement and magnification, reduction and minimalisation.

What would a city that "does not posses rights and everywhere gets crushed" be? The Inform(ing) City resembling nothing is nothing in itself – it is performative and exists only operationally – and contacts with such a city take place by deviating from bureaucratic and technological protocols, from all abstraction and idealisation.

The city is not only in our hands, but also under our feet. We have to translate the action of *informe*, its dynamics of demotion and deposition, into new urban attitudes. In an informing condition, the position of the urbanist, his attitude versus the city is translated into a performative violence. Informing introduces the city by its very utterance and by the sign of "crushing", in a manner of violent movement, deforming, disqualifying, and confounding.

The *informe* is an operation which consists of confusing, or rather confounding classification. Resolutely anti-idealist, this attitude undermines and reverses every attempt at sublimation

Informing works against the "ideal city" through confounding classification and undermining sublimation in urban planning methodology. Which are the consequenses of such an operation in our current practise?

For the sake of answering this question let follow the logic of another set of concepts relevant to the development of what I propose in this paper as a performative urbanism: multiple heterologuos genome, autopoïetic community and matrix. The crossing of biology and electronics informing my specific urban paradigms already exists: the genomic and electronic databases are denizens of cyberspace and, as noticed by Donna Haraway, one of the pre-eminent figures of the new cyber/cyborg-logy:

> *Lives are at stake in curious quasi-objects like databases; they structure the informatics of possible worlds, as well as the all-too-real ones.*

In her introduction to *The Cyborg Handbook*, Haraway mentions the case of *Mixotricha paradoxa*, picked up from Lynn Margulius' and Dorion Sagan's *Origin of Sex: Three Billion Years of Genetic Recombination*. This microscopic creature will help us to introduce the biological paradigm of the multiple heterologous genome and the autopoïetic community.

Multiple Heterologous Genome

Mixotricha paradoxa is a protist denizen of the hindgut of a South Australian termite, a formless, mixed-up, paradoxical bit of hair, (trichos). According to Margulius and Sagan, in the five kingdom classification of life, a protist is a member of the protoctista made up of micro-organisms and their larger descendants composed of multiple heterologous genomes.

M. paradoxa is a nucleated microbe with five distinct kinds of internal and external procaryotic symbionts, including two species of motile spirochetes, living in various degrees of structural and functional integration with their host, all the associated creatures living in obligate confederacy. Opportunists all, they are nested in each others tissues in myriad ways.

The ties often involved genetic exchanges, or recombinations, that in turn had a history dating back to the earliest bacteria that had to survive the gene damaging environment of ultraviolet light before there was an oxygen atmosphere to shield them.

Autopoïetic Communities

From Margulius and Sagan "symbiogenetic" point of view, Mixotricha's kind of confederacy is fundamental to the history of life: plants, animal and fungi are all descended from such beginnings. The story of heterogeneous associations at various levels of integration is repeated many times on different scales.

> *Clones of eukaryotic cells in the form of animals, plants, fungi and protoctists seem to share a symbiotic history ... At first each autopoïetic* [self-maintaining] *community member replicated its dna, divided and remained in contact with the other members in a fairly informal manner. Informal here refers to the number of partners of these confederacies: they varied.*

An autopoïetic community maintains itself informing through variation, multiplicity, motility.

*M. paradoxa'*s story is similar to a certain measure to that of the Internet, itself an assembly of nets interwoven with each other and preserving the heterogeneous associations at various levels of integration. Both are inventions for saving information, genetic or military, in anticipation of a catastrophe. Internet started as the Arpanet, an attempt to create military communication networks which would function even after nuclear attacks.

Martin Ray, a researcher in ecology, presented already in 1990 a self-reproducing programme provided with mechanisms of mutation and degradation, analogic to the natural processes of evolution. Ray's system is a part of a new branch of computer science known as artificial life, forcing us to consider electronic space, the cyberworld, as another inhabited world, populated by new species and their specific spatial relationships: self-reproductive programmes, avatars, cyborgs and so forth. The informing city has to adopt new kind of social and spatial combinations that include these new artificial species, their multiple heterologuos genomes and their poïetic communities.

154 · DOINA PETRESCU

Matrix

Matrix is – according to Jean-Francois Lyotard – an assemblage made up of unstable and changeable parts. As vehicle of the compulsion of repetition, it is able to maintain its own identity through time. Elements of the matrix make up a block, not a system. The role of the matrix is to dissimulate contradiction and generate simultaneity of logically incompatible situations; if contradictory elements co-exist in a sort of non-differentiation, the matrix is – still according to Lyotard – the difference itself. Matrix operates at the interface between real space and cyberspace, between the physical city and the electronic city, between local and global, reality and simulation. Matrix is – according to Peter Eisenman – a new universal form of an electronic paradigm concerning spatial organisation, replacing the grid which belongs to a mechanical paradigm. Through the matrix, architecture has to realise the possibility of the simulacrum within a physical being, a new idea of place. This location, both physical and simulated, is that of the inform(ing) city.

The interest in matrix rises because of its capacity to integrate negativity: made up of entropy, it changes degradation into dislocation. Matrix functions in an autopoïetic way but, without preserving any unity, it always keeps in touch with its exterior in an informal manner. As for negativity as such, Paul Virilio has expressed his anxiety concerning the dangers of unconditionally and uncritically adopting the technology of the contemporary society. He stresses the need to anticipate the negative effects of technical revolution and the future crashes of the contemporary technologies. But how to anticipate an accident or catastrophe, which, by definition, cannot be anticipated? As a response, I propose in this paper to develop, with such concepts as multiple heterologous genome and matrix, models and programmes integrating negativity within their structure and function. Therefore these two paradigms of the *informe* – multiple heterologous genome and matrix – cross and influence each other in this paper.

Possibilities of a Praxis

I will try to place these new concepts in an urban contemporary paradigm and discuss questions arising from the premises of the inform(ing) city: how to operate the matrix, with the matrix in the city, or in a multiple heterologous community, how to formalise (within) the *informe*?

The multiple heterologous community is a hybrid, anomalous, impure community. It is a community which, in the same way as that of *Mixotricha paradoxa*, is constituted of elements functioning in an obligatory confederacy, nested in each others tissues in multiple ways. Virilio has remarked, concerning the Internet, that functioning in the net implies a restructuring in individual groups leading to social disintegration. An autopoïetic community has the capacity to build a self-prosthesis as an answer to that disintegration. This kind of community knows how to develop prosthetic social assemblages: occasional confederations of real and virtual individuals and places, located for example on the electronic interface between the individual behind the computer terminal and the re-figured social space. In this re-figured space, the relation between the real and the virtual, the local and the global is incessantly informed through continuities and interruptions. The confederations establish themselves hrough connections and zapping. It is social space regulated by subjectivity.

Thus the subject and the subjectivity have become vectors of the *informe* in the contemporary urbanism. We must consider communities not constituted of physically and socially well-defined individuals, but of recombinant subjects. In this sense the number of individuals constituting the population of an urban entity will no longer be considered as a relevant urban parameter. In the new social and cultural space we have to consider also the disembodied subjectivity, subjects no longer corresponding to corporeal identities. It is no longer the body which divides but the subject.

Not by getting physically shifty, but by dissolving, fragmenting – by being many persons in many places simultaneously, by refusing to be one thing, by choosing to be many things. It is this fragmentation and multiplicity that characterise communities mediated and represented by the technological prosthetics of presence.

A community mediated by technological prosthetics of presence functions as a matrix at the same time present and tele-present, here and instantly elsewhere. It accepts, as a matrix, the simultaneity of situations that are logically incompatible. It is a community not belonging socially and legally to a place, but potential being everywhere and "getting crushed everywhere" – to put Bataille's *informe* again into play.

The whereness and whoness of such a community, usually controlled by governmental and regulatory structures, becomes problematic.

When we are talking about telework, for example, the relationship of proximity between places of work and dwelling, the number of work places and the active population – important urban requirements and quantificators – lose their meaning. Generally such questions as how to manage the disappearance of the socially and legally constituted individual in society or how to anticipate and manage the needs of such a community become urgent. Location and identification technologies raise the question of managing fictional identities and codification of imaginary territories. We could say that Freud was the first confronting such questions when codifying the territory of the unconscious and identifying and working with the multiple instances of the psychoanalytical subject. Psychoanalysis and literature in general may be domains that could influence urban planning methodology in a far more comprehensive way than before.

The multiple heterologous community and the urban matrix are characterised by textually mediated physicality. The interplay of textuality and sociality – as recounted by Francis Barker – is a narrative of ramification of the social locus of community from a predominantly public space to a series of spaces increasingly privatised. In the electronic environment the separation between public and private, the spatial closure, is not made of walls but codification and cryptage. The question of creativity in urban planning is related to the importance of textuality and, by consequence, to the necessity to integrate literary devices, discursive techniques, narrative strategies and semiotics, for example, into the urban planning techniques.

The contemporary urban planning methodology relates to real or virtual spaces and objects. The inform(ing) city is localised in multiple places and nodal objects –telephones and modem-computer combinations – replacing the so called nomadic objects. Nodal objects are both tools and places, and the contemporary architect has to manage the complexity of a space which "gets crushed" and moves into the objects at the same time objects move into the space.

The Role of the Architect in Informing the City

Genetics, as well as the communication and information systems, has taught us that maintaining exchange implies maintaining disequilibrium. Generating disequilibrium in a self-regulating entity, as our inform(ing) city is defined, necessarily activates new strategies of adaptation. According to this logic, the perturbations, accidents, troubling events are dynamising vectors of creativity. The inform(ing) city has to "get crushed" in order to be creative.

In her introduction to *The Cyborg Handbook*, Donna Haraway mentions James Lovelock's research on the atmosphere, approaching the pollution problem from the point of view of the atmosphere as an adaptation mechanism to an extension of the biosphere. According to Lovelock, perturbations had to be studied as part of a self-regulating system, in which compensatory changes, in response to toxins, could very well produce new dynamic steady states that could drastically change the species composition of the earth. In the same way perturbations in a self-maintaining and self-regulating urban entity could engage compensatory changes and produce new dynamic states that could change the urban species composition.

In an autopoïetic entity (such as an inform(ing) city) genetic accidents, provoked through perturbation, infection and pollution, would initiate predictable and unpredictable dislocations and even mutations in the very structure of the urban genome. The urbanists, local governments, and other public decision makers assume the position of initiator when they engage their subjectivity and act performatively in order to provoke a process of creation within the community. Such strategies give the act of urban planning an evential structure, enabling us to manage, and thus control, negativity. This also requires an active creative role on the part of the community acting as an informed body informing its own structure.

My concrete example comes from Romania, a former socialist country close to my own experience. Romania is a society that has known only one social and economic system regulated in a centralised and hierarchical manner and has now lived through the shock of the first years of change. It is a society forced to build its own prosthesis and initiate radical mutations within its structure. It embodies the experience of *Mixotricha paradoxa* on all levels: political, economic and civic. Romania has a multi-

tude of political parties having more or less the same message, overlap of the right and the left, hybrid institutions between public and private, and so forth. The most striking example of commercial hybrids is a form of private and incipient, a sort of multiple heterologous trade, local but also a metonymy of the new general economic system. It is localised in small units, caravans or kiosks of 4–6 m², functioning both independently and in chains, characterised by multiplicity, similarity in diversity, smallness, heterogeneity, selling diverse and divergent goods, anything and everything.

These kiosks have great commercial and physical dynamism. They are good opportunists, thriving on the freedom resulting from the lack of real estate legislation, but also benefiting from the necessity to establish a set of laws adapted to the evolution of the society. They pollute the urban environment and parasitise on other spaces, sometimes antithetically, living in various degrees of structural and functional integration with their host. This kind of commerce can function temporarily nested, for example, in a photo studio co-existing in a kind of obligate confederacy. The phenomenon is un-controllable and the future of the symbiosis unpredictable. The condition develops as a function of local negotiations in a continuous physical and economic process of differentiation fusing and diffusing symbiotic functions.

When making a proposal in the competition for the centre of Bucharest, our team took this heterologous trade as a model. Our solution consisted in disseminating, preliminary to any other urban changes, a net of trouble agents, germs of diverse urban functions, all over the area. These germs were expected to engage in a complex system of exchange and recombination in downtown Bucharest – which has inherited a megalomaniac and mono-functional urbanism – and to determine reactions of self-accommodation generating new recombinants and finally mutations in the entire structure of the city.

Here we face an inversion of the classical approach of the architect and urbanist forced to find answers to questionable urban situations. The approach is always directed towards the effect, not the cause, always delayed in answering the questions formulated by the city. We cannot answer a question that never stops evolving if we do not place ourselves as both initiators and performers, in the very movement raising this question. From here opens a passage from a projective, prospective urbanism towards a performative urbanism.

A strategy based on performativity is necessarily open to subjectivity and play. Urban methodology is not only a system of rules and prescriptions but also a field for experiment. Architects and urbanists have to informe cities by learning to explore and exploit the event and surprise, by letting themselves be surprised, by starting to nourish and subvert their profession and knowledge from inside. This, in itself, is the work of the informe.

From Simcity to Our City

Ron Kenley
Professor, École d'Architecture Paris la Seine

Introduction

The Conference has as its theme on the one hand creativity within the current view of the information society and on the other, the necessary effort for urban development and often renewal which takes place all over Europe.

Gilles Deleuze said that there can be no creativity without a necessity. There is no possibility of an idea as a creative act without a genuine necessity. He further defined an idea as potentials already engaged in a mode of expression. For the purposes of today's intervention I would wish to retain the terms of creativity, necessity and idea. To connect them engaged potential and mode of expression will be of reference.

In order to introduce Simcity as a step towards the creation of tools for participation in the process of urban development that engages creativity, I have mapped out the territories which are involved and their relationships. I will first define these territories, then use our work here at University of Art and Design Helsinki to describe Simcity for its potential as a tool for development in relation to two applications for Urban Pilot Projects in Helsinki and Lahti and finally offer the actions engaging the potential of the identified territories.

The Butterfly Diagram

The line of development of a scenario towards programme is interfered with at a number of levels. I called the figure a 'Butterfly Diagram'. The image seems to fit, as it refers to the flight path of the butterfly of unpredictable geometry between one attraction and another, always changing direction and intensity. At the same time, the open and closed wings alter the figure the butterfly presents to the world and it is certainly important to understand and use the diagram in a number of directions at all times. There are two other references for the figure of the diagram: one is the Gregory Ulmer's gear shift between Contrast, Analogy, Theory, Target and tale. The other is one of the patterns of change described by René Thom in his Catastrophe Theory and known apparently as the Butterfly.

Urban Ludic Culture

The diagramme operates in the absence of an Urban Ludic Culture, something akin to literature as a ludic culture for history[1]. It is to be seen as an empirical construction, built as the result of observation and experience and as such open epistemologically. As I hope to demonstrate, Simcity is a device that helps in the establishment of such a culture.

My plea through this work is for the recognition of the necessity to establish such a culture in the city, so that the production of knowledge based on a wider exchange of information is made possible and to see it as side benefits in the process of urban development. The importance of these benefits has already been recognised, for instance in the Endogenous Growth Economic Theory[2].

Scenarios

I use scenario as a vision, a dream, a story, a policy and even a plan. It describes and constructs a situation as a form for the city. This form is as told, seen from the point of view of an individual or a group. The studies that informed it are not in evidence any more than the intuition and the memories involved. As a form it is fictional and as a fiction it is accessible as a story. A scenario imagines and projects. Deleuze wrote in l'Epuisé:

> It is that the image is not defined by the sublime of its content, but by its form, in other words through its "internal tension", or through the force which it mobilises in

[1] I owe the term and the analogy to Constantin Petcou.

[2] Where investment in R&D leads to the changeing in unexpected ways of the concerned enterprise or production line: *"Where you can buy a factory and that produces 10 widgets a day, you can't a team of researchers and get 10 developments a year. And the more money you pour into research, the less you may get back. However, investment in knowledge leads to increasing returns in marginal products. If your team of researchers designs a prototype for the perfect widget, your factories can produce them, and you will sell thousands of them for the cost of the one development which putyou ahead of the competition."*
— Gladys Wu, Paul Romer

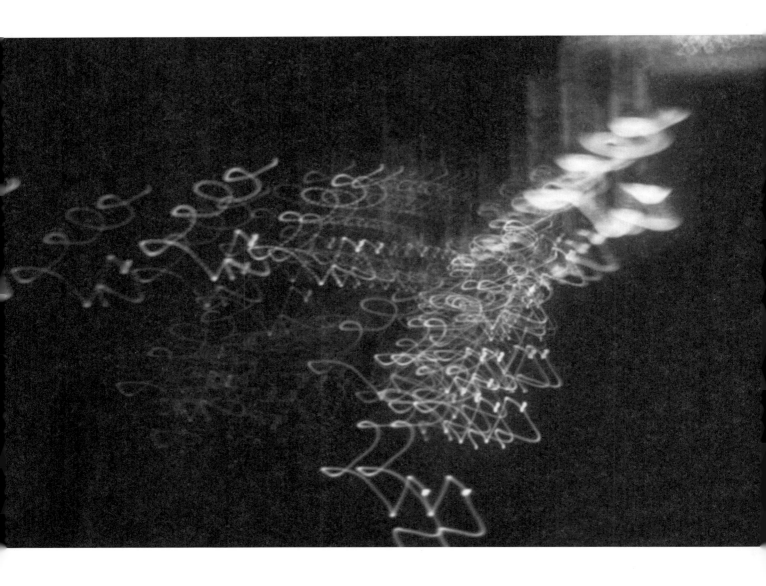

order to make a void or to bore holes, to undo the embrace of the words, to dry out the oozing of voices, so that it can disengage from memory and reason, little a-logical image, amnesiac, almost aphasic, sometimes keeping in the void, sometimes shuddering in the open. The image is not an object, but a "process". We do not know the power of such images, so simple are they from the point of view of the object.

The projective aspect of the scenario concerns the continuous transformation of image. The images are thus transported because projection is also talked about as a psychological colonisation of the real.[3]

3   Robin Evans in The Projective Cast

Thesaurus

The Thesaurus connects scenario to a story, a plot (or a drawing), a narrative (or a history, or a chronology), a plan, a scheme, a project and of course to a programme. The path is the alternance of meaning for the word and the synonyms for each meaning. Of course this particular path is not exhausted by my description, but it is an interesting verification of the diagram from another direction. How legitimate is such a path? It is authorised by the norm the Thesaurus embodies and as such it becomes a text enabling other texts, a 'tutor' text, which demonstrates use and makes information accessible.

The scenario is a common concern to the creative disciplines of writing, drawing and playing. The task is to make them resonate. The state of resonance makes communication possible and the transformation through change in the resonating registers in each disciplines. Custom, intuition, culture intervene broadly in the process.

In the case of Simcity, the scenarios are synonymous with tasks, with priorities as much as with limitations. They are there at the beginning of play (read development), structures fixed in their time span and a bias to development

Differences

What difference does the passage from one stage to another make in the transformation from scenario to programme? This is the territory of opposition, of inversion or translation from an existing or at any rate, preceding situation. Together with the explanation, it forms a sieve to the passage. It is possible to identify in the starting condition a set of qualities to attain**4**.

Explanation

The explanation for the Difference keeps the 'sieve' for the scenario well taut. It relies on other explanations of events and conditions which are already known and considered as reference. An explanation is a construction which uses another explanation through literal analogy. It tends to be fragmentary and not often easy to unify. It is a statement of the rules or laws which may well apply to the situation as explained. The explanation which is told functions like a narrative – it unfolds in time, it takes form, it in-forms. As in a scenario, the unfolding takes more than one route, with what-is-not-known being in turn continually posed, deferred, resolved – often only partially, repressed, forgotten or ignored, replaced with other not-as-yet-knowns.

We will enter by any point whatsoever; none matters more than another, and no entrance is more privileged even if it seems an impasse, a tight passage, a siphon. We will be trying only to discover what other points our entrance connects to, what crossroads and galleries one passes through to link two points, what the map of the rhizome is and how the map is modified if one enters by another point. Only the principle of multiple entrances prevents the introduction of the enemy, the Signifier and those attempts to interpret a work that is actually only open to experimentation **5**.

Part of the experiment, the hypothesis, the theory functions through repetition and literalisation. Simcity constitutes the application of simple rules in parallel to each part of the constructed model of the city. This is within the possible framework of scenarios and in reference to what we normally know and expect from municipal practice.

Parallels

There is a link between this territory and the preceding one. It is analogy. Analogy operates through displacement and figuration between domains or disciplines. Together with chance, it transforms method into invention**6**. At the same time, there is a difference between them, made up by the systems of reference. If explanation de-

4 Ulmer's Contrast qualifies this as an inventory of qualities for an alternative method and as argumentative writing.

5 Deleuze and Guattari quoted in Ulmer – *Teletheory*, p. 140. Part of the experiment, the hypothesis, the theory functions through repetition and literalization.

6 Ulmer quoting Justus Buchler's *The Concept of Method*

pends on the literal framing given by the reference, the parallel opens up the system to invention, to creativity. I think it is right that the connection of the two in the diagram is on the diagonal. In Simcity, parallels are drawn between conditions that apply to the 'ideal city' that we should all know and the divergence from that model under the headings of the variables that influence the development. The parallels allow the widening of the productive field by means of creativity. This is quantified at the other end of the second 'sieve', the project.

Projects

They are that which is done, that which is built, codified. The project transforms the idea into a constructed event, turns the creative act into material form. The projects establish 'zones', where a line is parallel to a wall, where an area describes a room and a turning circle a vehicle. Further, the design of a tram that can enter narrow streets changes the centre of the city (as in Grenoble), a tram-stop will be a place for information, ticket sales or shelter, and finally a continuous ground surface between pavement, road, shelter and tram make it accessible to babies in pushchairs, as much as to people with walking sticks or wheelchairs. The projects integrate all in the dependency instituted by the system they create.

A project or a design is synonymous with a plan. The plan is able to compose, trace, incorporate, co-ordinate and refer. The plan organises the event in its construction, determines the quantities and measures. It exists in thought, in art, in science, not to mention economics and the military. It is a tool for creativity. But it has different meanings and uses in each of the disciplines where it exists. It is beyond the scope of this paper to enter into an investigation of what the plan stands for. Suffice to say that it is an important convention and it involves the actualisation of the virtualities which constitute a lifetime of events or singularities[7]. The plan gives the event its own, proper reality.

7   Deleuze, immanence: a Lifetime.

Programme

At the opposite end of the scenario, the programme organises potential. Strategic and directive, while opening continuously, it organizes performance, it correlates ensembles, it enables development by recognising its process-like quality. I will propose that working towards the setting of a programme is the first task for any urban development in the creative city.

Simcity

Simcity 2000 and the Urban Renewal Kit are two complementary programmes produced by Maxis inc. of Orinda, California. They construct a computer model of cities using simulation technology, making close to 100 variables interact in a hybrid simulation, made up of cellular automata and system dynamics.

Cellular automata (CA) are used to calculate all the local variables and statistics. Each 'tile' on the map of the simulation (representing a square of 61m by 61m) is a stack of CA's, one for each of the variables that describes what is going on in that tile, including pollution level, crime level, land value, presence of electric power, and so forth. During each simulation cycle, each tile calculates all these factors based on its neighbours. Different CA's can affect each other; for instance, the pollution CA can affect the land-value CA, which in turn has an effect on the crime CA, and so on – in effect making a three-dimensional CA array. It is important to note that they relate different and diverse data in a way similar to city dynamics. The values in the CA's are also affected by global variables. The system-dynamics part of the simulation deals with the global, overall variables and functions, whether as the result of operator intervention, or from scenario considerations, such as demand for construction in different zones. These global functions drive the lower-level, spatially distributed CA's.

The models constructed by the simulation follow an economic structure of balance between public expenditure and taxes, with borrowing as option. As the mayor/player's executive power is fairly unlimited (within the budget), private investment is subsumed in the power of decision of the mayor. But the well-being of the city is influenced by many other variables which construct their own models internally and the entire simulation grows following the continuously changing relationship between the variables.

The core of the model is the balance between residential, commercial and industrial demand which are interdependent as well as dependent on the overall population size and even on an external national model.

Transportation systems and the travel distances between zones have a major effect on growth. Rail, buses and underground trains service the city as well as ports and airports. Car traffic moves along motorways and roads and adds to mobility but also pollution. Land value is affected by proximity to city centre, the size of the city; proximity to trees, water, parks, hills and lakes are a positive influence. Slums, poor services, pollution and crime lower land values. Electric power is necessary for all development. Power plants (of differing technologies, efficiency and life span) together with power lines are essential in Simcity. The population of Simcity is made up of Sims, electronic life forms that move in and out of cities. They have a maximum life span of 90 simulated years. They are divided into age groups (0–20, 20–55 and 55–90) and their well-being depends on working and living environment as well as health and education provision.

The industrial model determines what types of industries are in demand and desirable in the city. This is based on three controlling factors: external demand, tax rates and existing industries. External demand is made up of a historical model (US demand in the period 1900–93), a random element and a national model, where the effect of growth is studied in relation to neighbouring cities and the nation as a whole. Adjusting the tax rates modifies the demand and success rate of different industries and the ratio of existing industries aims towards a national balance. In Simcity 2000, high-tech and service industries are favoured because of their low pollution quality.

The financial model obtains revenue for the city through collecting property taxes, issueing bonds and enacting ordinances. Expenditure is mainly on infrastructure (building and maintaining), investment in zones and amenities and the enactment of ordinances. There are four economic trends in Simcity: recession, steady, boom, depression. They follow a cycle, but also random occurrences.

The water model is a major element of infrastructure. It is based on the construction of a system made up of water pumps, water mains, water towers, treatment plants and desalinisation plants. The amount of water available depends on the water table in the city as well as on the weather model, the seasons and the water features of the city, such as lakes and rivers. Treatment plants for sewage reduce pollution if as a provision they service the number of city inhabitants.

Microsims are micro simulations that track all individual structures and feed the information to the other parts of the model. They act like government departments in monitoring activity in a particular sector and transmitting the local information towards global change patterns. They are important in reflecting the quality and potential of such a simulation: namely the simultaneity of local action and global effect as well as global decision and local consequence between initiative, action and effect, recognising the influence of the player as a generative factor on the unfolding of any scenario.

Simcity in Arabianranta

The potential of using Simcity 2000 and its companion programme Urban Renewal Kit for the Arabianranta pilot project lies in its ability to promote a wider understanding and consideration of what is involved in the process of elaboration of a strategy for a city or part of a city until it becomes policy, as much as the consequences of applying the strategy to a model of the current situation.

For Arabianranta, a model representative of the current make up of the site was constructed and a simple scenario was built following the master plan for its development as a guideline. The 'players' are challenged to achieve the planning targets in the period stated for the implementation of the master plan. As the model evolves in this fictional framework, the possibilities proposed are to be evaluated and taken into account for the development of the area.

The simple, graphic three-dimensional appearance of the model makes it accessible to a broad range of possible players, spanning from school children to urbanists, architects and designers. This process of public involvement in the positive evaluation of a planning proposal is new and important in the systems of micro-responsibility and creativity it generates in a wide public. Awareness of the consequences of change and of the unexpected occurrence on a master plan is an important factor when considering alternatives and interim situations beyond any phasing of a project.

Finally, the freedom from commitment to form in order to explore potential – the game 'forms' the zones allocated by the player (as proto-mayor-urbanist-architect-designer) in relation to the complex variables it measures – encourages not only education through participation and dialogue with a wider public, but engenders a creative, mutually responsive climate in the search of new, contemporary and adaptable paradigms for planning and the renewing of our cities.

Will Wright, the creator of the simulation, describes Simcity 2000:

> *You have a certain amount of control, but then there's a certain amount of entropy in the system, and it's balanced just right between the two. It's life at the edge of chaos.*

Actions

By way of conclusion, I would like to refer to the research we are undertaking here, at the University of Art and Design in Helsinki, towards the creation of tools to assist in the process of urban development that cities like Helsinki or Lahti are concerned with.

Simcity in Arabianranta, Helsinki.

In a first stage of the research, we are constructing within the Simcity software a number of scenarios that are intended to encourage a broad participation. We have placed a Helsinki Arabianranta Scenario on the University server and invited some of the 100 Simcity sites we found on the Internet to attempt its development under the time and priorities conditions set by the current Master Plan. We are also proposing a demonstration of the possibilities of the game to the Municipality. We believe that this approach will permit when we are able to activate all the territories of the Diagramme:
- to planners to communicate quite directly with a large and/or interested public,
- to municipalities and administrations to experiment,
- the formulation of new dialogues in relation to the complexity of the city.

The Actors

1 The scenarios are the policy documents that exist or are proposed for the development of strategies. They are starting points. Municipalities, planning authorities and the interested public are engaged at this stage.
2 The game is played under different conditions particular to the public involved, effectively engaging a broad level of consultation. It becomes a device for negotiation between different priorities and approaches, framing complex territories and acting as a common language (lingua franca).
3 The resulting event is evaluated through the 'sieves' and links of the 'Butterfly Diagramme'. This is done within the conditions of Academic Research at the level of the University and the conclusions discussed as part of the development process with those involved in decision-making. At every stage, mechanisms of negotiation are devised and the mode of expression is sought in terms of the engaged potential.
4 Gilles Deleuze defined an idea as a potential already engaged in a mode of expression. Identifying ideas and their field of necessity allows, we believe the fabrication of concepts within the creative disciplines concerned.
5 Finally, strategic proposals can be made, or assembled out of the elements of potential towards a programme. It is important to note that the programme does not represent a fixed started point, but a continuously evolving device towards the actualisation of potential within and as a consequence of the forms developed by projects.

The Role of Computer Networks

The computers and the appropriate software act as agents to monitor activity irrespective of location, become communication devices and perform tasks in consequence of the demands made.

The interface is the device which makes the communication through the computer possible. To design the interface allows access to the electronic tools. In our work so far, we have favoured the use of existing parts of programmes for the combinatory and adaptive development or the processing of images. This requires the elaboration of a theory for the interface. The distinction between production and consumption is challenged by the definition of participation. The interface becomes more than a button on a screen – it needs to be a mediation via a concept[8]. The interface is then built out of theory (or explanation) and a 'tutor' text (or the result of the activation of the Diagram). The learning involved is measured through the invention of knowledge effects. The interface depends on two aspects: demonstration (for accessibility) and the direct access to information via a technological apparatus. Another kind of literacy ensues, unlimited in time, space, form, or content, but by the choices made in the constitution of each step. Here, we are looking to set up collaborations at the level of software design for the accessibility of the technological apparatus.

Like the luna-moth and other butterflies with eye-patterns on their wings, the position of the wings creates many patterns and figures. Their fluttering makes circles which intersect and follow each other in an invisible spiral of cycles. This is how the butterfly flies from one place to another and it may well be so that in our diagrammes of territories and actions we find a similar pattern. I would certainly hope so.

[8] Roy Parkhurst – Telegraphy in the Post (e)-classroom

BIBLIOGRAPHY
Buchler, J. (1961). *The Concept of Method.* New York: ColumbiaUniversity Press.
Evans, R. (1995). *The Projective Cast: Architecture and Its Three Geometries.* Cambridge (Mass.): MIT Press.
Ulmer, G. (1989). *Teletheory: Grammatology in the Age of Video.* NewYork: Routledge.

PROJECTS

The Tilburg Pop Cluster
New Strategies of Urban Cultural Development

HANS MOMMAAS
Senior Lecturer, Tilburg University

> *There is a very real crisis of urbanity itself. What do we think cities are for? What are the values that should regulate urban life? What does civic identity mean (or not mean) now?*
> — ROBINS 1993

> *But whose city? I ask. And whose culture?*
> — ZUKIN 1995

> *Which way is left for a cultural politics of difference?*
> — KEITH & PILE 1993

Abstract
Already for more than a decade, cities are experiencing a new phase of urban transformation. Fresh attempts are made to produce urban growth and revitalize the urban milieu. Pushed forward by an increasing inter-urban competition for new investments, jobs, inhabitants and purchasing power, leisure, culture and the arts have started to function as major resources for urban development. In the process, the inner city has become an alternative stage for "experience consumption", part of the

tourist, media and entertainment market, to be given shape and evaluated in accordance.

From the perspective of established dichotomies such as those between place and market, the community and capital, location and flow, the inhabitant and the tourist, culture and the economy, production and consumption, this transformation is generally evaluated as part of a process in which the local vernacular is put on sale on the market of consumption and pleasure, ignoring community interests and local needs.

It is doubtful whether such dichotomies are useful in understanding the full complexity of what is happening in today's inner cities, and in organizing alternatives for future developments. The measure, impact, and speed of today's flows of people, products, and ideas have made such an evaluation of space too linear and unproductive. How can we any longer differentiate between the inhabitant and the stranger in tomorrow's poly-cultural cities? Can we still think of communities as spatially fixed entities? In what sense can culture and the economy still exist in insulation from each other? In what sense can strategies of cultural planning still be based on singular identities and interests?

In this presentation, an illustration will be given of an urban pilot project which has the potential to bridge some of the aforementioned dichotomies. In combining a major popmusical venue for 3000 visitors in total, with a "Rockacademy" and a "Popfactory", the Pop Cluster, to be situated at the eastern corner of the inner city of Tilburg in the Netherlands, has the ability to establish a creative connection between interests of production and consumption, culture and the economy, place and market.

The Pop Cluster forms part of a wider portfolio of cultural strategies, used by the municipality of Tilburg, a former centre of textile production, to combat urban decline, and to reposition the city as a "Modern Industrial Town". The Pop Cluster, conceptualized as a techno-cultural workshop, is intended to function as an integrated instrument to promote social activation and integration, an atmosphere of cultural entrepreneurship, culturally guided urban regeneration, the creation of a new notion of place and innovative urban design. It is regarded not only as a pop venue contributing to the consumer vitality of Tilburg's city centre, but as a composite instrument of physical, socio-economic and cultural renewal.

As such the Pop Cluster might also function as an example for a new urban "politics of difference", targeted at a representation of a variety of groups of inhabitants and cultural professions in the inner city cultural habitat, thus enhancing its function as a forum of cultural creativity and confrontation/association.

The City as a Tool of Economic Development

The resemblance between the contemporary design and construction of inner city areas, and the cultural idiom of theme parks has already been remarked upon by a number of authors[1]. Both are dominated, it is suggested, by the language and perspective of the simulated experience. Central is the aim to transform inner city areas into centres of cultural and social vibrancy, in order for them to function as dynamic centres in an increasing inter-urban competition for investments, employment, inhabitants and visitors. In a constant competition with other sources of leisure experiences (such as the multi-media living room, the neighbouring inner city consumption areas, the suburban multi-functional shopping mall, and the actual theme park), more and more elements of the inner city infrastructure are drawn into the market oriented idiom of experience consumption: this development reaches from the lay-out and decoration of streets, squares, water and building facades to the local industrial vernacular and artistic resources.

This (re)discovery of the inner city as a potential source of experience consumption can obviously be related to economic transformations: to the de-industrialization of cities, the increase in demand for jobs, the uneven suburbanization of the population, and the decentralization of welfare state functions. City governments had to look for new economic revenues in order to combat economic decline and social requests. One of the potential resources discovered was the inner city centre, to be developed as an attractive, dynamic living, working, and socializing environment.

Also political dimensions are involved. Members of the local political elites are looking for new ways to modernize their city, partly to assemble their personal prestige and secure their political careers. Secondly, the Dutch government considers the urban environment as a major spearhead in national economic revitalization, vital to the competitive strength of the Dutch economy in a globalizing market. This is

---

[1] see e.g. Featherstone 1987; Urry 1990; Zukin 1991; Sorkin 1992

explained by cities' multi-dimensional character: they integrate a large pool of service oriented activities (accounting, banking, law firms, information technology, insurance, public relations, design, etc.), while embedding those in a milieu of knowledge (universities and polytechnics), health (sports facilities, environmental quality), culture (theatres, galleries), and consumption (distinctive retail spots in historical inner city areas)[2].

This regeneration of the inner city centre can, however, not be understood without also taking into account the cultural dynamics which quite significantly pre-date and transcende the discovery of the inner city as an economic potential. At stake is the renewed cultural thematization of urbanity, as part of a wider increase in cultural/symbolic sensibility. We can speak of an active search for new sources of inspiration and experiences of urbanity, carried along by the urban counter cultural movements of the sixties and seventies[3], entering the labour market and remaining attached to the urban in the eighties and nineties[4], but also stimulated by an expansion and intensification of consumer culture with its increase in symbolic sensitivity.

Three sources stand out. First, there is the almost mythical, early-bourgeois city of the 19th century. The popularity of the writings of Baudelaire, Simmel and Benjamin can partly be seen as linked to their contemporary function as potential sources of symbolic inspiration. At stake is the visual language of the mondaine commodity culture of the boulevards, theatres, Grand Magasins, Grand Hotels, Grand Cafes and department stores of 19th century cosmopolitan Paris, Vienna, St. Petersburg, London and New York[5]. Secondly, contemporary images of the "bubbling" city can be linked to the magic of American consumer culture, founded on the symbolic economy of the triangle of television, theme park and shopping mall. And thirdly, there is the "mediterranization"[6] of the city. Since its successful rebirth during the 1992 Olympic Games, Barcelona ranks high on the scale of European cultural cities. Central is the combination of public sociability and aesthetic liveliness, of cultural renewal, local historicity and bourgeois grandeur. But also older Mediterranean cities can function as potential sources of contemporary inspiration. In the city of Utrecht, plans exist to restore the old canals, in the 1960's turned into an inner city high-speed ring road.

2 cf. Sassen 1994

3 cf. Sennett 1970; Martin 1981
4 cf. Featherstone 1987, Bianchini 1993, O'Connor & Wynne 1996

5 cf. Berman, Girouard, Olsen

6 cf. De Cauter 1996

Alongside the canals, there will be outdoor cafes. [...] Also during the evenings, this will give the place its liveliness. [...] The new development makes you think of Venice[7].

7 Ontwikkelingsmaatschapij UCP 1995

In the 1980s and 1990s, this revitalized urbanity became a breeding ground for new interests amongst politicians, property developers and retail investors in the role of inner city areas as a resource for economic surplus. A quest developed for new talked-about museums (designed by Italian architects), for trend-setting city halls, spectacular festivals and grand urban vistas. This in the context of an elevated competition between cities to make themselves visible on the national cultural and tourist stage.

In the northern Dutch city of Groningen, at the time of the opening of the new Groninger museum (offered to the region by the national gas company, designed by a Disney inspired Mendini, and sometimes referred to as the "Groningen show tent"), local administrators were stating that the city finally had acquired the ability to lure visitors from the Randstad area to the North of the country, instead of taking the normal route down South. This was, however, a few months before the city of Maastricht, the "Romanic" city in the south-eastern corner of the Netherlands, opened its own high-prestige regional Bonnefanten museum, designed by Aldo Rossi. Recently the city of Groningen has answered this by opening the Waagstraat complex, a new inner city area of apartments and shops, also designed by an Italian architect. Now it is waiting for Maastricht to finish the much talked-about Ceramique district, a multi-functional, high prestige area with up market apartments, high quality shops, spacious atrias, and boulevards, situated adjacent to the river Maas.

Image development has a high priority on many urban cultural policy agendas. In cities that lack historical capital, new museums are built to house "modern" cultural capital (photography, film, architecture). Existing museums are renovated according to the latest architectural style. If necessary, museums are replaced and grouped together, a strategy also followed with theatres and cinemas, sometimes in combination with art, architecture and music academies, to form so-called cultural clusters. This is referred to as "packaging", in the context of the now popular "city marketing". With the same idea in mind, local municipalities of Rotterdam, Tilburg, Utrecht, and

Den Bosch established a distinctive festival policy, enabling a packaged presentation and management of their yearly festivals. The cities made this to gain their place on the market of experience consumption (high quality shopping, cultural tourism, day tripping, urban flanery), a market itself experiencing a major expansion and implosion.

Due to processes of time-space compression, carried along by developments in transportation and communication technology, more and more products and experiences have come into the reach of the leisure industries. This has resulted in an increasing competition for the attention of the consumer, which is speeded up by the recent downfall in the amount of leisure time amongst leading groups of consumers (high education, high double income households with partners between 25 and 45 years of age). Following Ian Chambers, Mike Featherstone (1987) has stressed how this expansion and condensation of the market of cultural experiences (or in terms of Giddens, this situation of cultural "post-scarcity") implied a qualitative shift in the organization of culture. Not only did it result in a intensified sensibility for and interest in the game of experiences, simulations, imagery, and presentation, but it also created a rapprochement of the arts and everyday life. The everyday physical environment of coffee machines, toasters and audio equipment, of furniture, clothing and the body became the object of an intensified aesthetic reflexivity, of design and beautification. We can witness a faster and more superficial circulation of images and styles, transgressing the former hierarchical boundaries between the arts, tourism, sports, consumption, the media, design, and leisure.

The Inner City as "Landscape"

From the perspective of established dichotomies such as those between place and market, the community and capital, location and flow, the inhabitant and the tourist, culture and the economy, production and consumption, this new phase of urban transformation is often evaluated as part of a process of putting the local vernacular on sale on the market of consumption and pleasure, ignoring community interests and the "needs" of local inhabitants. An elaborated example of this is delivered by the work of Sharon Zukin. Market here stands for "the economic forces that detach people from established social institutions". Place indicates "the spatial forms that anchor them to the social world, providing the basis of a stable identity"[8]. According to Zukin, the dichotomy between place and market can be traced back to the beginning of modern market capitalism, to the moment when the concrete marketplace (the spatial and cultural centre of the region) had to make way for the dynamic and abstract market which no longer had any direct relation with the local community. This produced the permanent problem of the regulation of the market, and the readjustment of the community to the changing norms of the market. Place and market entered into a conflict-ridden relation which each other, a relation difficult to be institutionalized. For Zukin, the contemporary inner city can be typified as a "postmodern liminal space, both slipping and mediating between nature and artifice, public use and private value, global market and local place"[9]. In a similar way, Castells spoke of the coming into being of "a space of flows, superseding the meaning of the space of places"[10]. Hallmarks of "place" (a local dialect, local spatial forms, local material cultures, local artistic creativity) are being subordinated to and made available for the supra-local dynamics of surplus production. The autonomous community has never been nourished by big cities or by big economic structures, Zukin remarks. However, "the continuing erosion of locality none the less raises a question about the future of the vernacular in postmodernity"[11]. If characteristics of place become subordinated to the abstract and changeable norm of the market, and the needs of inhabitants constantly loose out to the desires of tourists, what place will remain for the less economic powerful?

But while Zukin and others think it possible to conceptualize today's postmodern urbanity in terms of the dichotomy between place and market (inhabitants and tourists, culture and economy, community and mobility), others argue that developments have come to the point where these dichotomies are becoming redundant or at least less stable and productive. According to Keith & Pile (1993), the dichotomy between place and market presupposes a notion of spatial and cultural immanence which has become problematic. The dichotomy implicitly holds the promise of an undivided authentic community, purified of the false, superficial Mickey Mouse world of global consumer capitalism.

According to Keith & Pile, two problems occur. First, there is the question: "how can the authentic be authenticated – or, more properly, who is to authenticate the vernacular?"**12**. This is related to the second problem: characteristics of place and market continuously mingle, without necessarily influencing the truthfulness or the genuine quality of those characteristics. While images of "Burgundian" Maastricht, "modern industrial" Tilburg or "knowledge centre" Utrecht have been developed as part of marketing strategies, nevertheless, they may start to function as genuine elements in the construction and reproduction of urban life, at the same time an element of urban identification and prestige, as a resource of urban belonging and sociability. The question then is how "false" or "genuine", "fictitious" or "concrete", "illusory" or "real" these images are. Or more sharply: who is going to decide about that? Who is going to decide about the cultural and spatial authenticity of the historical façades behind which traditional functions have made room for new boutiques? Respect for "place", or subordination to "market"? And does it change something if it is not the retail sector, but museum culture, which takes over? There are a lot of potential conflicts of interest between inhabitants and tourists. However, at the same time it becomes more and more difficult to distinguish between the two in some unequivocal way. According to Urry (1990) we are witnessing the end of tourism, because in a certain sense we are all permanently tourists, strolling flâneurs on global boulevards of images, products, and ideas. Besides, how long should someone from Marrakech, Paramaribo or Amsterdam live in Groningen, Utrecht, Rotterdam or Maastricht to become an "inhabitant" of those cities? What about the inhabitants of Amsterdam, Rotterdam or Utrecht, living their lives in the adjacent new towns of Almere, Capelle or Houten? How many inhabitants experience their city, walk through their city, talk about their city, "gaze" at their city, as "tourists", evaluating their city as a field of possible experiences in a wider context of "famous" cities. And how many tourists, especially of the higher educated kind, like to submerge as local flâneurs in the everyday surroundings they are visiting? From the perspective of the dichotomy between place and market, there is the danger of paying insufficient attention to the versatile and ambiguous use made of cultural and spatial objects in an increasingly mobile and diverse urban environment. Increasing mobility has made the modernist

12 Keith & Pile 1993

pretention of an unequivocally regulated and planned environment more and more untenable. Place and market, culture and economy, local authenticity and global consumerism have become entwined in numerous ambiguous and unpredictable ways. Every pretention to be able to separate the two in some decisive manner will run the risk of ending up in artificial rigidity, in the long run only maintainable through the use of closed tv circuits and barbed wire. "The ideal of community privileges unity over difference, thereby denying the reality and value of irreducible differences between individuals and between types of people. It threatens to reinstate the structures of exclusion which operate in ethnic and other forms of chauvinism. It is founded upon a unitary ideal of subjectivity"[13].

Today, the construction of "place" inevitably takes place in a context which constantly forces openness, diversity, unpredictability and dialogue. Instead of thinking of places in terms of bounded spaces, according to Doreen Massey (1993), we should think of them in terms of visible movements in networks of social relations and understanding. This requires citizens to feel at home in a diversity of places and markets, and to enjoy the variety of identities and positions, without shying away to some nostalgic longing for small-town or suburban surveyability. Gellner (1995) called this "the importance of being modular". He used the phrase to stress the importance of being economically and politically flexible, something which requires cultural stability and homogeneity. Yet one could use the same phrase to stress another, perhaps more favourable, project, one of political and cultural flexibility and mobility, based on a foundation of economic security – which is always also a moral foundation of trust.

An Urban Cultural Politics of Difference: the Pop Cluster

According to Robins (1993), if increasing mobility threatens the integrity of cities, then, without doubt, this may also form the basis of new possibilities. The city seems to be the place par excellence to explore these new possibilities[14]. This will, however, require an urban politics which does not satisfy itself with taking the shortest route to the touristic market of experience consumption, but which tries to combine a place on that market with attempts to strengthen the local cultural vitality.

[13] Young in Patton 1995: 118

[14] cf. Sennett 1970

Needed is a cultural politics aimed at strengthening local cultural diversity; at a confrontation and mutual influencing of different cultural forms and activities. Such an open receptive politics should include the total domain of urban culture; from the classical arts and classical theatre, to architecture and design, fashion and popular culture, urban festivals, cafe and restaurant sociability, shopping mall liveliness and the public life on squares, streets and in parks. At stake is a cultural politics aimed at the formation of a multiform civic urban space. According to Swanson (1995) such a politics should no longer be based on an illusory set of shared interests: on traditional notions of community, integration or freedom, or on singular identities such as the professional, the inhabitant, the consumer, the tourist or the worker. That will only lead to new forms of rigidity and exclusion. Instead, the politics should be formulated "on the basis of a set of agreements, or perhaps rather a set of protocols, concerning the access to cultural resources whereby effective citizenships may be established within the space of public life"[15]. It should be a politics based on a nuanced sensibility for the diversity of social and cultural "affinities" people can nourish in and with the urban milieu. Next, these affinities should be supplied with enough resources to make it possible for them to be made visual and represented in the public space of the city.

Swanson herself uses this model to overcome the pathologization/idealization dichotomy of women's participation in urban consumption. Yet the model may also be extended to the field of cultural politics at large. The Tilburg plans to establish a new "pop cluster" may function as a good example of what this could lead to in the everyday practise of urban cultural planning.

The Tilburg new Centre for Popular Music (Pop Cluster) will result from the integration of three existing pop musical organizations, which originated from a diversity of Tilburg youth movements: Noorderligt, Bat Cave and the "Musician's Shop". Noorderligt is a "profit for non-profit" concert hall for pop music, which exists already for ten years, housed in a former cinema. It is the biggest pop venue outside the Randstad area (with around 100,000 visitors each year), and presents a broad range of pop music: rock, country, hard core, funk, metal, dance, techno, etc. The Bat Cave is a club, formed in 1985, for small-scale, innovative modern music, predominantly run by volunteers. The "Musician's Shop" (Muzikantenwinkel) concerns a pop

[15] Swanson, 1995: 204

collective, formed in 1984, today active in the support of some 275 regional bands. This support covers a wide range of activities from rehearsal facilities to presentation, recording, and clerical and financial aid.

The new organisation will be housed in a prestigious new building, especially designed for its function as a centre for rock-pop music and culture, adjacent to Tilburg's main inner city club and cafe area. The building will have a main hall with a capacity of 2200, a music cafe for 400 visitors, and a Bat Cave club for 250 visitors. Other facilities will include a giftshop, a restaurant and a ticketshop. Besides, the building will house rehearsal rooms, a recording studio, a video-clipstudio, and an information desk.

Here, heavily based on its possible role as a medium of urban renewal and vibrancy, rock-pop music and culture has (physically and symbolically) moved into the Tilburg centre of cultural attention. This will give the project the opportunity to cover functions which are normally kept apart.

Basic are functions of production and consumption. The project will operate as a concert hall where professional groups from all over the world will perform and audiences "consume" rock-pop (the organization envisages some 400 acts for approx. 200,000 visitors each year). At the same time, however, it will function as an important site of pop musical production, especially targeted at the local "amateur" market. For this purpose, the project includes the organisation of a Rockacademy, a

The planned Centre for Popular Music.

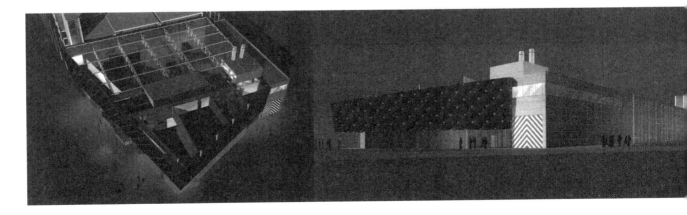

Summerschool and a Popfactory. A variety of networks will be established between these initiatives and a wide range of other cultural functions in the city. For the purpose of musical education, lines will exist between the Pop Cluster and the local Music Academy, involving teachers and students. At the same time links will be established between the Pop Cluster and local youth and community work. These links will enable the Cluster to tag into local musical youth scenes, at the same time producing a constant resource for musical renewal, and giving Tilburg youth the possibility to take part in the more productive dimensions of the pop cultural centre. Thus, links will be established between a professional inner city stage and suburban youth scenes, enabling the latter to represent itself in the centre of town in a variety of ways: from the consumption of music to the production and registration of it, including video production and project management. Moreover, shared pop cultural affinities, together with the multi-dimensional infrastructure developed, will enable the Pop Cluster to become a major resource in local social programmes, aimed at the economic and socio-cultural integration of marginalized youth.

Thus, the Pop Cluster, conceptualized as a techno-cultural workshop, will be able to cover and link a wide variety of functions, places and interests: functions of consumption and production, the global large scale pop musical market and local small scale pop musical creativity, inner city centre liveliness and suburban youth culture, commerce and culture, the private and the public, professionalism and amateurism, "tourists" and "inhabitants", urban imagery and cultural representation, "market" and "place". It will function as a composite instrument to promote social activation and cultural mobility, an atmosphere of cultural entrepreneurship, culturally guided urban regeneration, the creation of new notions of place and innovative urban design.

It is exactly this multi-functional, multi-faced character which makes the Tilburg Pop Cluster such an exciting project. Its position at the cross-roads of a variety of functions and systems makes the project able to mediate a variety of local/global and central/marginal circumstances.

If successful, the Pop Cluster might start to function as a spearhead in the development of a wider urban "politics of difference", targeted at a representation of a variety of local groups and professions and at enhancing the inner city cultural habitat as a forum of confrontation and association. Much will depend on whether the parties concerned – the project management itself, the local municipality, private parties, and the local social-educational infrastructure – know how to appreciate the composite and open character and how to exploit its opportunities. It will require a rather unorthodox kind of business operation, very different from the standard commercial and cultural project management.

Besides stimulating local cultural creativity and sociality, the Pop Cluster could enhance local economic development. Of importance here is not only the Cluster as a resource of consumption and urban imagery but as a site of small-scale innovative entrepreneurship. Moreover, in line with O'Connor[16], one might see the Pop Cluster as an important ingredient in an overall policy aimed at nurturing the local cultural sector in order to link its creativity – of milieu and business – to targets of economic innovation and development.

[16] see J. O'Connor: *Popular Culture, Reflexivity and Urban Change* pp: 72–98

BIBLIOGRAPHY

Castells, M. (1989). *The Informational City*. Oxford: Blackwell.
Chambers, Ian (1987). 'Maps for the Metropolis: A Possible Guide to the Postmodern'. *Cultural Studies* 1987, nr. 1.
De Cauter, L. (1996). *Archeologie van de kick*, Amsterdam: De Balie.
Featherstone, M. (1987). *Consumer Culture and Postmodernism*. London: Sage.
Gellner, E. (1995). 'The Importance of Being Modular'. In J.A. Hall: *Civil Society. Theory, History, Comparison*. Cambridge: Polity Press, pp. 32–56.
Keith, M. & Pile S. (1993). 'Introduction Part 1: The Politics of Place'. In M. Keith & S. Pile (eds.): *Place and the Politics of Identity*. London: Routledge, pp. 1–22.
Martin, B. (1981). *A Sociology of Contemporary Cultural Change*. Oxford: Basil Blackwell.
Massey, D. (1993). 'Politics and Space/Time'. In Keith & Pile (eds.): *Place and the Politics of Identity*. London: Routledge, pp. 141–162.
Robins, K. (1993). 'Prisoners of the City: Whatever Could a Postmodern City Be?'. In: E. Carter, J. Donald & J. Squires (eds.): *Space & Place. Theories of Identity and Location*. London: Lawrence & Wishart, pp. 303-331.
Rose, D. (1984). 'Rethinking gentrification; beyond the uneven development of Marxist urban theory'. In *Environment and Planning D, Society and Space* 1984, nr. 1, pp. 47–74.
Sassen, S. (1994). *Cities in a World Economy*. Thousand Oaks: Pine Forge/Sage.
Sennett, R. (1970). *The uses of disorder: personal identity and city life*. London: The Penguin Press.
Sorkin, M. (1992). *Variatons on a Theme Park. The New American City and the End of Public Space*. New York: Noonday Press.
Swanson, G. (1995). 'Drunk with the Glitter. Consuming Spaces and Sexual Geographies'. In S. Watson & K. Gibson: *Postmodern Cities and Spaces*. Oxford: Blackwell, pp. 80–99.
Urry, J. (1990). *The Tourist Gaze. Leisure and Travel in Contemporary Societies*. London: Sage.
Utrecht Centrum Projekt bv (1995). Het ruimtelijke funktioneel concept UCP. Utrecht: Ontwikkelingsmaatschapij UCP.
Patton P. (1995). 'Imaginary Cities. Images of Postmodernity'. In Watson & Gibson, pp. 112–125.
Zukin, S. (1995). *The Cultures of Cities*. Oxford: Blackwell.
Zukin, S. (1992). 'Postmodern Urban Landscapes: Mapping Culture and Power'. In S. Lash & J. Friedman: *Modernity and Identity*. Oxford: Blackwell, pp. 221–248.
Zukin, S. (1991). *Landscapes of Power. From Detroit to Disney World*. Berkeley: University of California Press.
Zukin, S. (1982). *Loft Living*. Baltimore: John Hopkins University Press.
Bianchini, F. & Parkinson, M. (1993). *Cultural Policy and Urban Regeneration*. Manchester: Manchester University Press.
O'Connor, J. & Wynne, D. (1996). 'Lef loafing'. In: *From the Margins to the Centre: Cultural Production and Consumption in the Post-Industrial City*. Arena: Ashgate.

Kirklees
The Development of a Creative Milieu

PHIL WOOD
Kirklees MC Cultural Services

Introduction

Although much of the attention around issues of creativity and cultural planning tends to focus on cities, small towns – of which Britain, and surely Finland, has many – do also have potential. Kirklees is the story of how one such town has moved from failure and decline to the threshold of success. It also discusses the particular role that artists and other creative people, in partnership with the local authority, have played in this change.

The borough of Kirklees is located in the central industrial belt of the UK, between Manchester and Leeds. This area was the cradle of the industrial revolution, and the landscape today combines – in stark juxtaposition – picturesque rural countryside, relics of past industrial glory and modern urbanisation. Whilst the borough has a population of 380,000, it is made up of a collection of small towns, each of which developed with the expansion of the textile and coal mining industries of the 19th century – and each of which have suffered as these industries have slumped into decline. The largest town, and administrative centre of the borough, is Huddersfield, with a population of 130,000.

The title of the council's recently-published cultural policy is Made in Kirklees, reflecting the fact that the local people have always had a strong inclination for creating things, whether it be pieces of cloth or engineering at their places of work, or works of art in their leisure time. The Kirklees area has, for example, more people actively participating in music-making through choirs and brass bands than anywhere else in the UK. Unfortunately, however, by the 1980s, this harmonious balance between work and leisure, art and life had broken down and the area was troubled by a profound social dislocation.

This was reflected in the local authority for the area. As I remember Kirklees Council in the mid-1980s, it was parochial, faction-ridden, narrow-minded, defensive and riddled with self-doubt: an institutional basket-case. The UK Institute for Local Government Studies came to study Kirklees and concluded that it had never come to terms with being formed as an unpopular amalgam of 11 small towns and districts and that whilst – with a population of 380,000 – It ought to have been a big hitter, its resources were turned inward and to negative ends. It was, they said, one of the most problematic local authorities they had ever encountered.

How then, in the space of 10 years, have we reached a state where I and my colleagues are now regularly invited to address national conferences on economic, social and cultural renewal?

Briefly, these are a selection of Kirklees' achievements over the last few years: the £20 million Alfred McAlpine Stadium, a 20,000-seat venue which won the UK Building of the Year award last year. The stadium hosts not only sports but also the arts, including R.E.M. in front of 70,000 fans, establishing it as one of the premier outdoor venues in the UK;

- the £6 million Lawrence Batley Theatre, a 625-seat venue, is a beautiful conversion of a 19th century chapel;
- the £1.5 million Kirklees Media Centre, which is the home of 20 high-tech media businesses including recording studios, an Asian women's magazine and the region's first Internet cafe;
- the Huddersfield Contemporary Music Festival, the UK's leading festival of modern music and living proof that challenging art and popular appeal are not incompatible. The festival provides a great opportunity to experience the latest trends in European art and has recently included visits from leading Finnish composers;
- Huddersfield has also been described as the Poetry Capital of Britain because of the extraordinary number of new writers who have emerged there over the last decade;

- the local arts scene is very lively, featuring opera, brass bands and folk dancing. Over recent years it has been enhanced immeasurably by the cultures of immigrant groups from the Caribbean and India;
- Kirklees has a 100% success rate in applying to the UK government for urban regeneration funding. In the last three years this has brought £75 million of new Government funding into the area, which has in turn released hundreds of millions of pounds of private investment;
- Kirklees is the most successful town in the region for winning funding for sport and the arts from the UK National Lottery, over £10 million in the last 18 months;
- the small town of Batley was honoured only last week with a national prize to acknowledge it as the town which had done most to integrate public art and sculpture within urban regeneration;
- finally Kirklees is the place which the UK Secretary of State for National Heritage described as being the cultural equal of Paris! Yes, Mr Stephen Dorrell really did say that – which is perhaps why he ended up as the Secretary of State for Health!

THE NEW ORGANISATIONAL CULTURE

The reason that artists and other creative people have been able to flourish in Kirklees is due in a significant part, I think, to the new organisational culture which was created in Kirklees Council during the late 1980s. As I have already said, the Council at that time was a profoundly uncreative organisation, and I believe much of the responsibility and credit for initiating the transformation is due to one man, the Council Leader John Harman, who took over in 1986.

So what is this organisational culture which has proved so conducive to creativity? It could be summed up with the following set of dichotomies. To my mind, Kirklees has moved from:

Centralism to Devolution

Responsibility for decision-taking has been spread throughout the organisation, releasing initiative in hundreds of people who previously simply took orders. The determination of strategic policy-making still does, and must, remain at the centre, but once officers are clear on the direction in which they are meant to go, they have great discretion to operate creatively.

Isolation to Partnership

Previously there existed neither trust nor respect between the council and other major institutions in the borough. The council was the elected body and believed it alone had the mandate to act on behalf of the people. Partnership was regarded negatively because it involved sharing power and resources. Gradually, however, partnership has proved to be the greatest success story of all because it has enabled the council to increase its ability to make things happen through pooling its resources with others to achieve things it could never have achieved alone.

Control to Influence

Previously, the council believed it could only achieve objectives if it controlled the planning and the delivery mechanisms. Mrs. Thatcher presided over a period in which the powers of local government were systematically eroded and Kirklees found it no longer had the power to control everything. It had to learn how to negotiate, compromise and exert influence over other key local institutions. As I have already said, the council has found that through partnerships and influencing strategies it can achieve far more than when it had absolute authority.

Leading to Enabling

Politicians used to think that the public exerted their power once every four years by electing them to office, and that within that period the public should shut up, sit back and let the politicians run things. The council has now realised that it cannot run people's lives for them. The council held most of the resources, but was too distant from the real issues which affect people's lives, whilst the people had most of the experience and the best ideas but did not have the ability to take action. The council now accepts it has a role to surrender power to the people and enable them through funding, resources, advice and information to become involved in the delivery of their own services.

Secrecy to Openness and Participation

The council used to believe that the less the people knew about what it was doing, the less opportunity there would be for them to complain. It now finds that consulting the people actually produces better and more efficient services, but is moving even beyond this stage to actively encouraging people to participate in the planning and delivery of its services.

Quantity to Quality

The council used to judge itself by the scale of the service it provided. By listening to the people, it has found that demand is far more diverse, discriminating and sophisticated than it ever imagined and people are much more interested in the quality of the service they receive.

Uniformity to Diversity

Because quantity mattered more than quality, the council for its own convenience expected people to adapt to the services it provided. It now believes that, on the contrary, services should be designed to meet the varied needs of the people. The council used to fear the ethnic, social and cultural diversity of its people – it seemed anarchic and expensive to cater for. It now recognises this rich diversity to be one of its principal assets and a source of much of the area's creativity.

Low Risk/High Blame to High Risk/Low Blame

In the past, both council officers and politicians avoided taking innovative measures for fear of retribution if they did not succeed. Now we are positively encouraged to have new ideas and take risks, and failure is not punished but is seen as a point on the route to success.

Conformity to Creativity

Because of the fear of failure, council officers conformed to an orthodoxy which encouraged taking the safe, easy and short term solution to any problem. Officers used to have their salary levels set purely upon the size of the empire they commanded and their time served in the organisation. They are now also judged on the levels of creativity and innovation they bring to their work.

The combination of these factors has made Kirklees move from failure to success.

THE ROLE OF ARTISTS

So how have artists and creative people been able to take advantage of this new spirit and begin to develop a creative milieu within Kirklees? The new leadership announced its new vision for Kirklees in 1988. The date is interesting because it coincided with Gorbachev's glasnost and perestroika and at times it felt very similar. The leadership set itself a set of targets for economic, environmental and community regeneration and announced that it was inviting partners to come forward with whom it could work. Many observers in the private and voluntary sectors at the time looked at the council's track record and said "thanks but no thanks", but local arts workers – perhaps because they felt they had very little to lose – took up the invitation.

Armed with a handful of statistics on the economic importance of the Arts and a few pious hopes, they tiptoed up the garden path of the council and tapped on the door that had always been so firmly bolted. To their amazement, it flew open and they were invited inside and asked to take a seat at the table. They explained that the new culture into which the leadership was trying to haul a reluctant council was in fact second nature to them and, if given the chance, they would prove it. The chance was offered and a group of arts workers under the collective banner of Cultural Industries in Kirklees were funded to produce an extensive 80-page study into "The potential of cultural industries and community arts in the social and economic regeneration of Kirklees".

The report and its 50 recommendations were well-received and adopted as a strand of the council's regeneration strategy. A little new money was found immediately to initiate some projects and bolster some struggling arts groups, but this is not really the point. Far more important was that arts workers and their methodologies were now accepted within the mainstream processes of the council. Once this had been accepted the serious money began to flow.

Having established in Kirklees a model of practice, and having scored a few successes, it was time to formalise the position in 1994 with the adoption of a cultural policy entitled Made in Kirklees. It is an ideas paper rather than a strategy and was written in order to establish a philosophical underpinning to our work. Firstly, it set out very clearly not to be an "arts plan". It seemed to me that many arts plans had done more harm than good by restricting culture to a ghetto rather than opening up new opportunities. "Made in Kirklees" was one of the first policies to adopt the cultural resources approach which has been developed and refined by Landry and Bianchini at Comedia[1]. This provides a set of measures whereby the unique cultural attributes of any village, town, region or country can be identified as the basis for policy-making. In our cultural policy, we draw a comparison between culture and our now commonly-held understanding of the natural environment as a rich, unique, dynamic but essentially fragile entity. Just as local authorities and communities have now come to recognise their roles and responsibilities regarding their local environment, we call for them to develop that same understanding of culture. Through our three corporate themes of "maintaining distinctiveness, celebrating diversity, and harnessing creativity" we have been able to gain a recognition of the symbiotic relationship which exists between culture and the local authority's mainstream aims of economic, environmental and community regeneration.

WHAT NEXT?

I want to turn now to the way forward for Kirklees. A conference was held in 1996 to review the progress made on achieving the council's vision for Kirklees. Held in the new stadium, it was a symbolic acknowledgement that we had actually achieved all the items on the original agenda and it was now time to open a new chapter. The leader in his keynote speech said the following:

> *My key idea is that physical regeneration is important but secondary. It is the outward sign that regeneration is taking place, but by itself it is not regeneration. Regeneration must be people-based.*

We have achieved an impressive infrastructure of popular and pioneering cultural facilities in Kirklees which by their physical presence alone are a testament to our success. But of equal importance is what they have done for the "collective psyche" of the borough. They have enabled people to believe in themselves and in the vision, and they have given Kirklees a profile in the outside world it could not have dreamed of 10 years ago. The economic spin-offs are easy to calculate, but I am also interested in exploring the social benefits which are starting to manifest themselves. There is a growing social cohesion between disparate parts of the district and different ethnic and cultural groups. There is much less of the corrosive carping which used to be the automatic response of the local media and business community to anything associated with Kirklees.

There are three themes which highlight the way forward in Kirklees. If the first was "people-centred regeneration", second theme is "creativity".

In Kirklees' cultural policy we make harnessing creativity a principal aim. Creativity, we believe, is likely to be a community's principal asset as we move into the next century. Creativity is being able to find solutions to the apparently insoluble problems of modern life; it is being able to do that which we thought we could not do. Renewal and regeneration strategies are increasingly driving our towns and cities into a cycle of beauty contests where the winner takes all. Like it or not, we must opt into this cycle if we want to see our dreams realised – and there is little to suggest that a change of government would alter this significantly. Winning in this process has now much less to do with physical location or proximity to natural resources. In a knowledge-based economy the winners will be those who are best able to develop attractive images and symbols and project these effectively with added value. The losers are likely to be those whose organisational culture and systems are too hidebound and inflexible to accommodate creative people and concepts.

You may think I am saying this as a prelude to announcing that the artists shall inherit the earth. Actually I am not, because I do not believe that artists have a monopoly on creativity. It is as likely to exist in business or the community – and even in local government administration. It is just that the British are rather unsettled by this idea and prefer to file creativity away under the arts, where eccentricity is acceptable. What I am saying about the arts is that they can help institutions such as local government to come to terms with – and feel more comfortable with – creativity. The more that planners, highways engineers and social workers are exposed to the arts the more they can begin to identify innovative tendencies in themselves. That is crucial because, believe me, it is only when the many, not the few, start changing things that long-term sustainable renewal can take place. Artists interfacing with local civic institutions in the way that they have done in Kirklees has been one of the important factors in helping the council come to terms with itself and begin to act effectively both in improving the quality of life of individuals and galvanising the district as a player on the national and international stage.

The project we are currently working on is Huddersfield – The Creative Town Initiative, a bid for funding under the European Regional Development Fund's innovative actions programme, which has been designed by the EU to entice local authorities into employing unconventional approaches to urban regeneration. We aim to build a working model, based around the Kirklees Media Centre and Huddersfield University, by setting up an "innovation hothouse" in which the traditional barriers between artists, inventors, academics, entrepreneurs, civic administrators, politicians and financial institutions will be blown away.

As a local authority our primary concern is to protect and nurture the distinctiveness of our own local culture and economy. However, we have come to the conclusion that this cannot be done in isolation from external factors. We believe the greatest danger to the viability of communities is not globalisation but a retreat into isolationism and protectionism and that, ironic as it may seem, the best way for communities to preserve their local control and identity is to become more competitive globally. This takes me to the last of the three themes which are driving Kirklees: "Thriving locally in a global economy".

An example of this has been our approach to the new information technology, where community artists in Kirklees have led the way in developing what I might describe as "technology with a human face" and "technology with a local face". Kirklees has moved quickly into telematics, multimedia and the Internet technology, identifying its potential for a whole range of social and economic benefits, but it was artists who pioneered it and artists who brought it out of the sphere of the computer nerd and gave meaning to it for the general public and local politicians. Inspired by Artimedia, a telematics company, the small town of Batley has become the first town in the UK to have all its schools connected to the Internet. Local people can record the history of their community in sound, pictures and text in the Batley multimedia archive; the technology has been opened to a wide range of groups, an example being a disabled persons' electronic village hall. Local businesses have benefited from training in international sales via the Internet. In its own small way there can be no better example of how we can and must resolve the apparent paradox of thriving locally in a global economy.

Hopefully this description conveys some of the sense of excitement we feel at the moment in Kirklees. If I were to try to define what living in a creative milieu feels like, I would say it is the feeling that anything is possible – where you can reach for the stars, and if you fall in the effort, you still have the chance to get up, dust yourself down and try again.

Gardens of Anchor
Urban Pilot Project Proposal for the City of Lahti

RIITTA VESALA
City Planning Project Manager, City of Lahti Finland

Introduction

Lahti, an industrial city of 95,000 inhabitants, is located about 100 kilometres northeast of Helsinki. The labour force in Lahti is mainly employed by the private sector in small and medium-sized enterprises (SME). Because of its dependence on private employers, Lahti has suffered severely from the economic depression of the 1990s and is undergoing major structural changes. The Urban Pilot Project that Lahti is applying for will have an encouraging effect as a sign of new possibilities and hope after a deep depression.

The site of the project, the so-called Anchor area, is a former industrial zone. It lies on the shore of Lake Vesijärvi, a little more than one kilometre from downtown Lahti. The industrial history of the city began right there in 1869 with the founding of a steam-powered sawmill. Lahti grew as an industrial town at the cross-roads of waterways, important roads and the railway. For more than a century the best waterfronts were in the use of industry and infrastructure; the area was left vacant only ten years ago. Since then Anchor has been the most important area in the city for strategic development.

The Gardens of Anchor project is part of a wider integrated action for regeneration of the waterfront – the birthplace of manufacturing in Lahti – into attractive, environmentally high-quality areas for housing, work and leisure. The main EU Objective 2 project in the Lahti Region is the renewal of the harbour of Lahti; the aim is to develop Lahti into a real waterfront city.

The heart of the area is an old red-brick industrial complex. It consists of three parts built in several phases. The oldest and most valuable structure is the Carpentry Factory built in 1908. The Glass Factory dates back to the 1920s, and the Grinding Factory was built in the 1930s. These unexploited buildings occupy a prime location on the shore but are falling into decay. Formal preconditions for repairing the old buildings exist, as they are listed as valuable historical monuments in the city plan. Many ideas have been presented for the future use of the buildings, but the key question - funding - has remained unsolved, and therefore no action has been taken. A private construction company owns the factories and the land, but neither the company nor the city can afford the renovation of this large complex.

Lahti is symbolised by its ski-jumps.

The Gardens of Anchor Urban Pilot Project activities will be a focus for the development of the Anchor lakeshore centre and a magnet for new activities. With the help of the pilot project the whole Anchor shoreline area will begin to live and gain attractiveness. The UPP will prevent a area of historical importance from degenerating into dilapidation and transform an untidy industrial centre, which has attracted vandalism and crime, into an active public area.

The proposed UPP further contains several elements which will help to solve the following key problems of the city of Lahti:

Image
Lahti is considered a modern inland city without a history. The lakeshore industrial buildings represent the most essential part of the history of the city.

Preservation of Cultural Heritage
Lahti will lose an essential part of its cultural heritage if the industrial buildings of the Anchor area are not repaired and taken into use in time.

Unemployment
New jobs must be found in sectors other than traditional industry or public services.

Age Structure and Level of Education of the Population
Lahti needs young educated people to create new types of permanent jobs.

STRATEGY AND IDEAS BEHIND THE GARDENS OF ANCHOR

The Gardens of Anchor project emphasises cultivation and growth intended for both human and natural resources. Within this umbrella concept there will be a number of "gardens" with specific activities and characteristics integrated into the preservation of cultural heritage and environmental issues. The Gardens of Anchor will be an innovative urban community with different kinds of synergetic activities, where modern people will want to live and work. The project forms a link between the past, the present and the future: history, events and exhibitions, research, product development and virtual activities.

Cultural Heritage, Spirit and Image
The Gardens of Anchor project is located at the key point of the Anchor area, in the empty historical buildings of the Anchor Centre. It will ensure the preservation of industrial buildings and bring the lakeshore area into life by creating a dynamic and attractive centre for studying, working, living and leisure. The place where the urban development began more than a hundred years ago will become the symbol of a new era.

Education and Future Jobs
The goal of the city administration is to raise the level of education and know-how in Lahti. The Gardens of Anchor project gathers together development potential and expertise already existing in some form in the city. The aim is to survive by means of innovation, networking and synergy. The most natural way to improve the level of education is to encourage students of Lahti Polytechnic to stay in Lahti after graduation. They would be the innovative entrepreneurs who will be potential employers for the less educated. International virtual enterprises will also become generators of new jobs.

The Gardens of Anchor will become a magnet for new enterprises benefiting from its image and services. The aim is to develop virtual know-how and lots of small enterprises in the Gardens of Anchor. The project will create new possibilities for network-based employment, small enterprises and co-operatives in the fields of e.g. information systems and arts and crafts. Lahti Polytechnic will link studies and employment by helping students create their own enterprises in the Gardens of Anchor already during their studies. Virtual jobs will be created in a form of a cyber forum. The cultural and research-related services of the Gardens of Anchor will make the place attractive to both researchers and the general public.

Resources

The higher education in the city consists of the Lahti Polytechnic and certain departments of other Finnish universities. The expertise and educational opportunities in Lahti are concentrated in five main sectors:

- environmental expertise
- product design and development
- training for the so-called learning society
- arts and crafts, design and multimedia
- congress and recreation, tourism and sports

We expect the future employment and business to be in these sectors, especially in networked and export-oriented sme's.

Gradual Implementation

Renovation will be a continuous process: at the first stage, some activities will commence in lightly renovated spaces of the Carpentry Factory. It is the most valuable of the Anchor buildings and in relatively good condition. Later on the pioneer activities will give way to cultural activities (the Concert and Congress Hall and the Cultural Centre for Children and Youth) in need of more comprehensive rebuilding. Additionally, gradual renovation offers relatively cheap work space for young entrepreneurs.

Building as an Educational and Employment Project

The number of jobs in the construction industry in the Lahti region has diminished about 60% since 1989. In the future, construction work will mainly be in renovation and restoration. The old factories of the Anchor area provide an excellent opportunity to educate building workers in the new skills of repairing old buildings in ecologically sound ways. Therefore, a tailor-made course for unemployed construction workers will be arranged, and these workers will later be employed in the renovation of the factory buildings.

THE GARDENS OF INNOVATION AND DISCOVERIES

Student Workshops and Small Enterprises

Lahti Polytechnic offers education in many fields with future potential, such as environmental planning, multimedia and design, as well as arts and crafts. In the Gardens of Innovation and Discoveries, Lahti Polytechnic can build co-operation between studies and business while facilitating the creation of new jobs through interdisciplinary teamwork and on-the-job learning. The Gardens of Innovation and Discoveries will offer the students practical skills and support so that after graduating they can work as entrepreneurs or in co-operatives in the Gardens of Anchor. The project will also include an arts and crafts section where the apprentice – journeyman – master tradition will be continued. Multi- and interdisciplinary teaching methods supporting networks and teams and promoting ethical, ecological, aesthetic, economical and technical alternatives for preserving the environment and human welfare are keys to this co-operation.

The Virtual Office Forum

Virtual work will increase in every sector. Cyber-Anchor is a virtual office forum, a new form of distance work, where the variability of the office is connected with networked solutions; both the educational and the business world of the city will be linked up to the project. Cyber-Anchor will be a pioneering activity of the Gardens of Anchor pilot project.

The virtual entrepreneurs of Cyber-Anchor form a co-operative, giving independent small companies and entrepreneurs an opportunity to work in teams. Thus Cyber-Anchor will have the efficiency of a larger corporation. The aim is to give young people opportunities to start virtual enterprises without large investments and risk.

The Euro-Study Centre

The Euro-Study Centre is a network of about 50 universities in 13 European countries and is co-ordinated by the European Association of Distance Teaching Universities. The aim of the association is to develop tertiary education and training through distance learning and international co-operation. The Lahti ESC will integrate its activities with those of Cyber-Anchor.

THE GARDENS OF ASSEMBLIES

Oppilastalo Oy is responsible for student housing in Lahti. It is a public utility company owned mainly by the city. It will build student housing in the upper floors of the old glass factory for 100–150 students; some new spaces will also be added. The idea is to combine residence, study and work. On the ground floor of the factory there will be such services as an exhibition hall, workshops and boutiques where products of the Anchor Centre will be sold. Student apartments will serve also as accommodation for participants in various courses and seminars arranged in the Gardens of Anchor.

THE GARDENS OF GREEN GROWTH

All recreational areas will be designed as a green garden with various species of trees, bushes and flowers. Benches and squares will provide an opportunity for quiet meditation and contemplation. The garden will be a refreshing oasis for the people of the city and visitors in the summer and a ground for sport and recreation in winter.

A comprehensive environmental programme will be developed for the Gardens of Anchor. The project will become a laboratory of ecological systems, giving an opportunity for research and examination of the newest technologies.

INNOVATIVE FEATURES OF THE GARDENS OF ANCHORPROJECT

Holistic Concept
The project integrates the past, the present and the future into a holistic concept of human growth; the Gardens of Anchor will become an environment bringing together learning, working, living and leisure and connecting people to information networks.

New Paths to Employment
The project integrates study with work in an innovative way, helping young people to establish their own enterprises.

Co-Operation
Co-operation between a number of local private and public organisations generates the power of growth and synergy and utilises available resources efficiently.

Renovation Process
An extensive renovation of the dilapidated industrial complex will be possible with a relatively small initial investment, as it will be done in stages and the new uses will form a continuous process.

All in all, if implemented, Gardens of Anchor will contribute to the new image of the city of Lahti and symbolise its development from an industrial town with a negative image towards an environmentally and culturally competitive centre.

The Creative Lahti Study
Student-projects at the University of Art and Design of Helsinki 1995–96

Due to its economic structure, Lahti was hit hard by the recession in 1991–1995. The public sector in the town is relatively small, and for example higher education is totally absent. Lahti's many small and medium sized industrial companies often work as subcontractors. When the order-books of the big companies grew thin, the subcontractors were the first to suffer. The markets of Lahti-based firms are mainly domestic, so they have been unable to benefit directly from the rapidly growing export trade. The unemployment rate in Lahti was a rather alarming 25% in 1995 and in 1997 still stands at 22%.

There are at the moment some weak signals of recovery. Lahti, being on the main railway line to the east, is creating a position for itself as a logistics centre between Finnish ports and Russia. A new highway from Lahti to Helsinki will be opened in the year 2000, shortening the driving time to the international airport to 45 minutes.

Luova Lahti (Creative Lahti) is a study and set of proposals by students of environmental design in collaboration with the city authorities. It is aimed at discovering potential and developing it to generate concrete projects. The following five themes taken together form a possible urban strategy.

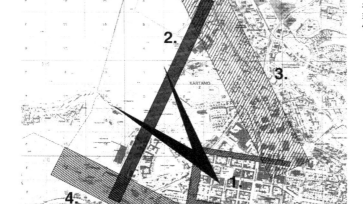

1. Living City Centre
2. Reclaiming the Waterfront
3. Alternative Cultures
4. Aestheticization of Sports

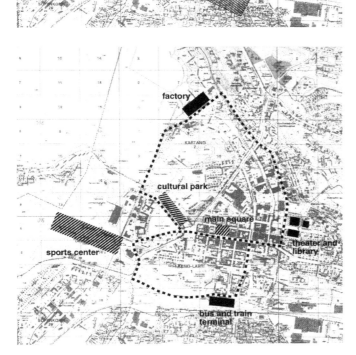

5. Traffic

THE CREATIVE LAHTI STUDY · 209

New telecommunications tower.
Jari Kinnunen and Ari Jääskö

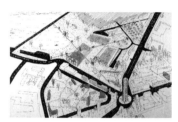

The new cultural park connects the city centre to the lake.
Jari Kinnunen and Ari Jääskö

1   See also Vesala, Riitta: Gardens of Anchor, pp 192–199

Asphalt shed student housing.
Antti Latvala

1. Living City Centre

The city centre around the main square is loosing its commercial attractiveness to inner-city shopping malls and, increasingly, to suburban, car-based shopping areas – a well-known development in many Western cities. Three areas of action were found to combat this trend.

1. The use of intensive programming and the enhancement of the quality of the public space to develop the main square and the pedestrianised main street to form a true events forum.
2. The commercial centre has a cultural fringe of churches, the City Library, the City Theatre, the Concert Hall and the Historical Museum. This fringe should be strengthened and given a clearer identity, especially on the lake side of the centre.
3. A new multimodal transport terminal should be built at the railway station. It would enhance accessibility and give a stronger "public face" to the whole town.

2. Reclaiming the Waterfront

The shortest route from the centre to the lake is at the moment underused; the view to the lake is cut by an old railway embankment. The relocation of the bus station opens the area to new uses ranging from sports to leisure, and including culture in a park-like setting.

The old Glass Factory is a link to the new Anchor housing district. The factory has a great symbolic value and is a natural centre for the whole waterfront area[1]. The old rail axis continues on to the main sports centre, providing a unique opportunity to connect sports events and the new lake-side programmes.

3. Alternative Cultures

On the eastern side of the city centre there is a collision between the historic urban grid and an industrial structure. Industry has largely gone and the area has become transformed into a supermarket district with a certain cultural mix. The character of the area is still undefined, and its alternative, free nature could be nourished by night-life programmes, youth culture, student housing and cheap workspaces.

4. Aestheticization of Sports

Lahti is the winter sports capital of Finland. It has hosted both European and world championships; the annual Salpausselkä games are of national importance. The main stage, Lahti Sports Centre, is very near the city centre. Big events are visible and already affect the life of the city. This connection between sports and urban life could be further developed as follows:

1. Extension of the skiing tracks to the Radiomäki hill next to the City Hall would create a new stage and allow the introduction of street skiing.
2. The Main Square could become a "skiing centre" for awards ceremonies, for example.
3. The Sports Centre itself should be intensively developed to solve practical problems like traffic and parking, but especially to create a distinctive aesthetics for the place and events.

New visual link between Radiomäkihill and the Sports Centre.
Jutta Kalmari

5. Traffic

A new central city line should be established to connect important areas within the Creative Lahti. It would make the developments more accessible, but could also grow to become a symbol of the whole regeneration programme. The new multimodal terminal would connect the Creative Lahti necklace to the surrounding region and further afield. The link could be a tram line, although the most realistic solution would probably be a specially designed minibus system with a clear marketing profile, good passenger information and inviting bus stops.

The abandoned railway line on the waterfront should be developed into a boulevard. Being an attraction in itself, it would also link new uses and make the whole lakeside economically more viable. The boulevard would also facilitate a very large car-free area between the city centre and the lake.

Two Creative Cases
The Cable Factory and the Glass Palace Media Centre

Panu Lehtovuori
University of Art and Design Helsinki UIAH

This paper presents two creative projects in Helsinki, the Cable Factory and the Glass Palace Media Centre. The selection criteria are not strict, and there are a number of other recent projects that would have also warranted documentation and analysis. Yet the Cable Factory and the Glass Palace are an illustrative couple: the Cable Factory is an almost established cultural forum, which provides an opportunity to discuss the dynamics of an unusual project with a long-term perspective. The idea of a media centre situated in the Glass Palace was first suggested in the early 1990s, but the project is only now being started: the organisation being built up and the premises redeveloped.

Both the Cable Factory and the Media Centre are projects which regular town planning, operating through separate functions, failed to predict, never mind produce. The 'creativity' of the projects lies in their programming: phenomena and cultural contents intermingling in a surprising manner. The aesthetics of the buildings and meanings construed over the decades in both cases interact with new programmes in an interesting and varied way. The third theme emerging on the basis of the data and the interviews is the development of the projects from the cultural margins into central institutions.

THE CABLE FACTORY

In 1989, Nokia Oy began to lease premises no longer required by the production of the Cable Factory in Salmisaari on inexpensive, short term contracts. The previous summer the City Cultural Office had taken charge of the leasing of the premises of Harakka Island, abandoned by the Finnish Defence Forces, to artists. The Cultural Office still received inquiries by artists, for the rent rate was rapidly rising in the business boom, and the Cultural Office started to forward them to Nokia. The flow of artists, various culture businesses, and sports organisations quickly filled the space. Nokia hired a consultant to negotiate over the contracts, and 20,000 m² was soon occupied. A special community of Cable Factory artists and other tenants was born.[1]

[1] Interview with Marianna Kajantie

A design competition had been organised in the winter of 1987–88 to plan the new Ruoholahti residential area. The competition and the following town planning measures failed to recognise the value or the potential of the Cable Factory. The plans fractured the factory, occupying it with municipal services of the future residential area, including school and daycare centre, and cultural services, including a conservatoire. The budget for this "basic redevelopment" was 350 million Finnmarks (59 MECU).

The redevelopment plan of the city would have emptied the entire factory and finished the community of artists. The Pro Kaapeli (Pro Cable Factory) organisation acting as the voice of the community launched an extensive defence campaign, choosing publicity and direct interaction with politicians as their means. Their central arguments included the unique, spontaneous nature of the community, and the value and atmosphere of the factory building itself, in particular the potential of the 110-metre-long marine cable hall. The overall attitude of the print media of those days (1989–90) was predominantly positive towards the community, but also somewhat sceptical: could something like this really be possible in Finland? The community was also a subject of a touching documentary, broadcast on the Finnish TV just before the City Planning Committee board meeting decisive concerning the future of the Cable Factory[2].

[2] interview with Jan Verwijnen

The following excerpt depicts the contacts to politicians:

TWO CREATIVE CASES · 213

The committee [of the Pro Kaapeli organisation]...has met politicians, negotiated with politicians and created the image of the community. The committee has introduced the factory to members of the City Board, and during the following weeks we intend to invite the representatives of political groups in the council, the Real Estate Committee, the City Planning Committee, and other political agents to the Cable Factory to see for themselves.

The committee submitted an address to the city cultural planning committee (the Donner committee), at which occasion the future of the Cable Factory was also discussed. The board of Nokia also received an address, on the basis of which the negotiations between Nokia and Pro Kaapeli will be continued.
— KAAPELI LINJA NEWS BULLETIN, APRIL 1990

In June 1990, the architects of Pro Kaapeli, Pia Ilonen and Jan Verwijnen, put together an alternative plan for the official version of using the Cable Factory. It reorganised the surroundings of the factory (the west end of Ruoholahti residential area) so that there would be no need to fracture the factory, yet build new housing and commercial space to the extent allotted in the town plan. The interior of the factory was organised to protect the long single space of the marine cable hall and provide an opportunity to arrange a wide range of events there. This plan, compiled in two weeks, was chosen as basis of realisation instead of the official version, which took years to make[3].

When the protection of the Cable Factory was secured, the city organised it as a company, which renewed the lease contracts largely at former conditions. The city limited its financial liability to the capital contributions, the building.

Institutions began to take interest in the Cable Factory as well. The Department of Architecture of the Helsinki University of Technology moved its arts instruction to the Cable Factory in 1992; the same year, the Free Art School moved inside the building into larger premises. Prominent architects designed both these redevelopment projects inexpensively, yet with high aesthetic standards. In 1992 of the 32,000 m² leased 25% was occupied by performing arts, 22% by studios, 18% by arts businesses, 15% by schools, 13% by commercial enterprises, and 7% by others[4]. These categories overlap,

3 Interview with Jan Verwijnen

4 Mäkelä et al. 1994

The alternative plan by Pia Ilonen and Jan Verwijnen 1990, 1991.

for the same premises occasionally hosted both commercial and non-commercial activities, and tenants changed every now and then. However, the list well depicts the heterogeneity of the Cable Factory: large and small spaces, individuals and institutions.

Today, there are several groups of performing arts operating in the Cable Factory (music, dance, theatre), three museums, and a large space for temporary exhibitions and various events. The community has developed freely, without guidance or any determined vision about contents. In 1996, the leased premises were occupied as follows: offices 7%, studios 13%, commercial studios 19%, sports 5%, museums 7%, music 5%, teaching 11%, temporary exhibitions and performances 15%, performing arts 3%, the Cable Factory's own use, storage etc. 15%[5]. Unfortunately, today's categorisation differs from that of the survey of 1992. The percentage of studios has decreased; however, museums create a new category.

The pioneering days are over now. The authorities no longer treat the Cable Factory as a special case and practical matters, such as ventilation and firewalling, require attention and investments. No one in charge at the Factory seems to have a strong vision of its future. The building is gradually being repaired to attain 'normal' standards: property maintenance takes a lion's share of the time and energy of the managers. The tenants have to fund the mortgages for the repair investments, which in the course of time will result in a rise in the rents.

The three state-funded museums (photography, theatre, restaurant) which operated in cramped spaces in the early days will obtain more space[6]. Moreover, the atmosphere is slightly scandalous, as the extension of the museums is supplanting the old tenants, who have repaired their premises at their own expense[7]. Yet the extension comes as no surprise, rather the museums are only now reaching the original target space[8]. The 'scandal' cries seem to emerge from the delicate balancing between studios and public services[9]. The demarcation lines between cultural production and financially more feasible commercial activities are also constantly under dispute. The management of the Cable Factory plans to devote some sections of the complex to studios only, i.e. zoning. The museums extending decreases the number of studios from 115 to 100.

[5] Annual report of Kiinteistö Oy Kaapelitalo

[6] interview with Auni Palo

[7] Helsingin Sanomat, September 22, 1997

[8] see Tyrväinen 1992: 28

[9] interview with Pia Ilonen

The leasing of the exhibition spaces has been outsourced to PopZoo Productions, a private events producer. The share of theatrical performances may increase slightly. A coordinator or PR officer would be necessary in order to market the Cable Factory under a single brand. The Marine Cable Hall is in its original condition and is crying for investments [10].

10 interview with Auni Palo

THE MEDIA CENTRE IN THE GLASS PALACE

Built in 1935, the Glass Palace was a part of the Helsinki Olympic Games project and it has been owned by the city from the very start. In the early days it housed a large restaurant with a palm tree lounge and various shops introducing new trends from the modern world. In the course of time, the building decayed, and the tenants changed: in the 1990s, they included cheap pubs and a bingo hall. In 1996 Finnkino decided to close down the Rex cinema as the 61-year-old theatre was no longer financially viable.

The Glass Palace was originally built to be "temporary", and the building was not protected until the 1980s. At the end of the decade, the city provided it with a large-scale redevelopment plan, similar to that of the Cable Factory. The plan included a public library, large facilities for youth, city PR offices, a space for temporary exhibitions, film theatre, etc; the budget was, depending on the choices made, 133 to 272 million Finnmarks (23–46 MECU).[11] The project was never realised, however.

11 Multi-purpose centre for the Glass Palace block 1988

Bio Rex with its auditorium and foyer was to be a key issue in designing the future of the Glass Palace, corresponding to the position of the Marine Cable Hall at the Cable Factory. Bio Rex is an interesting 1930s space, but is badly suited for the contemporary movie business, which requires wide screens, good sound quality, and small auditoriums. When the future of the auditorium was being discussed in 1990, Perttu Rastas, then manager of AV-arkki media art archives, proposed a media centre of video art and tv, which could be accompanied by new uses of the square adjacent to the Palace. The time was not ripe yet, as Finnkino still wanted to keep Bio Rex as a movie theatre.

The Cultural Office gradually furthered the idea of a media centre, making contacts with media agents and charting their potential interest in the project. In 1995, it

The Glass Palace in 1930s.

ordered a plan of renovation and redevelopment on idea level. This project, largely finished, was used as a basis for the European Union's Urban Pilot Project application in the summer of 1996. The following summer, after a lengthy selection process, the Glass Palace media centre received 2.7 MECU (some 15 million Finnmarks) for the renovation of the building and for starting the activities.

At the time of writing this paper, the Glass Palace is being renovated and restored. The Helsinki Real Estate Department has signed preliminary contracts for many spaces: the historical restaurant has a new owner and two national TV stations have made reservations. Along with the progress of the renovation, the organisation is likewise being created: the City Board decided to make the Glass Palace into a independent company, corresponding to that of the Cable Factory. Yet the city remains the owner, and the rent paid by the company is becoming a central issue with respect to the form and possibilities of the activity.

In the years to come, the surrounding neighbourhood of Kamppi will be transformed into a culturally significant area, instead of the mere bus and coach station it is today: the Glass Palace will be part of the new Culture Triangle, with the museum of contemporary art, Kiasma, and the multiplex and museums to house the Tennis Palace also currently being renovated, as its two other points.

In the following chapters I will draw conclusions and create hypotheses, based on these two projects.

HYBRID PROGRAMMES

The 'creativity' of the Cable Factory and the Glass Palace largely lies in their programming. The projects mix work and leisure, production and consumption, art and entertainment: they are hybrid programmes.[12]

> Hybrids are programmatic structures able to capture surpluses and fix them in specific topographies once the traditional urban organism becomes too rigid to operate efficiently within the unstable territory of flexible accumulation. Hybrid

12 cf. Hans Mommaas' contribution in this publication *Tilburg Pop Cluster* pp. 170–181.

The Marine Cable Hall.

programmes articulate between erratic economic flows and their consolidation as urban topographies, without the mediation of a unitary urban structure.
— ZAERA POLO 1994: 27

Zaera Polo regards hybrid programmes as means of late property capitalism to secure capitals and accelerate their circulation. The role of the Cable Factory and the Glass Palace is different: their hybridism is more of a cultural sort, even though the financial consequences still matter.

The so-called experts of planning and financing initially regarded the cultural programme of the Cable Factory unfeasible in every respect: the profits at best could only be a fraction of the renovation costs. The marine cable hall in particular was seen as having no practical use whatsoever by the 'hard' expert city departments[13]. Only a very special programmatic whole could at all consider occupying the building. Artists, however, were able to appreciate the "primitive" industrial space and see its studio potential. Large-scale, innovative arts productions and occasional, better-paying corporation events gained extra value of the marine cable hall atmosphere. This combination, consisting of permanent, uncontrolled studios and workshops as well as performance spaces suitable for temporary productions, has since proved also financially viable.

Despite its central location, the Glass Palace has more or less lived in oblivion for the last decades. Its large-featured interiors have become impractical; the glamour of cinema, exotic imports, and the modern way of life has withered away and become rather banal. The media centre consisting of a multi-purpose auditorium, media library, TV studios, as well as shops and restaurants serving the passers-by, is a hybrid programme, which both draws upon the image referring to 1930s modernism and its capability to renew it. In the media centre project, the cultural value of the hybrid was also a means to stand out in the international financing competition. The EU organ distributing the money had to consider the thematic richness of hundreds of proposals. The Glass Palace combination proved successful.

Yet in both cases the biggest risks and problems also seem to lie in the programmes.

13 Interview with Marianna Kajantie

THE DIFFICULTY OF CREATING A CULTURAL BRAND

> [The Cable Factory] *must be coordinated on a professional basis, with each cultural product suiting and supporting the brand. The future of the Cable Factory depends on the cultural products and the artists' studios.*
> — ISOHANNI 1993

The Cable Factory has failed to advocate its brand. After eight years in operation, of which five as a company, it still lacks a coordinated programme production. It lacks a clear, ambitious profile as an arena for events. Ideally, the ground floor exhibition and performance spaces would form a unit of their own, independent of the studios and workshops and financing its activities by box office income, project-fixed sponsorship, and public support. Now the artists occupying the upper floors are paying for the underused facilities[14].

A model could be the newly built commercial Hartwall-Areena multipurpose stadium. There the organisation of a dense events programme is a serious business, occupying a personnel of 20.

HOW TO ACHIEVE A TRULY PUBLIC SPACE?

The Urban Pilot Project application of the Glass Palace brings the social advantages of the project to the fore. The Glass Palace and the adjacent square is described as the social centre of Helsinki, a place where one can leisurely loiter without any presssure to consume. The social contents of information technology are hoped to improve. The Glass Palace is thought to provide an easy and natural way to get acquainted with new technologies and bring together the developers and content producers of the new technology and the general public.

> *An important aim will be to break down the privacy often associated with information technology and to develop the experience of information technology in a more social and collective manner.*
> — UPP APPLICATION 1996: 15

[14] Interview with Jan Verwijnen

At the moment (late 1997), achieving an open, public character seems uncertain. The Real Estate Department, who owns and leases the property, has made preliminary contracts with several tenants at market prices, which at such a central location are quite high, 235–350 Finnmarks per square metre per month (40–59 ECU). Rents like this can only be paid by large, well-established businesses who want centrally located, prestigious headquarters, and productive businesses depending on large customer flows. The former category includes the downtown studios of Finnish Broadcasting Company and MTV3, who have already reserved their spaces, and the latter the Glass Palace Restaurant. On the basis of the preliminary contracts, the Real Estate Department estimated the yearly tenant turnover of the Glass Palace to be some 9.5 million Finnmarks. Yet the committee discussing the activities and contents of the media centre worked out an estimate of five million Finnmarks resulting from the problems caused by the protection of the building, and in particular from securing the operation of the centre financially, reserving funds for its own productions and activities.[15]

The final turnover estimate was a compromise: on November 17, the City Board decided that the rent was to be 7.5 million Finnmarks (1.3 MECU) per year; however, should the turnover exceed 9.5 millions, the media centre would be obliged to pay 50% of the extra income to the Real Estate Department. For content producers of experiential new media, young businesses, media artists, and the like, the Glass Palace will be far too expensive, as feasible workshops can be leased at 25–40 Finnmarks (4–7 ECU) per square metre a little farther from the city centre. Even the concessionary rent, 155–225 Finnmarks per month per square metre (26–38 ECU) agreed for the city's own activities, such as the media library, is too high for this group. The idea of a media refinery with employers acting as 'patrons' for young experts trying to make it[16] might be a good solution. At the time of writing, the realisation of the media refinery is uncertain. So the risk of the Glass Palace becoming a commercial mainstream media mall with a library upstairs, still remains. The programme and character of Bio Rex will be a key factor in the destiny of the Glass Palace: should it wither, the dream of an open, public media house is in trouble. I continue by discussing the old or abandoned buildings themselves: the importance of location and a specific 'feeling' of the spaces in relation to new programmes.

15 Working group memo, September 15, 1997

16 Working group memo September 15, 1997

THE LOCATION IN THE CITY

For a long time, the Cable Factory was somewhat cut-off from the conventional 'culture Helsinki': in a seemingly desolate industrial area to where it was hard to travel. This was naturally a disadvantage: the lack of a taxi station, for example, was found to be a problem when it came to the new uses of the Marine Cable Hall[17]. On the other hand, distance and separation was part of the dissident atmosphere of the Cable Factory. Today, the Ruoholahti residential area is almost touching the factory, and the public transport connections are fairly good – the underground is only a 10 minute walk away – but the unrefined immediate surroundings still provide the factory with its original moody territory.

The Glass Palace has a different position altogether. It is in the middle of a public transport terminal, opposite a large department store, with a location that could not be more central. The new cultural monuments are under construction around the Palace, forming a potential 'culture triangle'. Yet the Media Centre is being essentially programmed on the basis of the inner starting points: electric connections to other cultural institutions and TV audiences are more important than physical ones. The splendid location seems to be no more than a piece of good luck for the project.

The existence of empty space is a trivial explanation when it comes to projects like these two. A suitable empty building yet seems to be a more important factor in explaining the success than any organic connection to the urban structure. Quite paradoxically, the TV studios of Finnish Broadcasting Company and MTV3, vital for the media centre, are an exception: they seek a central location, accessible to urban life according to the contemporary TV ideology. But the financial expectations based on the central location of the Glass Palace may risk the public, experiential nature of the project.

THE CABLE FACTORY: THE ATMOSPHERE OF WORK

It is easy to claim that any old abandoned commercial building off the city centre could never have provided a basis for a cultural project such as the Cable Factory. The building is formidable, attracting aesthetically sensitive tenants and visitors.

17 Tyrväinen 1992: 23

Jan Verwijnen, an architect closely connected to the early days of the Pro Kaapeli, explains the attraction of the factory as follows: "The powerful images of abandoned industrial buildings and sites that we now constantly meet in detective series on TV or in MTV's music videos show that these spaces are no longer meaningless but culturally very attractive."[18]. Another pioneer architect, Pia Ilonen, emphasises the atmosphere of work. "Protecting the Furnace Room was the last struggle, as it were. It, too, was won by Pro Kaapeli."[19]. The Cable Factory also has a symbolic value connected to the history of Finland, for the copper cable produced there made up a significant part of the war indemnity paid by Finland to the Soviet Union after the Second World War.

A new and unusual environment provided established cultural institutions such as classical concerts or art exhibitions with an impulse of renewal, and introduced new audiences: "The space gives you a feeling of great freedom, which truly forces you to deviate from the conventional concert practices"[20]. The large, raw space of the Marine Cable Hall provided possibilities for organising wholly novel productions, such as performing West Side Story in cooperation with Helsinki-based arts schools, or the Drive or Die spectacle. The Cable Factory has been an object for photographers and stimulated artistic ideas: the spatial experience and light of the Marine Cable Hall was an essential element of the impression evoked by Stefan Lindfors' first insect sculptures.

Maintaining the factory atmosphere and the traces of industrial production became a standard practice in renovating the Cable Factory, which probably was something new in Finland. Yet aesthetics were not the only reason for this: a total renovation would have been 5 to 10 times more expensive than the chosen method, realised in stages and with sensitivity. Good examples include Avanti's concert hall and foyer, the Kaapeli restaurant, and the space of the HUT Department of Architecture, realised with minimalistic partition walls made of glass. Yet at many spots the atmosphere has been covered under paint and gypsum boards. Fireproofing and ventilation also bring more 'normal', contemporary details to the premises.

---

[18] Verwijnen 1996: 129

[19] Interview with Pia Ilonen

[20] Lampila, quoted in Isohanni 1993

THE GLASS PALACE: 1930S MODERNISM IN THE MEDIA ERA

The Glass Palace is part of the white, elegant building stock designed for the 1940 Olympic Games. The Olympic Games was a project of modernisation, which provided Helsinki citizens with spaces required by the contemporary, sporty lifestyle – a swimming pool, a zoo, a fair centre, and tennis courts – plus contact with the aesthetic idols of such a lifestyle. The Glass Palace was central in this respect: it was a horizontal, dynamic building, anticipating the hustle and bustle of the future metropolis and the flow of cars passing by; it was a glass house shining light and neon in the night, right to the heart of the young, Continent-oriented cultural elite. Colonial and luxury products presented in the shop windows radiated cosmopolitanism and wealth.

It is interesting how this building, which for the agrarian Finland signified the future, was re-introduced as the symbol of information society Finland.

> *A departure point of the already completed idea plan is the restoration of this valuable building to its original, at that time visually radical appearance and the creation within the building of an easy and natural encounter point for cinema, the new electronic technologies and the public which meets the needs of the present day and of the future.*
> — UPP APPLICATION 1996: 9

Up till now, the virtual world of the information networks has developed independently, between the user and the screen. It has had relatively few public expressions: the impact has been limited to the idiosyncratic graphics of websites, computer games and science fiction freaks, which is to some extent visible in magazines, toys, ads, and trendy bars. It seems that the media centre is attempting to force the orthodox modernism of the Glass Palace into a public wrapping for the virtual world. It seems that net communities, producers of new media, and teleoperators alike approve of using references to transparency, speed, and mobility to their attributes and images of their own orientation to the future.

an amazing, splendid classical world of colour is surfacing in the interior, with golden and silver pillars supporting a cobalt ceiling ...
— ALLI ARCHITECTS, WORKING GROUP MEMO, SEPTEMBER 15, 1997

The competition over the use of Bio Rex is an illustrative example. While the media centre idea is being developed, two lease offers are pending concerning the Rex foyer and auditorium. The Rex Nova concept compiled by independent programme producers would convert the auditorium into a multi-purpose club and restaurant seating 1,000. This concept, which is truly 'contemporary', would clearly be both functional and financially viable, but it would also involve a major intervention regarding the architecture (terracing the sloping floor and discarding the cinema seats). The other concept would continue using the auditorium for various archive screenings and special series. Although this line of action is not considered financially sensible, it seems likely to be chosen on the basis of its spirit conforming to the original atmosphere.

Do we not long for chaos, fractals, mycelia, pluralism, blur? It seems that the Finnish information society is considered a child of modernity to such an extent that the Glass Palace serves as a good symbol.

FROM MARGINS TO INSTITUTIONS – ORGANISATIONS AND ECONOMY

Having discussed hybrid programmes in relation to the physical buildings they occupy, I continue by describing some aspects of organisation and economic feasibility of the projects.

The Cable Factory was born as an 'underground' movement, an independent community, which had to defend itself and find its own place. It belonged to the margins of space and culture, challenging all conventional practices[21]. Dynamic people and activism were central in the early stages. "The Cable Factory was a huge spaceship, which was gradually being repiloted." Creating the future required "tough work and small-scale lobbying"[22]. Coordinating activities on several fronts and practi-

21 Kopomaa 1997: 210–211

22 Interview with Pia Ilonen

cal matters demands organisation. The prominent figures of the artistic community were quick to organise themselves into Pro Kaapeli, created in 1989–90.

When the factory was taken over by the City of Helsinki from Nokia, the city founded an independent real estate company – whose shares are still owned by the city – to manage it. The city provided the company with the building as a capital investment. It pays a current rent for the site and finances its activities through its own income or its own loans. Today (1997), the established lease income is approximately 10 million Finnmarks (1.7 MECU) and the income from temporary events some 1 million Finnmarks (0.17 MECU). The degree of utilisation of the building is roughly 90% and the rents for the studios remain reasonable (32–50 Finnmarks per square metre per month). The company rents the site from the city (800,000 Finnmarks, 0.14 MECU) and pays property tax for the state. After these and maintenance expenses the profit is some 4 million Finnmarks (0.7 MECU). Unlike in many other corresponding cultural institutions, the restaurant is not a significant source of income for the Cable Factory. The stable financial situation of the Cable Factory derives almost exclusively from the sheer size of the building, the amount of leased space[23].

23 Interview with Marianna Kajantie

The development of the Glass Palace project from the margin to the centre is connected to the changed cultural role of the media centre idea. The development reflects the increase in information technology, new media, and in recent years publicity in 'cultural industry', as well as expansion of impact: as late as 1991 there was interest in the subject merely among a small group of insiders, but in the course of a decade, the information society has been chosen as a national strategy, communication and electronics industries have become central fields of economic activity, and positive attitudes towards technology have been made a main instrument in building national identity, with the Nokia mobile phone as the principal symbol. At the same time, the 'Media Centre' has turned from an alternative playground for young experts into an information and entertainment centre for the general public, with substantial economic value.

NEED FOR LEADERSHIP

The sectored implementation machinery of the city has been put to a severe test with both projects. Both the Cable Factory and the Glass Palace have been carried on through the city bureaucracy in a variety of packages, adapting the format according to the respective department. Year after year, innovators and promoters of cultural content have been forced to defend themselves against experts of technology and economy and their conditions. Within the city of Helsinki organisation, which is very much involved in both projects, cultural content has traditionally been represented by the Cultural Office. The other pools include financial profitability, represented by the Real Estate Department, and technical feasibility and safety, represented by the Building Department.

Different agents have different means within such a field. Wide publicity and public interest have traditionally been keys to the success of cultural innovations. The projects have been provided with an 'aura', which is likely to have affected the decisions. Publicity also has an international dimension. The Cable Factory is a member of Trans Europe Halles, an organisation of alternative cultural centres, whereas the Media Centre was financially supported by the EU.

An organisation which is as independent and strong as possible is another means to secure the continuity of cultural content. As described above, the Cable Factory real estate company is financially and functionally independent. According to the company regulations, the chairperson must be an 'eminent cultural character'. In the early days, the chair was held by Jörn Donner, a writer, director, and politician, and today by Lauri Törhönen, who is a film director and a professor. Yet the chairman has no functional responsibility for running the cultural centre, which may be reflected in the lack of profile. The Cable Factory is not personified into Donner, Törhönen, or anyone else.

The Glass Palace Media Centre has lacked an organisation of its own. The project has been carried out within the city organisation, and the innovators and the rebels have also been cast inside the city administration.

Yet the need for an organisation and a prominent advocator has been evident all the time. The names of the architects designing the renovation were publicised in the media, and consequently they have been contacted by people who want to lease spaces or realise projects: it is the architects who have been acting as the key figures. Moreover, they have been responsible for programming the project, instead of the commissioner (the Real Estate Department), who deals with the project as a techical restoration project[24].

Now, the organisation is being built up. Four models of administration were compared by a consult. The best alternative was found to be an independent company "practising media and film centre activities", running and leasing the building and maintaining the technology[25]. The difference between this system and the one realised at the Cable Factory is that the company does not own the premises, which means fewer risks and less liability for the management. On the other hand, the target rent turnover sets clear limits to the financial independence of the company. A prominent, responsible manager is being head-hunted for the media centre; at the early stage, the post is being held by Marianna Kajantie, the head of the Cultural Office, who has already been developing the project for a long time.

[24] Interview with Pia Ilonen

[25] Working group memo, September 15, 1997

MAIN EVENTS OF THE GLASS PALACE AND THE CABLE FACTORY PROJECTS

1988	The founding plan of the 'Glass Palace Block Multi-Purpose Centre'.
1990	The city's culture authorities make plans for the new use of the Glass Palace. Perttu Rastas (AV-arkki, today a curator at the Kiasma), presents the idea of a centre for audiovisual culture.
autumn 1991	City authorities accept a partial land use plan: the Glass Palace and the square to become a 'living room' for the city.
spring 1993	The city approves the preliminary renovation programme for the Glass Palace, scheduled for 1997–98.
1994	A proposal is made for the film and media centre, supported by the Centenary of the Cinema committee, among others.
1995	City culture authorities charts the potential interest of various agents, including the Finnish Film Board and Nokia Ltd, in the media centre project.
autumn 1995	Idea plan by Alli Architects. MTV3 starts regular broadcasts from the Glass Palace.
spring 1996	The city applies for EU Urban Pilot funding for the media centre. The Cultural Office decides to remove Kirjakaapeli (the public media library) from the Cable Factory to the Glass Palace.
autumn 1996	Finnkino closes Bio Rex.
winter 1997	The renovations begin. The project is commanded by the Real Estate Department designed by Alli Architects, and budgeted for 40 million Finnmarks (6.8 MECU).
July 1997	After a lengthy selection process, the media centre project receives 2.7 MECU (approx. 15 million Finnmarks) for renovation and operation.
autumn 1997	A company to run the Glass Palace is founded. Leadership is still being resolved. The estimated (compromised) rents expected by the city are 7.5 million Finnmarks (1.3 MECU) per year.

1987	The Cable Factory committee is set up by the City of Helsinki.
1987–88	Architectural competition of Ruoholahti plan.
1988	The prologue: the City Cultural Office rents studios at the island of Harakka in the premises no longer required by the Finnish Defence Forces.
summer 1989	Nokia Oy begins to lease out spaces now available in the Cable Factory. 20,000 m² is rapidly occupied.
spring 1990	The Free Art School moves to the Cable Factory.
May 1990	The final report of the Cable Factory committee is published.
June 1990	An alternative plan by Pro Kaapeli.
autumn 1990	The City Planning Committee approves keeping the Cable Factory as a complete entity in future town planning.
January 1991	The city of Helsinki and Nokia Oy sign a contract on dividing the factory.
January 1991	A new committee is set up: Pro Kaapeli architects (Ilonen and Verwijnen) compile a new use plan. Their expertise allows for quick decisions by the committee.
1991	Construction of Ruoholahti residential area begins.
autumn 1991	The part owned by the city is formed into a company.
autumn 1991	The company signs new lease contracts on largely former conditions.
1991–92	The West Side Story production realised as a joint project of Helsinki art academies is evidence of the potential of the marine cable hall.
spring 1992	Foto Finlandia photography event in the marine cable hall.
autumn 1992	The arts instruction of the Department of Architecture at the Helsinki University of Technology moves to the Cable Factory. The Free Art School receives new spaces.
January 1993	The rehearsal and performance facilities of Avanti Chamber Orchestra are opened.
spring 1993	The Museum of Photography and two other special museums move to the Cable Factory.
August 1993	Ruoholahti underground station is opened.
1994	A new restaurant opens in the High Voltage laboratory.
1994	Drive or Die megashow.
1996	The marine cable hall is occupied by various productions for six months in a row.
1997	The Centre of New Dance sets up in the Cable Factory, opening the first permanent theatre space in the building.
1997	Air conditioning system renovated.
1997	The restaurant owner terminates the contract as it is unproductive. The Cable Factory is seeking a new restauranteur.

WRITTEN SOURCES:
"Ajetaanko Kaapelilta ulos kunnon maksajia?". *Helsingin Sanomat*, September 22, 1997.
Isohanni, Tuula (1993). *Kaapelitehtaan kulttuurimiljöön säilytys*. A report commissioned by Kiinteistö Cy Kaapelitalo (Cable Factory Ltd).
Kaapeli Linja. The newsletter of Pro Kaapeli organisation, April 1990.
Kopomaa, Timo (1997). *Tori – marginaali – haastava kaupunki*. Helsinki: Suomalaisen Kirjallisuuden Seura.
Lasipalatsi-korttelin monitoimikeskus. Perustamissuunnitelma 27.10.1988. Publication 3/1988 by the Building Department of the City of Helsinki.
Lasipalatsin elokuva- ja mediakeskus. Working group memo, September 15, 1997.
Lasipalatsin Mediakeskus osakeyhtiön perustaminen. Excerpt from the agenda of the City Board, November 17, 1997.
Mäkelä, Laura; Vuorinen, Marja; Siurala, Lasse (1994). *Kaapelitehdas taloudellisen ja kulttuurisen muutoksen ilmentäjänä*. Helsinki: Helsingin kaupungin tietokeskus.
Tyrväinen, Paiju (1992). *Metamorphosis. From industry to arts production*. A diploma work report for the European Diploma in Cultural Management 1991–1992.
Verwijnen, Jan (1996). The Cable Factory – a story of another kind of interior renovation. In *Helsinki sisältä – Helsinki interiors*. Helsinki: Rakennustieto.

OTHER SOURCES:
Interview with **Marianna Kajantie**, the head of the Helsinki City Cultural Office, September 11, 1997
Interview with **Pia Ilonen**, architect, October 2, 1997
Interview with **Auni Palo**, Managing Director of Kiinteistö Oy Kaapelitalo, October 9, 1997
Interview with **Jan Verwijnen**, architect, November 24, 1997

Culturing the Mall
A Design Museum in the Heart of the City
Master's thesis project at UIAH

Edina Dufala

Museum buildings in many West European countries have been used as a key tool for developing the images of their host cities. However, museums themselves have also undergone through a fundamental transformation. From being temples of culture, they have become a central part of the modern city, offering multifaceted experiences alongside their collections.

Moreover, the notion of design is itself changing. At the moment it may seem as if museums, design shops and magazines are the sole intended targets for quality design products. This cannot be correct. Design is actually a central feature of culture and everyday life, and its scope is increasing.

Such considerations lie behind the proposal to relocate the Design Museum in the "Makkaratalo" building in the very heart of Helsinki. The Makkaratalo (lit. sausage building) is in itself an emblem the 6os "golden age" of Scandinavian design[1]. Situated here, the museum would effectively become part of an urban mall. This project nevertheless wants to avoid simplistic interpretations. The museum is seen as a place of passage, a cultural "anchor" swimming in the flows of people. It belongs to the public realm, where families and individuals can promenade, where it is possible to eat out and do shopping or browse in a bookshop, but it tries also to "culture the mall", to render the everyday goods and experiences in a different light.

[1] Editor's note. For more information on the Makkaratalo and surroundings see Quaderns 200/1995.

The "in-between-museum" square: the former parking deck is reprogrammed to form a space for events and an open-air exhibition.

The mart zone: the commercial underworld from which the museum derives its icons.

Suspended elements house independent programs such as the bookshop, cafe and movie complex.

The museum not only occupies the structural frame but, with a constructivist gesture, also breaks free of the stiff grid. It revitalizes the suspended movement of the ramp, spiralling higher and higher (as the collection of the museum itself is fed from each of the lower levels), like Tatlin's Third International Project.

Kowloon City
Destruction of the Wall of Identity,
(Re)Construction of a Public Place of Consumption

JACKIE KWOK
Associate professor, Hong Kong Polytechnic University
MICHAEL SIU
Lecturer, Hong Kong Polytechnic University

Abstract

Kowloon City in Hong Kong was a place full of political legends. In 1847, according to the Kowloon Extension Agreement, walls were built around some villages in the district and the walled area, Kowloon Walled City, was supposed to be excluded from the rule of the colonial government. Since the walled area status deprived it of social services (roads, water supply, sanitation), it formed a standing invitation to disreputable trades like illegal entertainment, drug trafficking and unlicensed medical care. It was one of the poorest squatter areas in Hong Kong, but the people who lived inside the walled area had a strong identity. The scene of the walled area was a complete contrast to the prosperous futurist look of Hong Kong at the waterfront.

In 1987, the Hong Kong government had decided to demolish the Walled City and build a park on the site. In 1993 the park was awarded a Diploma at the IGA Stuttgart EXPO '93 (International Garden Exposition) as a fine example of "integrating landscape with the unique history of the Walled City". Since the late 1980s, consumer industries have also flourished in the district, making it a simulated pseudo-public place of restaurants and shopping centres.

This paper attempts to examine the transformation of the sense of place caused by spatial destruction and (re)construction in Kowloon City. The principal questions are how radical changes destroy the local people's rootedness in place and how place becomes "the site of incommunicable otherness" disconnected from the community.

Kowloon City

As the plane descends, you can almost feel that you are touching the multitude of television antennae on the apartment house roofs and reaching the laundry poles sprouting out of the windows.
— WEI & LI 1995: 11

After 1997, this exciting experience of landing at the Hong Kong International Airport in Kowloon City will be history. The airport will be moved to Chek Lap Kok in Lantau Island. As the building height controls over large parts of Kowloon will be relaxed, most of the old apartment houses will be demolished to match the urban redevelopment. As the centre of Kowloon, Kowloon City District is included in this area of urban renewal.

Kowloon City District is the south-eastern part of Kowloon. Its area is 944 acres (382 hectares) with a population of 340,000 people (about 6.7% of the total population of Hong Kong). Kowloon City is not only the oldest area among the 21 constituencies for election inside Kowloon City District but also for the whole of Kowloon[1]. The City was originally a salt field and its history can be traced back to the Chuen dynasty (200 BC). Records show that the site was first used as a military and administrative centre in 1197 during the Sung dynasty. The officials and troops extended their authority over vast areas of what is now known as the New Territories[2].

[1] Kowloon City District Board 1994: 33

[2] Ho 1986: 19

Kowloon Walled City

The original Kowloon Walled City was built in 1843 right after the First Opium War. Its area was 70 Chinese acres, 1,000 by 530 yards (914 by 484 metres). The central position of the city was occupied by the "yaman". As the name suggests, the whole City was surrounded by walls, which were 6 to 12 feet thick and 25 feet high. In 1943, during the Japanese occupation, the walls were demolished to provide material for the extension of Kai Tak Airport. The special status of the area remained, however.

Basically, the Walled City shared with East Berlin the politico-geographical status of a town within a town. Under the Peking Convention of 1898 the Chinese retained jurisdiction and the use of the road from Kowloon to Hsinan. At that time the British

negotiator MacDonald stated that "it is not to be expected that the City of Kowloon will long remain outside British jurisdiction". The actual administration proved more controversial. Although the Hong Kong government had attempted to clear and resettle some residents inside the Walled City in 1933, 1948 and 1963, all the projects failed due to the protests of local residents and the objections of the Chinese government[3].

[3] Wesley-Smith 1973

In the late 1980s the Walled City had some 33,000 residents. It had a theatrical appearance of extreme antiquity: narrow streets and narrower lanes, frequent corners, changes of level, short flights of steps in the streets and irregular placing of the buildings. Its built structure consisted of 500 ten-to-fourteen-storey buildings which had 8,300 residential units. One thousand premises were for commercial use, including 87 illegal dental clinics, 74 medical practices, and a large variety of other businesses. Since the mid-1970s, the Walled City has been claimed to be full of pornographic activities, gambling, and drugs, as well as being a haven for illegal immigrants and criminals. Consequently, the Walled City was branded the "Cancer of Kowloon"[4].

[4] Mok 1990: 41

Demolition of the Walled City

Before the Sino-British Joint Declaration in 1984, the Hong Kong government seldom disclosed or described the problems of the Kowloon Walled City. Serious attention was never paid to improving living conditions, although a lot of residents and the Kowloon City District Board had been making complaints since the 1960s.

At 9.00 a.m. on 14 January 1987 the Hong Kong and Chinese governments suddenly announced their agreement that the historical Walled City would be demolished and turned into a US$7 million urban park: the Kowloon Walled City Park. The project was the first clearance in Hong Kong where the rehousing of residents was tied in with property compensation[5]. Since then, much has been heard of the poor conditions in the Walled City.

[5] Lino & al. 1982: 55

The Hong Kong government has never provided a concrete answer as to why the Walled City should be demolished. John Corrigal, the Government Land Agent, only

a Landing at the Hong Kong International Airport in Kowloon City: an impressiv experience for the tourist.
b Kowloon Walled City before demolition.

Before demolition of the Kowloon Walled City children played on the roof of a building inside the City.

claimed that "the project is regarded as an environmental improvement project". While relating the history of the place and the ambiguous reasons for its demolition, it can be noticed that the whole project consists of "miracles which cannot be spoken"**6**.

6 Chen 1995: 3

Quite surprisingly, people seemed not to care about the fate of this historical city. Many awaited with excitement the prospect of the "Cancer of Kowloon" coming down with a bang – an implosion. Because of safety reasons, the expectation was dashed by a low bidder – with a wrecking ball**7**. Actually, the demolition faced a lot of opposition from the residents. Asiaweek wrote on December 13, 1991:

7 Tam 1993: 38

> *Man Chong-chung, the chairman of the Kowloon Walled City Residents Association, reacted angrily that "even the Vietnamese boat people are better treated than we are... they're illegal immigrants and no force was used when they were repatriated. We're Hong Kong citizens and the government pushed us out of our homes."*

The Walled City Park – a New Wall of Separation

However, the Government did not care and the notorious landmark was demolished and changed into a park. Jonathan Yung, senior landscape architect of the government's Architectural Services Department (ASD), says that

> *each Hong Kong's new park project will stand out as an individual entity... The most common approach would be to use the historical background of the site. This will stimulate the memories of park goers on the one hand, and on the other, it will create more talking points amongst them.*
> — BUILDING JOURNAL HONG KONG CHINA, MAY 1996

William Greaves, senior property services manager in the ASD, also claims that

> *the park won't be a theme park... But it'll be a heritage park, with genuine stuff to appeal to the locals. I'd like to see a kiddie-sized kingdom on a genuine Ching dynasty site.*
> — RAM 1991: 19

In fact, the park design does not consider "historic memory" and "cultural landscape"[8]. The yaman and some historical items are put in the park for fun, but the design forgets the mentally important history of conflicts between the British government, the Chinese government and the people of Hong Kong. It does not provide information about daily life inside the walls within the past tens of years, either. The demolition of the real and continuous part of Hong Kong history and the appearance of the synthetic Chinese heritage park generate a confusing and unrealistic sense of space and time which allows little sense of continuity. It almost seems that people's perception of time would be "annihilated"[9].

According to Kevin Lynch the features of space "should be generated from thinking of how people relate to their surroundings"[10] and open space "should reflect the complexities of [people's] daily social life"[11]. Kowloon Walled City Park only serves as a major tourist attraction – a marker[12]. Every day tens of coaches carry non-residents and foreign tourists to visit the park. The constructions inside the park and the activities conducted there are totally isolated from the local residents' daily life. The only scene are people taking pictures in front of various Chinese Ching dynasty architectures. Thus, the park is prepared as a "stage" which only allows visitors to perform well-determined activities within the fixed opening hours and constantly supervised by the guards. It is a stimulated hyper-space and utopia with restricted access and determined meaning.

After the demolition of the walls during the Japanese occupation, the relationship between residents inside and outside the former wall had grown closer. Although it may be true that the Walled City was an underworld haven for criminals, the residents around it got services from its unlicensed doctors and bought things from shops along its boundary[13]. Today, the wall exists again. It not only re-separates the spaces of Kowloon City, it also (re)constructs the living style inside the city.

When descending southwards from the Kowloon Walled City Park, one encounters a confusing urban collage. Opposite the Carpenter Road Park there are many traditional shops selling bread, Chinese tea, clothing, medicine etc.; there are also small local cafes. The range of merchandise reveals the concrete content of the everyday life of the inhabitants. But when one comes to the Kowloon City Plaza, the street

8 Hsia & Liu 1995:30
9 Harvey 1989:241
10 Lynch 1975:789
11 Lynch 1979: 415
12 Culler 1988: 159
13 Tam, 1993, p. 36

scene changes abruptly. The highly designed shopping mall is completely alien to the adjacent environment. When walking again southwards, one encounters a specialised restaurant street, Fok Lo Chuen Road, and its extension to the adjacent streets.

We will discuss closely this configuration of urban spaces and examine its effect on the change of lifestyle in the area. Let's first look at the oldest and also the most unplanned part, Carpenter Road.

Carpenter Road

As already mentioned, the atmosphere of the road is extremely casual. Shop owners freely reshape the street space, which is officially meant for circulation. The pavement becomes the place where goods, clothing and bread alike, are displayed and stored. A modest everyday sense of life is easily perceptible. The aged buildings match well with the old-fashioned, non-designed, local shops; the boundary between home and street is not strict, so from the home above the residents have an easy and simple access to the street below for daily living supplies and transportation to work. On the opposite side of the street there is even a park for rest, relaxation, and socialising.

Compared to the Kowloon Walled City Park, the construction of the Carpenter Road Park created less opposition from locals. Although the two parks are near each other, their functions are totally different. The Carpenter Road Park is popular, though it has never been claimed to be a great urban planning project like the Walled City Park. This modest greenery serves as a common ground for movement and communication. The park can be said to work, on the lines of Kevin Lynch, as an

> *uncommitted land susceptible of many uses, it extends the individual's range of choice and allows him to pursue his satisfactions directly, with a minimum of social or economic constraint. Private purpose can be pursued [there] without elaborate prior planning or community intervention.*
> — LYNCH 1965: 397

Also the notion of "fit" could be brought in: according to Lynch, it is

Kowloon City: the oldest area among 21 constituencies for election inside.

the degree to which the form and capacity of spaces, channels, and equipment in a settlement match the pattern and quantity of actions that people customarily engage in, or want to engage in...
— LYNCH 1981: 118

The spatial performance of Carpenter Road is very appropriate to the basic set of desired behaviours in the neighbourhood. However, the situation is deemed to change as the society grows richer. People seek diversity and variety; in our so called post-modern age, diversity and variety mean precisely consumerism.

Kowloon City Plaza

Consumerism tries in every way to give shape to a shapeless place which is yet apt for many uses. Kowloon City Plaza, with its colourful collage facade, announces a new lifestyle in this oldest district of Hong Kong. The design of the Plaza is a complete contrast to the environment. The building itself not only invades the architectural construction by pushing it far beyond its own normative limit, it also alters the habitual visual perception of space and the daily life rhythms of the neighbourhood.

Although the whole building intends explicitly to transform itself into a huge metaphor of funfair, the design of the entrance is purely functional, allowing no other activity than circulation. Inside, the columns are all decorated with colourful, flashing, mobile neon lights, glossy floor tiles, and polished wall finishes. Floors are linked by running escalators, and transparent bullet lifts constantly move up and down. An additional structure hangs from the ceiling in the middle of the central void and is again decorated with flashing neon lights. Halfway up the Atrium hangs a stage; underneath is an open food court stuffed with colourful dining furniture. This busy and carnivalesque design is complemented by noisy pop music. The whole setting encourages the rapid flow of things, food and people.

When discussing the metaphoric operation in design, Diana Agrest claims that when architecture is organised according to other cultural codes than the enclosed historic or classical mathematical ones, it enters into the horizon of design[14]. In the case of Kowloon City Plaza, consumerism imposes intentionally a hyper-system of

14 Agrest 1991: 32

configuration of funfair onto the classical architectural codes. The restless setting of the interior not only drowns the architecture, it also destroys the spirit of carnival defined as a blunt enjoyment of the body. People are actually acting "normally" in the world of consumption. They have to follow submissively the paths highly controlled by the electrical/mechanical rhythm of the escalators and the bullet lifts. People inside the plaza are not the "flâneur" defined by Baudelaire: the plaza does not provide "the endless imaginative possibilities for strolling, daydreaming, watching and being watched"[15]. Instead, they are consumers, they are there to learn and to consume ceaselessly the new trend of commodities. Living in a consumer society, leisure life is no longer rest and relaxation in an open space that allows free movement. For an individual, it is rather to actualise the socially programmed free time behaviour in a restrictedly designed space.

Enclosed in this space of exuberant light, sound and movement, people are overwhelmed with the impact of the dramatic, illusive experience of pleasure. In this fictionalised non-space, people who are actually living in the "real" space of the streets gradually see that at least part of their life has to be "exciting". Things to do in leisure time have to be, as Rojek puts it, an

endless search for novelty and variety but leave nothing memorable.
— ROJEK 1995: 109

Instead of offering the access to basic wants, space now has to offer

unrealistic wants of total satisfaction and fulfilment.
— IBID.: 113

Fok Lo Chuen Road

As Kowloon City opens to the people living outside it, either as a tourist marker or as a consumer paradise, consumption industries develop within the district. The most striking of these developments are the specialised restaurants which came to flourish among groceries, Chinese pharmacies, and small shops selling basic clothing and daily life utensils. Cuisine from all over the world – Korean, Taiwanese and Japanese

[15] Rojek 1995: 91

a   Kowloon Walled City Park: people perform well determined activities within the fixed space.
b   Kowloon City Plaza next to the residential buildings built in the 60s.
c   Carpenter Road: a street of everyday life that belongs to the grassroots class in Hong Kong.
d   A local bakery in Carpenter Road.

food, western bars – are found within the space of two to three adjacent streets; a Greek restaurant appears next to a traditional paum shop.

However, most of the restaurants on Fok Lo Chuen Road promote luxurious, expensive Chinese dishes, such as bird nest and shark fin. They employ similar facade design, bright colourful neon light, to attract clients and popularise the expensive food associated with the life of Chinese aristocrats and high bourgeoisie. According to Mennell[16], gastronomy means the art and science of "delicate eating". To accomplish the refined art of eating, not only has the meal to be expensive, but one has to be correctly dressed and familiar with the restricted manner of attending the dining table. On Fok Lo Chuen Road everything except the food ingredients has been vulgarised. People dress in T-shirts and shorts, talk loudly when paying thousands of Hong Kong dollars for the Japanese-style raw fish, lobster from Boston or Chinese shark fin soup. The setting of the restaurants is very congested, and even the smallest corners are stuffed with dining furniture.

16 1992: 270

The absence of polished manner, the ignorance of a correct dressing code, together with the popular, undefined setting of the interior of the restaurants reveal the shallowness of the culinary culture. Diners think that the content of the dish is more important than the aestheticisation of the atmosphere and the dining behaviour. For them food in abundance and variety is the sole sign of wealth instead of the distinction in habitat: environment and manner.

Conclusion

The residents of the Kowloon City are facing great changes in their environment: the demolition of the Walled City, the implantation of the Kowloon City Plaza, and the process of specialising the district as a centre for international cuisine. From a critical point of view, Kowloon City is a typical place following the track "programmed" by the

a Carpenter Road Park: residents and local Filipino servants taking rest inside the Park.
b Carpenter Road Park: a common ground for movement and communication.
c The entrance of Kowloon City Plaza: the design plain and wholly functional.
d People dress casually when enjoying an expensive seafood dinner in the congested interior of a restaurant.
e Specialized street of restaurants: Fok Lo Chuen Road.
f The exuberantly decorated interior of Kowloon City Plaza.

consumer economy. The real space of everyday life is gradually becoming mixed with a non-space of hyper-reality and exuberant wants. The everyday space which once wa clear in the sense of direction, area, shape, pattern, volume and distance[17] has now disintegrated into a hyper-real sphere of perception and imagination.

When R. Hewison says that "history becomes a contemporary creation, more costume drama and re-enactment than critical discourse"[18], he is critically judging the illusive operations of the heritage industry on history. Imagine what Hewison would say about the Hong Kong government wiping out the whole community of the Kowloon Walled City, then erecting the walls again, and constructing an abstract aesthetic tourist-marker on the emptied terrain. A private developer tries to confuse the neighbourhood by the kaleidoscopic design of the Kowloon City Plaza, which encourages people to surrender the common sense of daily life to depthless simulacra of carnival.

Just as the "Machine to Live In" of Le Corbusier was a "UFO" opening up the modern way of living, the Kowloon Walled City Park and the Kowloon City Plaza are again two UFO's that have landed on the grassroots community of Kowloon City. They urge the local residents to believe alien things to be their history; they also reprogram the sense of community and the value system of the people. Now life should be exciting, exciting meaning to constantly buy and eat all that is not necessary. Crowded in an enclosed, flashy place to buy trendy clothing, and crowded in a congested place to eat expensive food – that is what consumerism trains us for and what a post-modern leisure life is programmed to be.

However, no matter how sophisticated the renovation and redevelopment programme of the district may be, the users – commonly assumed to be passive and guided by established rules – may not follow every step of the programme. As mentioned by Lynch: while you can design a house, you can never design a city[19]. The ways people take rest in the Carpenter Road Park, operate their small shops next to the park, eat and dress in the restaurants in Fok Lo Chuen Road, and generate business around the Kowloon City Plaza, all prove that individuals can go "as far back as the age-old ruses of fishes and insects that disguise or transform themselves in order to survive"[20], even in a programmed city.

[17] Harvey 1989:203

[18] quoted in Harvey 1989: 62

[19] 1981: 105

[20] de Certeau 1984: xi

The rebuilt wall for Kowloon Walled City Park.

As stated in the title of this paper, the urban redevelopment projects in the Kowloon City are the destruction of the wall of identity and the (re)construction of a public place of consumption. When the programmes of redevelopment and consumption meet the responsive operation of the users inside the district, a "culture" is formed. The present paper has only traced in detail the ways by which the daily-life experience is changed by the redevelopment. However, it is important to say that the critical viewpoint is not the only one possible. We may yet discover how creatively the users commit their lives to the programmed spaces and ultimately alter the rules of the game. Cities are too complicated, affect the lives of too many people and are subject to too many cultural variations to permit any direct analysis. We, as lucid viewers of urban culture, should always consider also the other side of the coin when tackling any problem; only in constant questioning can we see the dynamics and vitality of city life.

BIBLIOGRAPHY

Agrest, D. (1991). *Architecture from without: Theoretical framings for a critical practice*. Cambridge: The MIT Press.
Building Journal Hong Kong China (May 1996). 'Landscape and Identity', pp. 32–35. Hong Kong.
Chen, C. W. (1995). *Two to three items which I know: The mythology of Taiwan building and planning*. Taiwan: Cultural Strategy Conference 1995.
Culler, J. (1988). *Framing the sign – criticism and its institutions*. London: University of Oklahoma Press.
de Certeau, M. (1984). *The practice of everyday life*. London: University of California Press.
Harvey, D. (1989). *The condition of postmodernity*. Oxford: Blackwell.
Ho, S. F. B. (1986). *Redevelopment of Kowloon Walled City: A feasibility study*. Hong Kong: The University of Hong Kong.
Hsia, C, J. & Liu, K. C. J. (1995). 'Settlement preservation and community development'. *Hon-seng Magazine 74*, pp.47–56, Taiwan.
Kowloon City District Board (1994). *A better Kowloon City*. 3rd edition, Hong Kong: Kowloon City District Board & Kowloon City Home Affairs Committee.
Liao, K. S., Wong, J. K. H., & Wong, J. Y. C. (1982). *Needs and aspiration of the Kowloon City Residents on Community Building Aspects in the Kowloon City District*. Hong Kong: Public Affairs Research Centre, Chinese University of Hong Kong.
Lynch, K. (1965). 'The openness of open space', In T. Banerjee and M. Southworth (eds.) (1990). *City sense and city design: Writings and projects of Kevin Lynch*, pp.396–410. Cambridge: The MIT Press.
Lynch, K. (1975). 'Grounds for utopia', In T. Banerjee and M. Southworth (eds) (1990) *City sense and city design: Writings and projects of Kevin Lynch*, pp. 789–810. London: The MIT Press.
Lynch, K. (1981). *Good City form*. Cambridge: The MIT Press.
Lynch, K. and Carr, S. (1979). 'Open space: Freedom and control', In T. Banerjee and M. Southworth (eds.) (1990). *City sense and city design: Writings and projects of Kevin Lynch*, pp. 411–417. London: The MIT Press.
Mennell, S. (1992). *The sociology of food: eating, diet and cultur*. London: Sage.
Mok, B. H. (1990). 'The Kowloon Walled City under demolition: Streets, mental health and social support of the residents'. *Hong Kong Journal of Social Work*, 24, pp.41–51.
Ram, J. (1991). 'Conservation and the Walled City'. *Asian Architect and Contractor 21(11)*, pp.18-20, Hong Kong.
Rojek, C. (1995). *Decentring leisure: rethinking leisure theory*. London: Sage.
Tam, A. (1993). 'Organic demolition: Walled City comes down'. *Asian Architect and Contractor 23(6)*, pp.33–36, Hong Kong.
Wei, B. and Li, E. (1995). *Culture shock: A guide to customer and etiquette*. Singapore: Times Book International Series.
Wesley-Smith, P. (1973). 'The Walled City of Kowloon: Historical and legal aspects', In G. D. Basto, H. Litton and J. Dear (eds.). *Hong Kong Law Journal 3*, Hong Kong Law Journal Ltd.

Urban Lighting in the 21st Century
New Strategies for New Uses

CARL GARDNER
Writer, Consultant

Introduction

Light is the main means by which any city is experienced visually. At night our experience of the city relies almost solely on artificial lighting. So far, exterior lighting has been largely neglected as a creative medium within the modern city. Its potential is increasingly being realised, however.

The new forms of urban lighting I want to discuss have a specific social and economic context.

1. The growing trend across Europe is to exclude cars or limit their access to city centres. City centre streets are increasingly defined as being for pedestrians only.
2. A fragmentation of the conventions of time, due to new technologies and flexible working, can be observed. The conventional 9–5 working day is breaking down.
3. The night-time economy, "the 24 Hour City", is growing.
4. Cities increasingly strive for differentiation and new civic identities to gain a competitive edge.
5. The inner-city crisis is becoming more visible. The middle class is fleeing to the suburbs resulting in the "doughnut effect". Crime rates and fear of crime are increasing.
6. A rather mid-to-long-term factor is the climate change. The shift of climatic bands northwards, due to global warming, could create more favourable conditions in northern Europe and extend the night-time use of city streets for longer periods of the year.

This socio-economic context has not as yet been seriously addressed by most city lighting plans.

The Functions of Urban Lighting

Urban lighting can play a number of roles[1]. These functions are not mutually exclusive but overlap considerably. Neither can lighting achieve all these objectives alone.

Despite the wide range of potential roles for urban lighting, to date 90% of investment and research has been given over to ensuring traffic safety. We are at the cusp of change in that respect, as cars are gradually being excluded from city centres. However, as we shall see, this development is leaving a legacy of totally inappropriate lighting for other urban activities involving pedestrians.

Looking at the other possible functions, urban safety has been the focus of considerable attention in the UK context. Just look at the dozens of studies which claim to prove that crime can be reduced by some 30% and people's fears of crime considerably lessened with the installation of brighter street lighting. My only comment is that brighter or more street lighting doesn't necessarily mean better urban lighting in the qualitative sense.

Similarly city beautification and specific night-time vistas also have an increasing purchase in the UK, particularly in the context of the various comprehensive, city-wide lighting plans that have emerged in the last six years. Obviously beautification and illuminating itineraries also contribute to the sense of place and the civic identity of dwellers.

Lighting conceived as an art form and light spectacles are special cases. They are usually temporary and geared to particular events, competitions, etc. However we should encourage the development of light-art on a more permanent basis, as potential foci for night-time itineraries (see below).

The encouragement and extension of pedestrian use of urban space and the stimulation of the night-time economy are the most neglected functions of urban lighting. I believe most thought and attention needs to be addressed to the improvement of these.

1 THE FUNCTIONS OF URBAN LIGHTING

- To ensure traffic safety
- To reduce crime and the fear of crime – to create a safe, secure night-time environment
- To enhance a city's architecture and monuments – so-called city beautification
- To create night-time vistas and illuminated itineraries
- Lighting as an art form, light sculptures, etc. These are usually temporary, due to maintenance issues and vandalism
- Public spectacles and special events à la Jean-Michel Jarre
- To create a sense of distinctive civic identity
- To give structure and form to urban spaces
- To encourage and extend pedestrian use and increase the range of urban night-time activities
- To stimulate the night-time economy

The Unsuitability of Road Lighting for New Pedestrian Uses

As already intimated, the dominant form of urban lighting, designed for traffic safety, is highly inappropriate for pedestrian use. This is due to the following reasons.

1. The common 9–12 metre lighting poles are too tall and completely lacking in human scale.
2. The main criterion of road lighting is horizontal illumination on the road surface. However, pedestrians benefit more from the vertical illumination of walls, etc.
3. Road safety demands maximum uniformity of illumination, which produces an all-over evenness and is very boring.
4. Road lighting sources – low and high pressure sodium and mercury sources – offer poor to mediocre colour rendering.
5. Direct high-level overhead lighting with visible lamps creates a harsh and ugly effect with poor modelling of the night-time environment.
6. Road lighting, designed for maximum efficiency, is by its nature utilitarian and functional, with no aesthetic qualities.

By contrast, the requirements of pedestrians are almost diametrically opposed to the above design parameters. Comfort and visual interest are the main objectives.

1. More human-scale lighting fixtures, 3–4 metres maximum, produce far more intimate, comfortable conditions.
2. Pedestrians require only minimal horizontal (floor) illumination for safety purposes but are better served by good vertical illumination of wall surfaces, art objects, faces and bodies, etc.
3. A diversity of lighting levels, above a certain minimum, helps to create highlights and greater visual interest.
4. Light sources with good colour rendering – namely fluorescent and metal halide – offer realistic viewing of art objects, food, merchandise and skin tones.
5. Indirect lighting with no visible glare from lamps can create a softer, more diffuse and friendly effect.
6. Prominent, illuminated foci, such as fountains and sculptures, within the visual field help create points of reference to orient pedestrians in the night-time landscape.

The Rise of the Urban Lighting Plan

One of the most effective and interesting attempts to bring all urban lighting – street and area lighting, architectural lighting, lit advertising signage, etc. – under one common vision, are the urban lighting plans which first gained popularity in Edinburgh in Scotland and Lyon in France around 1989–90. The City Lighting Plan tries to co-ordinate all forms of lighting to give the city a distinctive night-time identity. Plans vary from city to city or town to town, but many include the following features.

1. Proposals for specific lighting treatments of key buildings and monuments on main roads and visual axes, to make the city as a whole "legible".
2. Proposals for lighting of a different character (e.g. different colour temperature) for areas with a specific historic or architectural feel.
3. Recommendations for maximum luminance for particular areas, according to their importance within the city as a whole, to avoid competitive "light wars" between neighbouring commercial properties.
4. Recommendations on architectural lighting techniques, for the education of building owners.

Some lighting plan specialists also advocate the creation of the post of City Lighting Manager to oversee and help implement the plans. Others feel that lighting ought to be brought under municipal planning law. Proposals on new forms of pedestrian street and area lighting to replace the outdated systems left over from the days of road traffic could well fall within the scope of such plans.

The Experience of Lyon

The Lyon lighting plan, dating back to 1989, was part of its overall competitive strategy to retain its position as the country's second city and to compete with cities like Montpellier and Toulouse in France and Geneva, Strasbourg, Milan and Barcelona in the broader Mediterranean region. The city has the advantage of a semi-Mediterranean climate, a strong architectural legacy and superb topography, set as it is on two

below: Hanna Vainio's performance during the Helsinki Light Festival 1995 at 'Kaivopuisto' Park was a 'Light-Sound-Fire-Dance'.

rivers with steep, high hills on either side. However it has no legislative framework controlling private lighting schemes.

One of the most important measures the city has implemented is municipal subsidies on electric power for those property owners lighting their buildings within the plan's broad framework. According to Henry Chabert, the city's deputy mayor, and one of the main figures behind the plan, the last few years have created a general culture and understanding among businesses and the public at large, of the important role lighting can play in the city's revival.

One important planning measure the city of Lyon took, was to light the main through traffic routes in the city with (orange) sodium lighting while the side-roads are lit in (bluish) white mercury vapour. This helps orientation and gives a hierarchy to streets and roads in the night-scape.

New forms of pedestrian-friendly light fitting were developed. Especially worth mentioning is the light fitting by the French designer Jean-Michel Wilmotte. It is used in several city centre areas. Its scale is human (4m high) and its form and appearance are modern. The fitting uses a concealed metal halide lamp with good colour rendering and employs the principle of indirect illumination from a matt-white reflector. The effect is bright but also soft and diffused.

Thirdly, several pedestrian and semi-pedestrian streets in the city centre employ a great deal of vertical illumination of facades, using close offset high-pressure sodium fittings. This contributes enormously to the lit ambience of the street-scene. Older, direct high pressure down-lights mounted on the walls at first floor level, will gradually be phased out as the indirect technique is developed. Several of these streets feature an illuminated focus at the end of the street – a fountain in one case, a lit building in another – which give a sense of orientation and destination to pedestrians.

Also, many key buildings, including the cathedral of Fourviere on the hill, the communications tower alongside, the Hotel de Ville, the Opera, the Credit Lyonnais tower and many of the bridges, are dramatically illuminated, using sophisticated techniques. This gives a real visual richness to the night-scape and creates a strong identity for the city. Direct buried up-lights in the pavements are used to illuminate the trees. This is an opportunity which Paris by contrast, with its dozens of tree-lined boulevards, has sadly missed.

The city has invested in several innovative lighting techniques and installations, such as the matrix of mini-fountains lit by fibre optics in the Place des Terreaux, designed in collaboration with the artist/sculptor Daniel Buren. In conjunction with the lighting of the more traditional Bartholdi fountain and the four impressive facades around the square, the effect is probably one of the most dramatic in any comparable square in Europe. Light levels are such that traditional road or area lighting has been totally avoided.

The effects of Lyon's overall urban improvement strategy – including the lighting plan and associated projects and installations – have attracted more people to Lyon at night to dine, promenade, etc. It is impossible to quantify the exact contribution of lighting alone, but it is surely an important factor in the stimulation of the city's burgeoning night-time economy.

Small Can be Beautiful, Too

Good urban lighting is not confined only to large, affluent cities. The central square of Tilft – a small town 6 kilometres outside Liege in Belgium – is lit by a series of 4m high light fittings of a similar design to the Lyon model. The fitting again uses a metal halide lamp, for pleasant white light, with good colour rendering. The lamp is concealed within the column, light being transferred up to a horizontal reflector (in faceted aluminium) via a "light-pipe" made from special 3M light-retentive acrylic.

Again the effect is very soft and reassuring, with no harsh lamp glare within the field of view. The re-lighting of the square has also encouraged local restaurant owners and hotel keepers to light their own buildings, which creates much-needed vertical illumination of the surrounding facades.

There is one further innovative feature: a cobbled, one-lane traffic access road runs across one part of the square. This is subtly signalled by a series of small blue, fibre-optic "landing lights" recessed into the edge of the road, powered by two metal halide "light boxes" concealed within a brick and stone wall/bench. This discrete but attrac-

URBAN LIGHTNING IN THE 21ST CENTURY · **265**

tive technique makes the boundary of the traffic area perfectly clear but does not spoil the view across the square.

Conclusion

I make two final points. The first concerns "light pollution" and "sky-glow", which is now becoming such a nuisance to those who wish to view the night sky. It may be asked, do we really need more lighting of any kind. Don't lighting plans simply encourage more lighting and further pollution? I would say that it is not lighting per se that creates the problem, but badly designed and installed lighting. A broader awareness of good lighting, instilled by the popularisation of lighting plans, will help this problem, not exacerbate it.

Secondly there is the issue of energy efficiency and conservation. Again some people will say that more lighting is a waste of energy and shouldn't be encouraged. Lighting is a very small part of our overall energy consumption, however. Air conditioning and wasteful, inefficient electric systems of other kinds are much greater offenders. The problem is that lighting is highly visible and as such serves as a scapegoat for our unwillingness to tackle other forms of CO_2 creation. The small amount of energy used on urban lighting is well worth the cost in terms of the amount of pleasure, security, aesthetic enjoyment and civic pride it can produce.

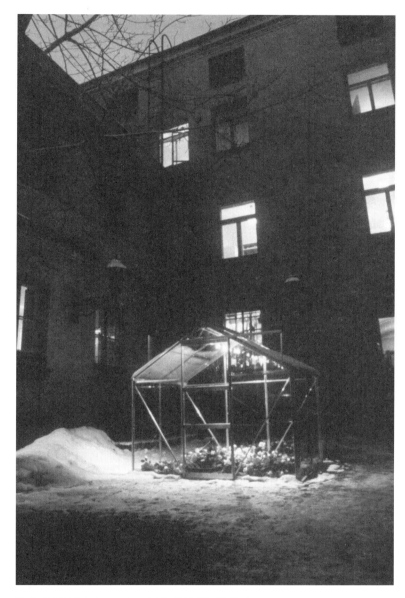

Kaarina Katajisto's 'urban greenhouse' at the Helsinki Lightfestival 1995.

The lit construction site of Helsinki's Museum for Contemporary Art, Kiasma.
Light installation by Viholainen and Pehkonen at the Helsinki Light Festival 1997.

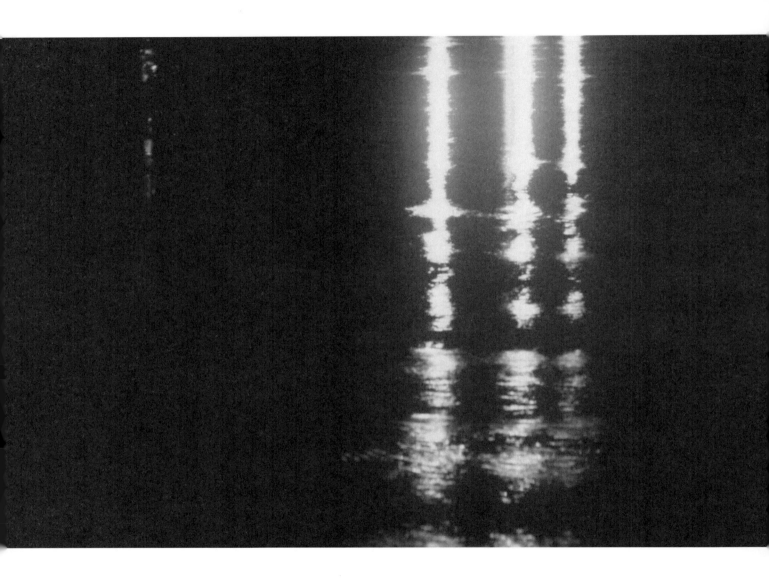